AF600239

THE CLERICAL OBLIGATIONS OF CANONS 138 AND 140

THE CATHOLIC UNIVERSITY OF AMERICA
CANON LAW STUDIES
No. 272

The Clerical Obligations of Canons 138 and 140

A HISTORICAL SYNOPSIS AND A COMMENTARY

BY THE

REVEREND JOHN THOMAS DONOVAN, PH.B., S.T.L., J.C.L.
Priest of the Archdiocese of Milwaukee

A DISSERTATION

Submitted to the Faculty of the School of Canon Law of the Catholic University of America in Partial Fulfillment of the Requirements for the Degree of Doctor of Canon Law

THE CATHOLIC UNIVERSITY OF AMERICA PRESS
WASHINGTON, D. C.
1948

NIHIL OBSTAT:

EDUARDUS J. ROELKER, S.T.D., J.C.D.
Censor Deputatus

Washingtonii, D. C., die XXVIII Martii, 1949

IMPRIMATUR:

✠ MOYSES ELIAS KILEY, S.T.D.
Archiepiscopus Milwaukiensis

Milwaukiæ, die XXXI Martii, 1949

PRINTED IN THE UNITED STATES OF AMERICA
BY THE SERAPHIC PRESS, MILWAUKEE, WIS.

To My Mother
in Memory
of My Father

TABLE OF CONTENTS

CHAPTER III

CHAPTER IV

CHAPTER V

CHAPTER VI

CHAPTER VII

FOREWORD

The obligations of clerics stand clearly defined in Book Two, Title the Third of the Code of Canon Law. In some twenty canons there are set forth legislative aids for the safeguarding of clerical dignity. This dissertation is concerned *ex professo* with only two of this number, Canons 138 and 140.

Like a golden thread through the works of the Fathers and other spiritual writers there runs the theme of clerical worth. Clerics stand in a special relation not only to God but also to the faithful. Thus it is that no single act performed by a cleric remains an isolated or insignificant act. This is doubly true if the act is invested with any publicity at all. It has repercussions either for good or for evil. There are certain things which clerics cannot do, for while "all things are lawful, not all things edify." Clerics are to be men of sound learning, for faith comes from hearing and they are to preach the word of God. But what is of greater importance, they are to be examples of outstanding moral integrity. Pope Pius XI has said that priests are to be not merely guides for the laity, but models of Christian life and of Apostolic virtue. *Qui lux est, luceat.* Priests may preach, but the faithful are more profoundly influenced by the well-chosen and highly persuasive phrases of example and proper clerical decorum.

Canons 138 and 140 are concerned with what are often termed "negative clerical obligations." These canons forbid to clerics certain things that are unbecoming, foreign to the lofty state into which first tonsure has initiated them. These things are forbidden not because they are intrinsically evil, but because they are unbecoming to clerics precisely as clerics, that is, as persons dedicated to God's service. The object or the action itself, and the attitude of the people towards it are the dual factors which determine whether or not a thing is unbecoming to clerics. It may be an occupation, a game, or some recreational event. In some cases the attitude of the people will be universally critical. Again, it will be a relative thing, varying with the communities, so that what is frowned upon in one place, may be held as becoming to clerics in another. This must clearly be kept in mind. When the writer states that something is unbecoming to clerics generally, he allows full room for those exceptions which after all give special weight to every law and rule.

The reader will note immediately that there has been a departure from the format which works of this type usually assume. The historical background of each of the six elements in canons 138 and 140 has been joined with the canonical commentary. Thus, each chapter stands as a separate and complete unit. This has been adopted in the interests of coherence and for the convenience of the reader, who will thus be enabled more easily to locate a particular point either in the history or in the commentary.

The writer takes this opportunity to express his sincere gratitude to His Excellency, the Most Reverend Moses E. Kiley, Archbishop of Milwaukee, for the opportunity of graduate study in Canon Law; to the Faculty of the School of Canon Law for their patient and scholarly direction and assistance; to his family and friends; and to all those, especially his fellow priests, who have aided in any way in bringing this work to completion.

CHAPTER I

INTRODUCTORY REMARKS

Saint Paul the Apostle, model of priestly zeal and comportment, has set forth an inspirational motto for all clerics in his Second Letter to the Corinthians: "We give no offense to anyone, that our ministry may not be blamed. On the contrary, let us conduct ourselves in all circumstances as God's ministers..." (II Cor. 6:3-4). It is an accepted axiom that each set of rights is balanced by a corresponding set of obligations. So it is with the clerical state; while the Code of Canon Law recognizes the dignity of the clerical state and claims certain rights and privileges for it (cc. 118-123), it also notes certain obligations that are incumbent upon all who enter that state (cc. 124-142).

The fact that clerics are set apart particularly for the service of God entitles them to special reverence; it also imposes on them a peculiar and pressing obligation to nurture sanctity, both internal and external. "You are the salt of the earth...even so let your light shine before men, in order that they may see your good works and give glory to your Father in heaven" (Matt. 5:13, 16) — this is the injunction of our Divine Lord. Its counterpart in positive ecclesiastical law is found in the canon which reminds clerics that they are to excel the laity in the internal and external holiness of their lives.[1]

This responsibility of the clerics is the chief source from which these obligations flow. It is the foundation of those special obligations which are found in the decretal law, in the decrees of the councils, in the Council of Trent

---

[1] Canon 124; cf. also Pius IX, Litt. encycl., *Qui pluribus*, 9 nov., 1846, and Pius X, *Serm. ad Pont. Seminarii Gallici in Urbe alumnos*, 9 dec., 1906 — *Enchiridion Clericorum* (Romæ: Typis Polyglottis Vaticanis, 1938), nn. 308, 797.

particularly,[2] and in various constitutions of the Roman Pontiffs. These obligations for the most part look to those acts which give external manifestation of clerical holiness of life. The entire title in which canons 138 and 140 are contained deals mainly with external conduct. At the same time it treats of internal acts as the necessary complement of many of the exercises which this title imposes; all its regulations are calculated to promote that correctness of intention, that inward purity and holiness of life, without which outward manifestations of piety are a mere sham. Canon 138 prohibits those things which are unbecoming a cleric; canon 140 places definite bounds to the extent and type of clerical entertainment and recreation.

Article 1. Comprehension of the Term "Cleric"

The etymology of the word cleric is to be sought in the Greek κλῆρος and its Latin equivalent, *sors,* which is rendered in the English by "lot," "portion," or "inheritance."[3] A cleric is one who has chosen the Lord as his inheritance, who has made the words of Psalm 15 a reality: *"Pars mea Dominus."* The cleric desiring in a very special way to serve God has left behind all worldly attachments. His lot, his future lies with His Lord, in service to Him and to his own fellow creatures for love of Him.[4]

In the first century and a half of the Church's history the term *clerus* was applied to the entire Christian com-

---

[2] Sess. XXII, *de ref.*, c. 1; sess. XXIV, *de ref.*, c. 12.

[3] C. 1, D. XXI; c. 7, C. XII, q. 1, where the source given is St. Jerome, though some scholars question this source — Raus, *Institutiones Canonicæ* (2. ed., Lugduni: Typis Emmanuelis Vitte, 1931), n. 54, note 1.

[4] Reiffenstuel, *Jus Canonicum Universum* (5 vols. in 7, Parisiis, 1864-1870), lib. III, tit. 1, n. 2 (hereafter cited Reiffenstuel); Beste, *Introductio in Codicem* (ed. altera. Collegeville, Minn.: St. John's Abbey Press, 1944), p. 164 (hereafter cited *Introductio*); Haring, *Grundzüge des katholischen Kirchenrechtes* (3te Aufl., 2 vols., Graz: Verlag von Ulrich Moser's Buchhandlung, 1924), p. 123; Chelodi, *Ius Canonicum de Personis* (3. ed., curavit P. Ciprotti, Trento: Libreria Moderna Editrice, 1942), p. 173 (hereafter cited *De Personis*).

munity.[5] Toward the end of the second century, as the result of a comparison instituted between their priesthood and the priesthood of the Old Testament, Christian writers, among them Saint Irenæus, Hippolytus, and Tertullian, began to use the term as referring properly and exclusively to the sacred ministers of the Church. In the *Novellæ* of Justinian all priests, deacons, and lectors are indicated by the term "clerics."[6] As shall shortly be seen, the term from that time on was used to designate the sacred ministers of the Church, and was not again applied to the laity.

From a consideration of canons 108, § 1, and 968, § 1, as found in the Code of Canon Law, a cleric may be defined strictly as a baptized male who has been dedicated to the divine ministry by reason of the reception of at least first tonsure. Although tonsure is not an order, but rather a preparatory step to orders, it is, according to canon 950, to be included under the term *ordo*. Since baptism is necessary in the recipient of valid orders, it is necessary also for the recipient of first tonsure. One author notes from canon 108, § 1, alone that a cleric may be defined as one who, though set apart from the lay state by the reception of first tonsure, does not as yet enjoy any ecclesiastical power. He is destined for it, however.[7]

Religious are also subject to the common clerical obligations which are binding on all clerics; this subjection arises by virtue of canon 592, which states that, unless the context or the very nature of the matter indicates otherwise, all religious are bound by the canonical clerical obligations. It was not always as clearly stated as this. In pre-

---

[5] I Peter 5:3. St. Peter speaks of the attitude which the *seniores* were to adopt toward the faithful: "Neque ut dominantes *in cleris*, sed forma facti gregis ex animo."

[6] Berutti, *Institutiones Iuris Canonici* (6 vols., Vol. II, Pars I [*De Personis et de Clericis in Genere*], Romæ: Marietti, 1943), p. 74 (hereafter cited *De Personis*); Wernz-Vidal, *Ius Canonicum* (7 vols. in 8, Romæ: Universitas Gregoriana, 1928-1943), Tom. II (*Ius de Personis* [3. ed., 1943]), n. 52.

[7] Sipos, *Enchiridion Iuris Canonici* (3. ed., Pécs: Ex Typographia „Haladás R. T.," 1936), p. 105 (hereafter cited *Enchiridion*).

Code law when one attempted to determine whether or not *monachi* and *regulares* came within the orbit of these obligations, it was necessary, first of all, to resolve the question whether they were clerics or lay persons. If their early origin and institution alone were considered, they would be numbered among the laity, for they had no power in the Church, either of orders or of jurisdiction. This helps to throw light on the definition of a cleric as given by Sipos. Further, they were punished for their grave crimes with the penalty of excommunication, and not with deposition or degradation as were clerics. However, if viewed in the light of later concessions whereby the way was made open to sacred orders, they were properly called clerics, and hence were bound by the obligations.[8]

Another pre-Code author held that monks and regulars occupied a middle place between clerics and lay people; in so much as they were regulars they could not be called lay, but since they shared in the clerical rights and privileges, they were clerics and were burdened then with the attendant obligations.[9]

A religious according to the Code is anyone of the faithful who has undertaken not only the observance of the common precepts but also the observance of the evangelical counsels through the vows of obedience, chastity, and poverty in an approved religious society, whether it be lay or clerical, for men or for women. These vows while necessarily public need not be perpetual, but may be of a temporary nature to be renewed at intervals determined by the constitutions of the particular religious institute.[10] There are within the Church groups whose members are not religious in the strict sense of the Code. These members belong to societies which profess a common life in imitation of religious. They are under the government of

---

[8] Vecchiotti, *Institutiones Canonicæ* (19. ed., 3 vols., Augustæ Taurinorum, 1886), I, 155 (hereafter cited *Institutiones*).

[9] Sebastianelli, *Prælectiones Iuris Canonici* (Vol. I, 2. ed., Romæ: F. Pustet, 1905), I, 6 (hereafter cited *Prælectiones*).

[10] Cf. canons 487; 488, 1° and 7°; and 1308, § 1.

a superior, and live according to approved constitutions, but do not take the customary three public vows.[11] These men and women are also bound to the clerical obligations through canon 679, § 1. Under such a heading come the Oratorians, Sulpicians, and Salesians, to mention but a few. The Third Orders Secular, although they live according to rules approved by the Holy See, are not members of the religious state properly so called, and are not affected by the provisions of these canons.[12] Schaefer,[13] without offering any specific example, makes mention of societies whose members would not be held to the obligations, since they are not religious in the proper sense of the Code. One of the constituent elements of the religious state is a stability which *de facto* is lacking in these societies, for their own vows are so temporary that they could not be renewed for life.

The members of military orders are not religious either, in the canonical sense of that word, since they take only the single vow of conjugal chastity. An exception to this is found in the Order of Saint John of Jerusalem (Knights of Malta) and the Teutonic Order whose members take the three vows. By reason of an indult given by Pope Leo XIII (1878-1903), the members of the first order take only simple vows.[14]

Under the provisions of the pre-Code law, when there was question of a *materia favorabilis* or of a *materia odiosa vel pœnalis*, the word cleric took on a different significance. In those matters which favored the cleric the word was taken in a general or broad sense to include all persons who were publicly pledged to God. It included not only those who had received first tonsure, but also monks, regulars, and nuns, and also the novices of any religious institute

---

[11] Canon 673, § 1 and 2.

[12] Canon 702, § 1.

[13] (Also Schäfer) *De Religiosis ad Normam Codicis Iuris Canonici* (3. ed., Romæ: Typis Polyglottis Vaticanis, 1940), p. 61-62 (hereafter cited *De Religiosis*).

[14] Schaefer, *De Religiosis*, p. 63.

which was approved by the Church.[15] This interpretation was in keeping with a very ancient legal principle later incorporated in the *Regulæ Juris* of Pope Boniface VIII (1294-1303): *"Odia restringi et favores convenit ampliari."*[16]

When it came to penal matters and the application of penal sanctions to clerics, the word was taken in a stricter and less proper sense. It was then used to designate only the lower secular clergy and did not include cardinals, bishops, canons, or anyone constituted in ecclesiastical dignity; nor did it include regulars unless it was otherwise expressed or was clear from the nature of the subject matter. Bishops were not subject to the sentence of suspension or of interdict unless expressly so mentioned.[17] Wernz (1842-1914), who wrote immediately before the promulgation of the Code, and an author frequently consulted by the Commission preparing the Code, held that in the rubric of the title, *de vita et honestate clericorum,* the word cleric was to be taken in the wide sense, so that it extended to all clerics in major and minor orders, to regulars of both sexes, and to tertiaries living in common.[18]

The present law does not admit of this double distinction of clerics, *sensu strictiori et sensu lato.* It communicates to religious and novices the common clerical privileges;[19] from the application of the *latæ sententiæ* penalties of suspension and interdict, it exempts cardinals and

[15] Reiffenstuel, lib. III, tit. 1, n. 11; Vermeersch-Creusen, *Epitome Iuris Canonici* (6. ed., 3 vols., Mechlinæ-Romæ: H. Dessain, 1937-1946), I, n. 232 (hereafter cited *Epitome*).

[16] Reg. 15, R. J., in VI°.

[17] Reiffenstuel, lib. II, tit. 1, nn. 14, 16, 17, 19; Ferraris, *Prompta Bibliotheca Canonica, Juridica, Moralis, Theologica, necnon Ascetica, Polemica, Rubristica, Historica* (8 vols., Romæ, 1885-1892, Vol. IX, ed. Ian. Bucceroni, Romæ, 1899), sub v. *clericus*, art. 1, nn. 19-22 (hereafter cited *Bibliotheca*).

[18] *Ius Decretalium* (2. ed., 6 vols., Romæ et Prati, 1906-1913), II, n. 174.

[19] Canon 614.

bishops alone, unless the law expressly denies this exemption.[20]

All religious as well as the members of such societies as live in imitation of religious are included under the term "cleric," and are bound by those canons which determine the clerical obligations.[21] The general rule is that, unless the subject matter or the context indicates otherwise, all those and only those who have received at least first tonsure are embraced by the word "cleric." It is to be noted that before the reception of first tonsure, seminarians, postulants, and novices are not subject to these obligations. The conduct of such while they are on vacation or on leaves of absence is a problem whose solution rests with their immediate superiors in the seminary or the religious house.[22]

Article 2. The Possible Rôle of Custom

Any consideration of the demands which law makes upon those whom it binds, any treatment of the obligations that arise from membership in a self-contained society, must be so arranged as to provide opportunity for a view of the relation which exists between custom or unwritten law and written positive law. Within the pages to follow a critical consideration is to be given to a number of negative clerical obligations, which obligations under certain clearly defined conditions rule out for all those who are included in the term "cleric" all unbecoming trades and professions, and, in addition, certain types of games and recreation, both in public and in private. The law as it stands forbids these things; the question may be raised, however, is there anything which might militate against

---

[20] Canon 2227, § 2; Berutti, *De Personis*, p. 74.

[21] Coronata, *Institutiones Iuris Canonici ad Usum Utriusque Cleri et Scholarum* (2. ed., 5 vols., Romæ: Marietti, 1939-1947), I, 216 (hereafter cited *Institutiones*).

[22] Brunini, *The Clerical Obligations of Canons 139 and 142*, The Catholic University of America Canon Law Studies, n. 103 (Washington, D. C.: The Catholic University of America, 1937), p. 3.

the severity and solidarity of the law to render its binding force less permanent or less extensive?

To answer such a question one must treat of the subject of custom, for it is custom, the consistency of action on the part of a community coupled with the consent of the lawgiver, which can influence the written law. One must look then to its nature, its qualities, and its divisions, and to whatever other of its essential notes that need to be considered. Since it is not unreasonable to believe that clerics for the most part little intend to introduce in these matters a custom that is either in accordance with or beyond the law, the main light will be focused on custom against the law *(consuetudo contra legem);* it is the formal negative object of this last division of custom to legalize the non-observance of existing law.

A. Definition of Custom Prior to the Code

In that vast wealth of legislation which is known today as pre-Code law, the product of long centuries of judicial and legislative activity, one looks in vain for a definition of custom which would match the precision of the definition set forth by present day authors. This fact, however, should cause no apprehension, for like the law on other important points the law on custom has admitted of gradual development. The early Church recognized custom as an agency of law; in fact, the obligation produced by custom was so strong that it was felt that, just as prevaricators of divine law were punished, so ought also to be punished those who disregarded or looked down upon the customs of the Church. This severity may be explained by the fact that in those times no clearly defined distinction was made between custom and tradition.[23]

Gratian (+ca. 1157) was the first to give clear recognition to the threefold division of custom: *iuxta, præter et*

[23] Guilfoyle, *Custom,* The Catholic University of America Canon Law Studies, n. 105 (Washington, D. C.: The Catholic University of America, 1937), pp. 4, 6.

contra legem. He mentioned also that custom was not the work of a single individual, but came rather from an ecclesiastical community; no specific examples were given, however, wherein one might come to a conclusion as to what the term "community" might include.[24] Attention was also given by Gratian to the reasonableness of custom and to the necessity of a certain time element constituting it.[25]

The Church's first official teaching on custom was contained in the first authentic compilation of the laws of the Church, the Decretals of Pope Gregory IX (1227-1241), promulgated in 1234. The use of the word *consuetudo* was canonized. The definition contained in the Decretals was that of Gratian, who in turn had borrowed the concept quite literally from Justinian (527-565) and Saint Isidore (+636): "*consuetudo autem est ius moribus constitutum.*"[26]

Although there was a great interval of time between the reign of Pope Gregory and the period of the better known pre-Code authors and commentators, such as Reiffenstuel (1642-1703) and Schmalzgrueber (1663-1735), during it no substantial change was made in the definition.[27] The general topic of custom, however, was given considerable treatment, especially by Suarez (1548-1617), who wrote at great length on this point. His treatment greatly influenced the writers not only of his own time but also of the centuries that followed.[28]

The real development and full discussion were in the fields of the efficient cause of custom, the reasonableness of

---

[24] C. 8, D. C; cc. 3, 11, D. XI; c. 12, D. XII.

[25] C. 1, D. XI; c. 3, D. VIII; c. 7, D. XII.

[26] Cc. 1, 2, 8, 11, X, *de consuetudine*, I, 4; c. 5, D. I; St. Isidorus, *Libri XX Etymologiarum*, II, c. 10 — Migne, *Patralogia Cursus Completus, Series Latina* (221 vols., Parisiis, 1844-1864), LXXXII, 131 (hereafter cited *MPL*).

[27] Schmalzgrueber, *Ius Ecclesiasticum Universum* (5 vols. in 12, Romæ, 1843-1845), lib. I, tit. 4, n. 1 (hereafter cited Schmalzgrueber); Reiffenstuel, lib. I, tit. 4, n. 6; Wernz, *Ius Decretalium*, I, n. 187.

[28] *De Legibus seu Legislatore Deo*, Lib. VII, cc. 1-7 (hereafter cited *De Legibus*) — *Opera Omnia* (28 vols., ed. Vivès, Parisiis, 1856-1861), Vols. V-VI, *De Legibus seu Legislatore Deo.*

custom, and the time required for prescription. Cicognani,[29] in speaking of the definition of custom, states that the definition as given prior to the Code can be retained. He notes that its nature would be more precisely and clearly determined according to the meaning of canon 25 if some indication were given of the necessity of the consent of the competent authority.

B. Definition of Custom in the Code

It is to be admitted that the present law does not itself define custom, although the question of custom is given a separate title in the First Book.[30] From the essential elements which are all clearly stated in this title, commentators were able to fashion a definition which contained all the necessary ingredients. Van Hove (1872-1947) defined custom as *"ius legale populi moribus accedente legislatoris consensu introductum."*[31] This definition, which seems to have been incorporated verbatim from the work of an earlier author,[32] appeals also to Michiels, who adds to it a phrase indicating the strictly legal mark of custom, namely that of unwritten law; to *ius legale* he adds the qualifying *"non scriptum."*[33] In this form the definition has been accepted by authors who wrote after the appearance of the Code. Many of these writers do not formally define custom, but rather discuss the individual canons as they appear in the Code.

---

[29] *Canon Law* (authorized English version by O'Hara and Brennan, 2. ed., Philadelphia: Dolphin Press, 1935), p. 644.

[30] Lib. I, *Normæ Generales*, tit. 2, canons 25-30.

[31] *Commentarium Lovaniense in Codicem Iuris Canonici,* Vol. I, tom. 3, *De Consuetudine, De Temporis Supputatione* (Mechliniæ-Romæ: Dessain, 1933), n. 2 (hereafter cited *De Consuetudine*).

[32] Bauduin, *De Consuetudine in Iure Canonico* (diss. canonica, Lovanii: Universitatis Catholicæ Typographi, 1888), n. 5 (hereafter cited *De Consuetudine*).

[33] *Normæ Generales Iuris Canonici* (2. ed., 2 vols., Lublin: Universitas Catholica, 1929), II, 6 (hereafter cited *Normæ Generales*).

C. Terms Not to Be Confused with Custom

By way of negation it is also possible to come to a clearer understanding of what is meant by custom in its legal canonical sense. Authors warn against confusing *usus* and *mores* with custom, for these terms indicate a natural inclination or a habitual manner of acting, and do not necessarily introduce an obligatory norm of action. Examples of this are found in canons 98, § 5 (on Communion in another rite), and in 136, § 1 (on the clerical tonsure).[34]

Custom is not to be confused with *tradition,* which has a wider connotation than does custom in that it may and often does include written law. This misconception, however, is rarely found after the time of the Decretals of Pope Gregory IX.[35] For a not inconsiderable period the terms *prescription* and custom were confused, this being due in great measure to a somewhat general misunderstanding and lack of agreement on what was expressed by the phrase, *consuetudo legitime præscripta.*[36]

Development through the centuries which gave sharp outline to the respective rôles of each of these concepts resulted in a clearer presentation of each, from which it was apparent that they had nothing in common save the consideration of use and time. For in custom, unlike prescription, good faith is not required, nor is a title necessary. In custom the consent of the legislator must be obtained; not so in prescription. In order to introduce a custom there must be a community capable of receiving a law; an individual could profit through the agency of prescription.[37]

---

[34] Guilfoyle, *Custom,* p. 79; *contra,* Crnica, *Commentarium Theoretico-Practicum Iuris Canonici* (2 vols., Sibenik: Typis Typographiæ „Kačić," 1940), Vol. I *(Normæ Generales et de Personis),* p. 48 (hereafter cited *Commentarium*).

[35] Reiffenstuel, Lib. I, tit. 4, n. 23; Sipos, *Enchiridion,* p. 57; Cappello, *Summa Iuris Canonici in Usum Scholarum* (3 vols., Vol. I, 3. ed., Romæ: Apud Aedes Universitatis Gregorianæ, 1938), I, n. 108 (hereafter cited *Summa*).

[36] C. 11, X. *de consuetudine,* I, 4.

[37] Canons 25-26; Guilfoyle, *op. cit.,* p. 80; Cocchi, *Commentarium in Codicem Iuris* (8 vols. in 5, Taurinorum Augustæ: Marietti, 1932-1942), lib. I (5. ed., 1938), n. 133 (hereafter cited *Commentarium*).

D. Canon 5 and Custom Against the Law

In this dissertation, and then only as a secondary consideration, attention is to be given to the pressure which *consuetudo contra legem* might exert when a group capable of receiving a law would act against the specific provisions of the general law as embodied in canons 138 and 140. The relation of custom to particular law, i.e., plenary, provincial, or diocesan, will be treated only in those rare cases in which such references will be in order to furnish pointed exemplification for special points under consideration. The teaching on the validity of custom against the law will become evident from the observations to be made shortly upon: (1) the consent of the competent authority; (2) the community legally capable of introducing a custom; (3) the reasonableness required in a custom against the law; and (4) the time required for the introduction of such a custom.

Canon 5 brought order out of the confusion and legal disorder which prevailed in regard to the customs in existence at the time of the advent of the Code. It accomplished this by fixing the status of existing custom in relation to the Code; also by letting the way open for the establishment of new customs according to the principles which it invoked. One section of this important transitional canon rules that those customs which are against the general law, but which are neither centenary nor immemorial, are to be held as suppressed. In the present consideration it makes little difference that the Code should qualify this suppression when it adds *"nisi expresse Codex aliud caveat,"* for in the canons on the negative clerical obligations one searches in vain for any of the phrases commonly employed in the Code to give continued life to a custom which would otherwise, without this phrase, be held as suppressed.

The first part of the canon speaks of those customs, universal or particular, which have been expressly reprobated *"tamquam iuris corruptelæ."* Nowhere among the canons that deal with clerical obligations does one find mention of the reprobation of any such customs. The phrase "expressly reprobated" is interpreted to mean that customs so referred to are never again to be resurrected, for they stand as forever unreasonable.[38] Michiels opposes this view, as he seems to hold that this reprobation does not outlaw the custom forever, but that it constitutes a prohibitory clause. What is now a *"corruptela iuris"* may cease under different circumstances to be a perversion and distortion of law, and may thereupon be introduced validly.[39] This view certainly appears as tenable, for although the Code expressly states that such customs are not to be allowed to revive in the future, this prohibition is directed against these customs in their nature of corruptions and distortions of the law; if the proper changes are made, they may be reintroduced. The elimination of the objectionable element has removed them from the category upon which the condemnation rests.

Canon 5 further speaks of customs which are not expressly reprobated. Among these are the customs which had been in existence for one hundred years at the time the law of the Code came into force, as well as those customs which are called immemorial. This latter term refers not to customs whose beginning is unknown, but indicates those customs contrary to which nothing has been done, said, or heard within the memory of those yet alive. Such a custom may actually be either of a longer or of a shorter duration than one hundred years. In the Code these two types of custom, centenary and immemorial, are generally treated as equal.[40] The ordinary in his prudent judgment may allow these customs to remain, as long as there is ground for a reasonable fear that a greater train of evils would follow from their abolition. It is to be remembered that the ordinary does not endow these customs with legal status. He merely tolerates them.[41]

[38] Coronata, *Institutiones,* I, 8; Beste, *Introductio,* p. 5; Cocchi, *Commentarium,* lib. I, n. 89; Wernz-Vidal, *Ius Canonicum,* I, n. 99.

[39] Michiels, *Normæ Generales,* I, 78.

[40] Guilfoyle, *op. cit.,* p. 75.

[41] In the light of the definition furnished in canon 198, § 1, the authorization for tolerating such customs is also enjoyed by major superiors of clerical exempt religious.

E. Consent of the Competent Authority

There can be no doubt that some form of consent is required of the ecclesiastical superior in order that the transition may be effected from a *consuetudo facti* to the *ius consuetudinarium.* Canon 25 demands this consent.[42] This approval is given to a constant practice introduced originally by a group which under law stands recognized as capable of such action. The manner of consent is not mentioned in the law, so recourse must be had to the teaching of the canonists. Here one finds that it is generally held that this consent must be manifested externally, that presumed or interpretative consent definitively is insufficient, as would also be a merely internal consent, whose real existence fails to find the proper sign for presentation in the external forum.[43]

This consent must be real and external. Required consent may be positively or specifically given by the superior. It may also be given negatively. Such is the case when disapproval is withheld, even though the superior is free to indicate his disapproval. *"Qui tacet, consentire videtur."*[44] Prior to the Code there was great disagreement as to whether or not a type of consent known as legal consent was in itself sufficient to give legal essence to custom. It is now commonly held that it does suffice.

F. The Competent Authority

When speaking of the competent authority one must keep in mind the distinction instituted between special and legal consent. If it is a question of legal consent, the rules to be followed are those found in canons 27 and 28, where mention is made of the legal elements of reasonableness and prescription. In practice, as regards special consent, only

---

[42] "Consuetudo in Ecclesia vim legis a consensu competentis Superioris ecclesiastici unice obtinet."

[43] Michiels, *Normæ Generales*, II, 31.

[44] Reg. 43, R. J., in VI°.

the Roman Pontiff can give such consent to a particular or general custom against a universal law of the Church or against a particular law which he himself has made for a certain territory. An example of a particular law of this kind is had in the special ruling given at the personal order of Pope Benedict XV (1914-1922) whereby all clerics (religious as well) were forbidden to attend moving picture shows in the city of Rome. The penalty was suspension *a divinis*.[45]

In the matter of particular law, only the author of that law can give consent to the custom. A bishop, for example, can approve custom against synodal enactments; he cannot approve custom against provincial law. Since he lacks legislative power there, no metropolitan can approve a custom which flourishes in the diocese of any of his suffragans.[46]

G. The Community Capable of Introducing a Custom

In the Middle Ages and approximately the following four centuries, it was the accepted teaching that only a community which had the capacity to make laws for itself could introduce a custom. The *causa efficiens* of custom was the consent of the community. This theory prevailed through the period of the decretalists, in fact, up to the beginning of the sixteenth century. The eventual change in this view came about primarily through the teaching of Saint Thomas (1225-1274), who held that if a people (community) did not possess the power to make laws, then custom took its force from the approbation of the lawgiver.[47] Suarez insisted that the legal heart of cus-

---

[45] Vicariatus Urbis, *decr.*, 25 maii 1918 — *Acta Apostolicæ Sedis* (Romæ, 1909-), X (1918), 300 (hereafter cited *AAS*).

[46] Van Hove, *De Consuetudine*, n. 69.

[47] St. Thomas, *Summa Theologica* (6 vols., Taurini: ex Officina Libraria Marietti, 1937), I, II, q. 97, art. 3, *ad tertium;* cf. also Kinane, "The community capable of introducing a custom" — *The Irish Ecclesiastical Record*, V. series, XXXVII (1931), 521-524 (hereafter cited *IER*); Reiffenstuel (lib. I, tit. 4, nn. 11, 110-115) quoted but falsely applied this principle taken from St. Thomas.

tom was the consent of the ruler. Only a perfect community could introduce a custom, and a perfect community was one which was at least capable of receiving a law.[48] All agree that the possession of legislative power was not required in the community which introduced the custom; this represents the constant pre-Code view.[49] It is also the teaching of the present law.

The question which remains for solution is one which takes the reader back to approved authors, for the Code says nothing on this point. The question is: what communities are capable of receiving a law? Lack of unanimity among present day authors mirrors the difficulties encountered by pre-Code writers in their efforts to find a satisfactory solution for this problem. In looking for a common denominator some have stressed the idea of a corporate community (autonomy),[50] some attached prime importance to the idea of stability and perpetuity,[51] while for others the necessary element was the factor of a moral union.[52] Van Hove in his attempt at a solution for the problem claims that community to be capable of receiving a law, and therefore capable also of introducing a custom, over which presides a superior who exercises a public office, that is, an office ordained to the common good.[53]

From weighing the mass of material substantiating the various schools of thought on this point, one may offer the

---

[48] *De Legibus,* lib. VII, c. 9, nn. 9-11; for further explanation of the term *perfect* confer Van Hove, *De Consuetudine,* n. 76.

[49] Bauduin, *De Consuetudine,* n. 80; Wernz, *Ius Decretalium,* I, n. 190; Michiels, *Normæ Generales,* II, 42.

[50] Augustine, *A Commentary on the New Code of Canon Law* (2. ed., 8 vols., St. Louis: B. Herder, 1918-1924), I, 108 (hereafter cited *Commentary*).

[51] Toso, *Ad Codicem Iuris Canonici Commentaria Minora* (5 vols., Romæ: Marietti, 1918-1927), Vol. I (2. ed., 1921), p. 84 (hereafter cited *Commentaria Minora*).

[52] Maroto, *Institutiones Iuris Canonici ad Normam Novi Codicis* (3. ed., 2 vols., Romæ, 1921), I, n. 252 (hereafter cited *Institutiones*); Cappello, *Summa,* I, n. 112.

[53] *De Consuetudine,* n. 81.

following as possible conclusions in which the majority would be in common agreement.

1. A private person or a family cannot introduce a custom.
2. The universal church, a province, a diocese, and a city may certainly introduce a custom. The Code seems to recognize this power in cathedral chapters and collegiate chapters.
3. The clergy being a community in the sense of a plurality of persons united by some common bond can introduce a custom against the general or particular law of the Church.[54]

The harmony of agreement is not as evident when authors treat of the possibility for a parish to introduce a custom. A parish probably may introduce a custom which formally may obtain the force of law.[55]

The material element of custom is found in the repetition of certain acts. When there is question of the formation of a custom that runs counter to the law, these acts need not be consciously performed as acts which stand in opposition to the law. Canon 27 does not set up any such demand. However, there must be a certain pattern of uniformity and likewise a frequency of acts, for uniformity shows the steady mind of the community, and frequency its determination.

The exact number of acts required cannot easily be determined by means of any fixed and uniform rule. In the earlier law various opinions held that number to be as low as two or four. These opinions did not enjoy any longevity. Michiels, quoting a decision of the Sacred Con-

---

[54] Cicognani, *Canon Law*, p. 646.

[55] Vermeersch-Creusen, *Epitome*, I, n. 138; Michiels, *Normæ Generales*, I, p. 140-142; Bouscaren-Ellis, *Canon Law, a Text and Commentary* (Milwaukee: Bruce Publishing Company, 1946), p. 39 (hereafter cited *Commentary*). The opposite view is held by other well-known authors, among them Coronata (*Institutiones*, I, n. 39) and Cappello (*Summa*, I, n. 112).

gregation of the Council, indicates that circumstances and the nature of the acts, i.e., if they are sufficient to show the intention of the people, must determine the necessary number.[56]

These acts must also be continuous, that is, uninterrupted by contrary acts. The expressed displeasure of the authority which is competent to furnish the requisite special or legal consent likewise interrupts the necessary continuity, and thus necessitates a new starting point for the needed course of legitimate prescription. The acts are also required to be public, for custom essentially constitutes a norm for the juridical and social life of the community, and as such must be perceptible to all.

H. The Reasonableness of Custom Against the Law

Regarding the reasonableness which must invest any custom, the Code law states unequivocally that any custom against divine law, natural or positive, is not reasonable, and as such, according to canon 27, § 2, cannot prejudice the existing law.[57] Any custom reprobated by the law itself falls, by that very fact, into the category of unreasonable customs. In addition to these concepts, in pre-Code law the traditional teachings of the canonists maintained that any custom was unreasonable if it upset ecclesiastical discipline, if it opposed the liberty of the Church, if it proved an occasion of sin, or if it was dangerous in any way to the common good.[58]

These are the factors which negatively indicate the character of reasonableness in custom. Over and above that, custom must, in the judgment of some, contribute

---

[56] *Normæ Generales*, II, 55-57.

[57] "Consuetudo quæ in iure expresse reprobatur, non est rationabilis."

[58] Cc. 3, 5, 7, X, *de consuetudine*, I, 4; c. 49, *de sententia excommunicationis*, V, 39; Hostiensis (Henricus de Segusio), *Commentaria in Quinque Decretalium Libros* (5 vols. in 3, Venetiis, 1581), lib. I, tit. 4, n. 3 (hereafter cited *Commentaria*); Reiffenstuel, lib. I, tit. 4, nn. 34-37; Cicognani, *Canon Law*, p. 650.

either positively or generally to the common good. As on a number of other points in connection with custom, the Code is silent as to this requisite. Apparently it did not wish to settle the controversy. In custom against the law, which would be the type possibly introduced by the clergy against the rulings contained in canons 138 and 140, a general utility seems to suffice. The fact of opposition, whether or not it be consciously such on the part of the community, is a reasonable indication that the community explicitly or implicitly considers the law burdensome. It deems that the common good will be helped by means of a release from that law. In these canons, however, it seems difficult to visualize how the common good would be benefited by any custom which would supplant the law which they contain.

Cicognani writes that a particular custom against a universal law of the Church can be admitted as reasonable only with difficulty. This might be deduced from canon 5, for this canon did not favor customs then in existence before the Code, and may be taken as proof that the Church does not now favor customs of this type.[59]

I. Prescription in Custom Against the Law

The basis for this requirement is found in the decretal *Quum tanto* of Pope Gregory IX.[60] Although this decretal referred to general laws, its application was extended to custom against particular law as well, both by the pre-Code and the post-Code authors. The law now demands that any custom *contra vel præter legem* run for forty continuous and complete years. This time is to be determined according to the rules outlined in canons 34, § 2, and 35. Against an ecclesiastical law which contains a clause prohibiting future custom, the time requisite to establish custom is extended to one hundred years. Prior to the Code the opinions exhibited great variety; some held that no definite lapse of

---

[59] Cicognani, *Canon Law*, p. 654; Van Hove, *De Consuetudine*, n. 97.
[60] C. 11, X, *de consuetudine*, I, 4.

time was really necessary, but that in each case the decision was left to the judge; others held that a lapse of forty years was required, this being the common view until the end of the seventeenth century. A third group was of the contention that ten years would be sufficient for custom to prevail against the law; in this group were Reiffenstuel (1642-1703), Pope Benedict XIV (1675-1758), and Bauduin (1860-1942), to mention but a few. The controversy was settled by the Code.[61]

The demands of canon 27 may still be met even if in some given instance the full course of prescription has not run. A special consent may be given. When the legislator gives this consent the acts of the community stand approved though actually the complete course of time prescribed by law has not run. There must be some duration of time before this special consent may reasonably be given. The duration must be sufficiently long to produce that multiplicity of acts which is demanded for the material element of custom.

---

[61] These opinions are treated at some length in Guilfoyle *(Custom)*, p. 62.

CHAPTER II

THE PROHIBITION AGAINST THE EXERCISE OF UNBECOMING TRADES AND PROFESSIONS

PART I. HISTORICAL CONSPECTUS

What appears to have been the first evidence of canonical legislation in the matter of clerics and their exercise of unbecoming professions is found in the 4th and 5th canons of the Council of Arles (314).[1] While directed primarily against the laity, *a fortiori*, it bound clerics also. Lack of explicit inclusion may be explained by the fact that at that time there may have been few clerics actually engaged as charioteers or as members of theatrical groups *(theatrici)*. The same century witnessed legislation on this same point in the East. At the Council of Laodicea (343-381)[2] clerics were forbidden to practice the art of magic, to be enchanters, or to be astrologers *(mathematicos vel astrologos)*. They were likewise forbidden to make or carry those superstitious charms and symbols which were connected with the practice of these arts.[3] The Council of Paris (829) stated the general mind of the Church when it stressed the

---

[1] Canon 4: "De *agitatoribus* qui fideles sunt, placuit abstineri eos a communione." — Mansi, *Sacrorum Conciliorum et Amplisissima Collectio* (53 vols. in 60, Parisiis, 1901-1927), II, 471 (hereafter cited Mansi). The word *agitator* here means charioteer. — *Thesaurus Linguæ Latinæ* (8 vols., incomplete [to M partially], Lipsiæ, 1900-   ), I, col. 1329; Forcellini-Corradini-Perin, *Lexicon Totius Latinitatis* (4 tomes in 15, Padua, 1864-1887), Tom. I, pars 1, p. 146 (hereafter cited *Lexicon*).

Canon 5: "De theatricis et ipsos placuit quamdiu agunt a communione separari." — Mansi, II, 471.

[2] Although this date is commonly accepted by modern authors, Fulton (*Index Canonum* [4. ed., New York, 1883], p. 63) recorded a few of the variant dates as proposed by earlier authors.

[3] Canon 36 — Mansi, II, 569; Bruns (*Canones Apostolorum et Conciliorum Seculorum* IV-VII [2 vols., Berolini, 1839]), I, 77 (hereafter cited Bruns), gives the Greek text of the canon, adding that in the versions of Dionysius and Isidore there is no reference to astrologers *(mathematicos vel astrologos)*.

evils inherent in such practices.[4] One finds no law on these matters in the West; it seems that the Eastern mind was by temperament given more to a display of interest in the things of the so-called spirit world than was the Western mind.[5] The penalty for the violation of the law is of interest: *"ejici ab Ecclesia."* There is reason to feel that this penalty was excommunication. Though this expression was used only rarely in the early Church, the same terminology was used much later by the Holy Office in speaking of the excommunication of a certain group.[6]

The sixty-six bishops of Spain and Gaul who gathered at Toledo (633) for the IV Provincial Council of Toledo ordered that no bishop, priest, or deacon was to consult a magician, diviner, or soothsayer. The penalty, the most severe thus far, called for the offender to be stripped of whatever dignity or honor he enjoyed; further, it ordered that he be sent to a monastery for penance. If this was the canonical fate of the clerics who consulted magicians, one may well imagine that greater prohibitions outlawed the practice of these arts by clerics.[7]

In the year 698 Emperor Justinian II (685-711) presided over the famous Trullan Synod, often referred to as the *Concilium Quinisextum*. The Synod took its name from the fact that it was meant as a continuation of the V and VI Ecumenical Councils. Those councils had formulated dogmatic decrees only; they had not published any disci-

---

[4] Canon 9: "Extant et alia pernitiosissima mala quæ ex ritu gentilium remansisse non dubium est, ut sunt magi...incantatores...quos divina lex inretractabiliter puniri iubet" — *Monumenta Germaniæ Historica* (188 vols., incomplete, Hannoveræ, 1826-), *Leges in 4°*, Sectio III, *Concilia Aevi Karolini*, Tom. II, pars II (recensuit A. Werminghoff, 1908), p. 669 (hereafter cited *MGH*).

[5] For an interesting chapter on the subjects of Astrology and Magic, one may consult Cumont, *The Oriental Religions in Roman Paganism* (Chicago, 1911), pp. 163-195.

[6] *AAS*, XIV (1922), 593.

[7] "...ab honore dignitatis suæ depositus, monasterii pœnam excipiat ibique perpetuæ pœnitentiæ deditus scelus admissum sacrilegii luat." — Bruns, II, 232. A somewhat similar and earlier law is found in the I Council of Orleans (511), c. 30 — Bruns, II, 166.

plinary canons. Among the disciplinary canons which the Trullan Synod then enacted was one which forbade clerics to own taverns or inns.[8]

In the period from Gratian's monumental *Concordia Discordantium Canonum* (ca. 1140)[9] to the time of the Council of Trent (1545-1563), the legislation as found in the canonical collections and commented upon by the decretists and decretalists was almost without exception a repetition of the papal and conciliar rulings. This is true not only of the subject of forbidden professions and occupations, but of the other negative obligations as well. The major decretists did no more than repeat the position of Gratian in their various summations. This was true of the *Summa* of Roland Bandinelli, a disciple of Gratian, and a distinguished canonist who later became Pope Alexander III (1159-1181).[10] It was particularly true of the work of Paucapalea, whose work preceded that of Bandinelli,[11] and of Stephen of Tournai (+1203), who wrote after 1160.[12] There is found here little which is not also found in the *Summa Decretorum* of Rufinus (ca. 1190).[13] Mention could scarcely be made of the *Decretum* of Gratian without referring to the *Glossa Ordinaria,* the work of Ioannes Teutonicus (+1245-1246). This work was completed over a two-year period, from 1215 to 1217, and was put into its

---

[8] Canon 9: "Nulli licere clerico *cauponariam habere tabernam.* Si enim in cauponam ingredi non est permissum, quanto magis aliis in ea ministrare et quæ non licet ipsi tractare" — Mansi, XI, 946; Bruns, II, 40. While this Synod specifically increased the depositary of Greek canon law, the Latin Church did not accept the whole body of its legislation, although individual canons were later accepted by some of the Popes. — Hefele-Leclercq, *Histoire des Conciles* (10 vols. in 19, Paris, Libraire Letouzey et Ané, 1907-1938), III, 561-581 (hereafter cited Hefele-Leclercq).

[9] Cf. Kuttner, "The Father of the Science of Canon Law" — *The Jurist,* I (1941), 2-19.

[10] Thaner, *Die Summa Magistri Rolandi, nachmals Papstes Alexander III* (Innsbruck, 1874), p. 132.

[11] Schulte, *Die Summa des Paucapalea* (Giessen, 1890).

[12] Schulte, *Die Summa des Stephanus Tornacensis* (Giessen, 1891).

[13] Singer, *Die Summa Decretorum des Magister Rufinus* (Paderborn, 1902) (hereafter cited *Die Summa*).

final and present form by Bartholomew of Brescia (+1258) about 1245, with but a few minor changes.

The single decree which Gratian had on this topic was taken from the 90th canon of the Trullan Synod.[14] The wording varies slightly, but in no manner was there any substantial change in the law: the cleric could not own a tavern, nor could he engage in such menial tasks as serving the customers. To whom it was not allowed to do a lesser thing, to him likewise it was not allowed to do a greater thing. The word *ergastium* was employed for the more commonly used term *taberna.*[15] In commenting on this law, Saint Raymond of Pennafort (+ 1275), compiler of the Decretals of Pope Gregory IX, pointed to the lamentable fact that many evil and immoral practices had taken place in these taverns.[16]

The Decretals of Pope Gregory IX (1227-1241) contained a letter of Pope Honorius III (1216-1227), his immediate predecessor, a letter under date of May 12, 1218.[17] This letter was addressed to a certain Everard, Bishop of Amiens. The Holy Father had been informed that a few clerics of the latter's diocese had been acting as tavern-keepers; others had been occupied in purely secular affairs. Yet these clerics wished to avail themselves of their clerical privileges. It may be noted that Gonzalez-Tellez (+ after 1673) identified these *tabernarii* as those who conducted the shops (taverns) in which wine was sold.[18] The Holy Father ordered that if these clerics (among them the shop-

---

[14] C. 3, D. XLIV — *Decretum Gratiani Emendatum et Notationibus Illustratum una cum Glossis* (2 vols., Romæ, 1582).

[15] Found also in the Friedberg edition — *Corpus Iuris Canonici* (ed. Lipsiensis 2. post Aemilii Richteri curas...instruxit Aemilius Friedberg, 2 vols., Lipsiæ: Tauchnitz, 1879-1881), I, 157 (hereafter cited Friedberg).

[16] *Summa* (nova ed., Veronæ, 1744), lib. III, tit. 4, 3.

[17] C. 16, X, *de vita et honestate clericorum,* III, 1; A. Potthast, *Regesta Pontificum Romanorum inde ab anno post Christum natum MCXCVIII ad annum MCCCIV* (2 vols. in 1, Berolini, 1874-1875), n. 5784 (hereafter cited Potthast).

[18] *Commentaria Perpetua in Singulos Textus Quinque Librorum Decretalium Gregorii IX* (5 vols. in 4, Venetiis, 1699), lib. III, tit. I, cap. ult., n. 2 (hereafter cited *Commentaria*).

keepers), after having been warned, did not give up their secular offices and pursuits, they would lose their clerical privileges. With the third warning unheeded, the privileges were lost *ipso facto*. Such a punishment was always preceded by a canonical warning.[19] This triple warning was to come from the immediate superior of the offending cleric; it was to be specific and definite.[20]

Boniface VIII (1294-1303) also promulgated a law relative to those arts which were not in keeping with the dignity of the clerical state; in this law was found the attitude of the ecclesiastical authorities of the time toward the secular stage.[21] The canon forbade clerics to act as *ioculatores, goliardi,* and *bufones*. This represented the incorporation of new terminology. From the context and from a study of the literature on the secular stage of this period, it is evident that the word *ioculatores* here referred to the theatrical profession.[22]

---

[19] *Glossa Ordinaria,* ad c. 16, X, *de vita et honestate clericorum,* III, 1, sub v. *tertio.* According to the gloss of c. 21, C. XII, q. 2, sub v. *admonitio,* the penalty of excommunication was preceded by this triple warning; not that of deposition, however.

[20] Panormitanus (Nicholaus de Tudeschis), *Commentaria in Quinque Libros Decretalium* (5 vols. in 7, Venetiis, 1588), ad c. 16, X, *de vita et honestate clericorum,* III, 1, nn. 5 & 7 (hereafter cited *Commentaria*). Cf. also Boich, *In Quinque Decretalium Libros Commentaria* (ed. recognita, Venetiis, 1576), *Commentaria* ad c. 16, X, *de vita et honestate clericorum,* III, 1, nn. 1-3. For a further treatment of the *monitio trina* and the *excommunicatio* consult the glosses and the commentators on c. 45, X, *de vita et honestate clericorum,* V, 39.

[21] C. un., *de vita et honestate clericorum,* III, 1, in VI°.

[22] *Glossa ordinaria,* ad c. un., *de vita et honestate clericorum,* III, 1, in VI°, sub v. *ioculatores.* Nicoll (*Masks, Mimics, and Miracles; Studies in the Popular Theatre* [New York: Harcourt Brace and Co., 1931], 145-160) notes that the word is found as early as the fourth century, but only as an adjective; it took on substantive form in the ninth century. The word *ioculator* (minstrel) did have some association with the stage, though this aspect was better expressed by the word *histrio,* which by then had come to mean actor. The majority of the *ioculatores* (with whom the *mimi* and the *histriones* were commonly identified) were nothing but ballad-singers and makers of romance. Thomas de Chabham, a dean of Salisbury (ca. 1213), spoke of the *ioculatores* as a group forming a part of the *histriones,* and stated that it was their duty "to sing of the gestes of the princes and the lives of the saints."

The word *bufones* included comic actors and singers. Literally the word means toad or frog. The name was then applied to comic actors in that frequently their rôles demanded that they leap about the stage after the manner of these animals. The *goliardi* were really a class of the *ioculatores,* and were known as the wandering scholars; unfortunately, many of their number were unfrocked clerics.[23]

The *Constitutiones Clementinæ* of Pope Clement V (1305-1314), which appeared in 1314 (and which obtained the force of law under Pope John XXII [1316-1334] in 1317), furnish a final citation on this point.[24] The decretal in question aimed at establishing a punishment for those clerics who publicly and personally served as butchers and dealers in meats, as shop- and tavern-keepers. The forcefulness of the prohibition led the glossator to believe that any cleric who disobeyed in this matter made himself guilty of a mortal sin.[25] The decretal included in its scope the exempt clerics, provided that they had committed the delict in a non-exempt place, for in that event they were subjected to the jurisdiction of the *diœcesani.* These were a group of prelates who enjoyed under their local ordinaries a limited jurisdiction to be exercised in certain clearly defined matters. Exempt religious were not included under this law if the delict had been committed in an exempt place. It was necessary for the incurring of the penalty that the clerics acted publicly and personally as tavern-keepers, butchers, etc.

---

[23] Article, "Goliardi"—*Enciclopedia Italiana di Scienze, Lettere ed Arti* (35 vols., Milano: Istituto Giovanni Treccani, 1929-1937), XII, 495-496. Wernz mentioned that these new classes of actors produced abuses within the Church: "contra novos abusus medii ævi contra clericos bufones et goliardos...novæ quoque leges promulgatæ sunt...."—*Ius Decretalium,* II, n. 213.

[24] C. 1, *de vita et honestate clericorum,* III, 1, in Clem.

[25] *Glossa ordinaria,* ad c. 1, *de vita et honestate clericorum,* III, 1, in Clem. sub. v. *commercius.*

There was also much conciliar legislation. Great influence derived from these councils for the future development of this law, although the major collections of law of the thirteenth century were most important. Hungarian bishops in their national synod at Gran (Esztergom) in 1114 passed a law forbidding clerics to act as tavern- or shopkeepers.[26] The Council of Prague (1346) spoke out against clerics acting as butchers.[27] The Provincial Council of Cologne, held two centuries later in 1536, commented that the early Church would most certainly be alarmed could it witness the sad condition existing at the time, namely, that of clerics acting as tavern- and inn-keepers. The Council declared that these clerics were bound to their places night and day as if they had no homes of their own. The lawmakers considered it a most sordid employment and one which was to be given up at once.[28]

The prohibition against clerics as active participants in the field of theatrics was found in two councils, which decreed the deprivation of the clerical garb as a penalty for these clerics, if, after having been duly warned, they still continued on in such a capacity.[29]

The Council of Trent (1545-1563) did not carry any direct reference to the particular problem regarding the exercise of unbecoming professions by clerics. This comparative dearth of matter is satisfactorily explained when one realizes that the Council did not change the extant law on clerical obligations, but rather furnished added importance, new force, and supplementary direction to the body of clerical law which had been handed down from the earliest centuries.

---

[26] C. 59 — Mansi, XXI, 112; Council of Constance (1300), c. 4 — Mansi, XXV, 30; Council of Prague (1346) — Mansi, XXVI, 83; Council of Benevento (1378), c. 50 — Mansi, XXVI, 645.

[27] Mansi, XXVI, 83.

[28] Mansi, XXXII, 1230.

[29] Council of Salzburg (1310), c. 3 — Mansi, XXV, 227; III Council of Ravenna (1314), c. 10 — Mansi, XXXV, 544.

Part II. Discipline of the Code

Article 1. Some Unbecoming Trades and Professions

As has been stated previously, canons 138 and 140 are inspired by the twofold purpose of safeguarding the decorum of the clerical state and of preserving its members from troublesome distractions which might impede their fruitful activity in the sacred ministry. Canon 138 proposes a partial listing, not an exhaustive enumeration, of the things which clerics are to avoid. The first section of the canon, which admits generally of a fivefold division, treats of unbecoming trades, professions, and occupations—all indicated by the phrase *"indecoræ artes."* In its proper sense the word *ars* is taken to denote a certain, determined way or method of action; in its wider and less proper sense it is applied indiscriminately to any occupation or employment of mind or body. It is precisely in this latter sense that it is used in this canon, with special reference to bodily employment.

These forbidden occupations, according to Augustine, comprise all professions or trades which in the common estimation of the people are exercised only by a low class of men, or which involve a lowering or degrading of the clerical state.[30] This wording is a bit harsh, for among the listed occupations forbidden to clerics and priests there are some which are now exercised by people of quite honorable status. What Augustine apparently meant was that at the time of their original condemnation these trades were engaged in by people of lesser repute. For determining just what these forbidden professions may be, one must look to the conditions of the times, to the general reaction of the faithful (and other upright people) of any given locality, and also to the decisions of the local ordinaries, whose right to act in these matters rests firmly upon their general right and duty to govern their dioceses in all spiritual and temporal matters.[31]

---

[30] *Commentary,* II, 87.

[31] Canon 335, § 1.

The authors who touch upon the subject of clerical obligations give only passing treatment to it; for the most part they only restate the law in the words of the Code. The lack of further specification in the Code itself shows that it was the mind of the Church to allow further treatment to be given to these points by diocesan statutes. Such statutes would have the advantage of being able to legislate for the particular exigencies of the dioceses, for one may assume that a profession forbidden in one area might in another area be entirely licit. The occupations which the authors do list as forbidden are those which had been ruled out as far back as the Decretalist period. This is clearly a law which did not change over a period of four centuries. The proscribed professions were those of saloon- or tavern-keepers, butchers, public executioners, clowns, and actors.[32]

The complexities of a highly mechanical and industrial civilization, the mushroom growth of large population centers, and the presence of other forces have increased proportionately all occupations, trades, and professions. Thus the number of possible forbidden professions has grown. In our own day there are forbidden to clerics many professions which were unknown in centuries past. Just which of these are not to be engaged in by clerics is to be determined by the application of the norms mentioned above. To the occupations expressly forbidden by *law* in his time, Reiffenstuel added several which were forbidden in consequence of existing *custom*, namely, those of laborer, carpenter, and tanner.[33] Present day attitudes in most communities would also rule out the permissibility for clerics

---

[32] Schmalzgrueber, lib. III, tit. 1, n. 45; Crnica, *Commentarium*, I, 155; Toso, *Commentaria Minora*, II, 102; Sipos, *Enchiridion*, p. 135; Beste, *Introductio*, p. 189; Augustine, *Commentary*, II, 87; St. Alphonsus, *Theologia Moralis* (ed. novissima, 4 vols., Romæ, 1905-1912), lib. IV, n. 189; Blat, *Commentarium Textus Codicis Iuris Canonici* (5 vols. in 7, Vol. II, pars 1, *De Personis* [2. ed., Romæ: ex Typographia Pontificia in Instituto Pii X, 1921]), II, pars 1, n. 77 (hereafter cited *Commentarium*).

[33] *Ius Canonicum*, lib. III, tit. 1, n. 127.

to practice these professions. Professions most certainly forbidden to clerics are those of prize fighting and wrestling. There seems to be no cause in virtue of which clerics would be justified in following these professions. Either of these sports, preferably boxing, can be indulged in rarely, and then only as a means of exercise or recreation.[34]

In smaller communities, in farming areas, or in sections removed from urban influences it would not be forbidden for priests to join with others in the constructing or repairing of church buildings. The priest could even undertake to do the work himself, if his priestly duties are not thereby slighted, and if no scandal could reasonably be taken from this activity. This same would hold true for repairs and improvements made about the grounds. In these matters due consideration is to be given to the presence or absence of skilled workers, to the financial condition of the parish, and to other pertinent factors. If a priest made minor repairs on the church property for the relaxation and enjoyment it afforded him, he would not be acting against the ruling of canon 138.

Sebastianelli mentioned that priests are forbidden to perform menial tasks in the homes of the laity.[35] This was undoubtedly what one of the Sacred Congregations had in mind when it forbade clerics to minister to lay people, especially if these were women. The word used was "*ministrare*" which had the meaning of "to serve" or "to wait upon."[36] In our own day there appears to be no immediate

---

[34] On the relation of these sports to the *privilegium fori* confer McGrath, *The Privilege of the Forum*, The Catholic University of America Canon Law Studies, n. 242 (Washington, D. C.: The Catholic University of America Press, 1946), pp. 59-60.

[35] *Prælectiones*, I, p. 32; Lombardi, *Iuris Canonici Privati Institutiones* (2. ed., 3 vols., Romæ, 1901), I, p. 339.

[36] S. C. Ep. et Reg., encycl., 16 mart. 1697 — *Codicis Iuris Canonici Fontes, cura Emi. Petri Card. Gasparri editi* (9 vols., Romæ [postea Civitate Vaticana]: Typis Polyglottis Vaticanis, 1923-1939; [Vols., VII-IX, ed. cura et studio Emi. Iustiniani Card. Serédi]), n. 1817 (hereafter cited *Fontes*).

cause for concern on this score, for clerics have neither the time nor the inclination for such service.

The Council of Trent[37] ruled that no secular cleric, although well qualified by reason of age, knowledge, and necessary moral endowments, was to be promoted to sacred orders unless there had been assigned to him an ecclesiastical benefice. This benefice was to be sufficient to maintain him. It should not be necessary for him to beg or to work at some unbecoming profession in order to obtain a livelihood. This point was reiterated shortly after the Council by Pope Saint Pius V (1566-1572), who thus showed that some clerics had continued to engage in such trades and professions. The cause for such action was not indicated.[38]

In our own country for the most part the clergy are well taken care of. In some poorer areas, however, the pastor's salary has not been increased to meet the higher cost of living. It would seem that in such instances the ordinary should investigate the matter carefully and make the proper adjustments so that, following the mind of the Council of Trent, there would be no possible reason why a priest should engage in these unbecoming professions.

The Sacred Congregation of Bishops and Regulars in a letter to the Apostolic Vicar of Capaccio ordered that on the next diocesan visitation the Vicar was to make it clear to his clergy that in the future no one in sacred orders was to act as a carrier of the public mail *(munus publicorum tabellariorum)* or to serve as public messenger *(munus cursorum)*.[39] While a cleric in an isolated instance, such as a time of great emergency, might serve as a mail carrier, an apostolic indult would be required for him to serve in

---

[37] Sess. XXI, *de ref.*, c. 2 — *Canones et Decreta Sacrosancti Oecumenici Concilii Tridentini* (ed. novissima, Romæ: ex Typographia Polyglotta, 1882), p. 142 (hereafter cited *Canones et Decreta*).

[38] Const. *Romanus Pontifex*, 14 oct. 1568 — *Fontes*, n. 129; also S. C. Ep. et Reg., encycl., 16 mart. 1697 — *Fontes*, n. 1817.

[39] *Caputaquen.*, 29 apr. 1586 — *Fontes*, n. 1406.

the capacity of postmaster, since such an office would be considered a public office. The provisions of canon 139, § 2, would then apply.[40]

On the assumption that a case of real necessity might arise, a cleric, in order to obtain the necessities of life, could take to some becoming trade or profession. This should be only for such time as is necessary to remedy the situation. The Sacred Congregation for the Propagation of the Faith ruled to this effect, adding that under no circumstances would the cleric be allowed to practice an *unbecoming* trade or profession. The cleric to whom this permission was granted was to make certain that some portion of each day be given to the exercise of his duties in church.[41]

A number of dioceses, both in the Americas and in Europe, have set up special bureaus whose function it is to arrange for pilgrimages of the faithful to the better known shrines of Christendom. Certain religious orders also have these bureaus. In 1936 a decree of the Sacred Congregation of the Council forbade clerics and religious to become involved in those things which look to the technical preparations for such pilgrimages.[42] From this it is clear that, although priests and religious may be appointed by their respective superiors to head these bureaus, they are to allow capable lay people to make the actual arrangements for travel, for hotel accommodations, and the like. The decree, it is true, speaks explicitly only of priests and pilgrimage groups. By analogy and from argumentation based on the purpose of the decree, it may be said to extend also to those priests and religious who organize vacation trips to travel here or abroad for purposes of special study. While it appears that there is no objection against accompanying such a group as instructor, chaperon, or spiritual director — or perhaps in all three capacities — the details

[40] "Sine apostolico indulto officia publica, quæ exercitium laicalis iurisdictionis vel administrationis secumferunt, ne assumant."

[41] *Decr.*, 13 apr. 1807, § 7, 14 — *Fontes*, n. 4691.

[42] *Decr.*, 11 febr. 1936, n. 5 — *AAS*, XXVIII (1936), 168.

and preparations of the trip should be handled by others within the group. The spirit of the decree is to safeguard clerical dignity and decorum. If in ventures as praiseworthy as pilgrimages the priest is not to make the technical arrangements, surely he is not to perform similar functions in trips which, at least objectively considered, are less praiseworthy.

Article 2. The Priest and Hobbies

Many priests find their legitimate recreation in the moderate and reasonable pursuit of some hobby. These hobbies vary with the talents, tastes, and personality of each priest. One hobby which seems to enjoy considerable popularity among the clergy is that of photography. Not infrequently one finds a priest who has followed this hobby for years, perhaps from his college and seminary days, and has become quite proficient in this art.

Could such a one conduct a photographic shop or studio in his own home or in the rectory? Several distinctions are in order. If he merely developed negatives and made prints from them for his friends, and charged [them] only enough to meet his initial expenses, he would certainly be within the law, for it seems that this is just another expression of his hobby. If he took portraits, however, and advertised for work, this would be forbidden, both on the score that it would be for profit and also because scandal might easily arise. This would especially be true if members of the other sex were numbered among his customers. The types and techniques employed would have to be wholly consistent with the norms of Christian modesty. However, if he took these portraits only for his relatives and a limited circle of men friends, and there were no publicity involved, this would be all right. Again, when he is reimbursed for the pictures, he should not take more than what is required to pay for the materials used, unless it were clear that the person intended to use this opportunity to present something by way of gratuity to the priest.

Should the case arise in which the priest were actually in need of financial help, either for himself or for his parents, he might ask a moderate fee for his work. A previous dispensation should have been obtained. The fine arts, among which it is safe to include the art of photography, if well and properly exercised, are not forbidden to clerics, provided the clerics, save in exceptional circumstances, do not receive money as profit for it.[43]

What is to be said of clerics engaging in farming? Some authors seem to allow it only if the cleric be under constraint to do so in order to obtain the necessities of life; the usual precautions must also be taken lest his priestly work suffer.[44] There are others who do not place this condition of necessity for the lawfulness of a priest engaging in farming. It is sufficient if his office and ecclesiastical rank and status are not thought less of due to this type of work.[45]

Both groups of authors appeal to Saint Paul in defense of their views, although they do not cite any specific texts. It seems safe to assume that the texts are those from I Thessalonians 2:9, II Thessalonians 3:8, and in particular Acts 18:3, where reference is made to Saint Paul working as a tent maker. As conditions are today, in order to forestall scandal and also to preclude any considerable loss of valuable time, this farming would have to be on a very limited scale, perhaps like the war-time "victory gardens." The recent advances in farm technique, the use of machinery, and the emphasis given agriculture in the curricula of many universities have all tended to set forth farming as a science, with the result that the farmer must spend

---

[43] "Se un sacerdote puo esercitare l'arte fotographica" — *Il Monitore Ecclesiastico* (Romæ, 1876-), XXV (1913-1914), 419.

[44] Oesterle, *Prælectiones Iuris Canonici*, I (Romæ: In Collegio S. Anselmi, 1931), p. 77 (hereafter cited *Prælectiones*); Cocchi, *Commentarium*, lib. II, pars 1, n. 5.

[45] Ferraris, *Bibliotheca*, sub v. *clericus*, art. III, n. 51, quoting c. 3, D. XCI; Vecchiotti, *Institutiones*, I, 398.

much time with his work. The average cleric could ill afford to expend this amount of time away from his ministry; were he retired from the active care of souls, then the case might be different.

There seems to be no objection to a priest's raising fruits, vegetables, and poultry for his own use. Could the priest employ others to run a farm for him, having them market the products raised on the farm? It would be licit for him to do this. It would not be licit, however, if the produce were raised *solely* with the intention that it was to be changed by hired help, e.g., grapes made into wine and then sold for profit. This seems to be forbidden not only as something unbecoming to the clerical state, but also as a type of trading known as artificial or industrial trading.[46]

At least in certain parts of our country, in farming areas particularly, it would not be held by the faithful as unbecoming or scandalous if a priest put up for sale, at a so-called "roadside stand," some of the surplus products which by way of hobby he had raised, the proceeds to go to the parish funds, or even to himself, should conditions warrant. As a precautionary measure it would not be unwise to consult the local ordinary before acting. The county authorities should also be consulted, for often a license is required for the operation of such a stand. The priest himself should not act as clerk in the disposing of these products.

Article 3. Employments Forbidden to Seminarians

On the 5th of May, 1935, the Apostolic Delegate sent a letter to the ordinaries of this country on the general subject of seminarians on vacation. This letter lists certain employments forbidden to clerics and seminarians. These

---

[46] Schmalzgrueber, lib. III, tit. 50, n. 18; also Blat, *Commentarium,* II, pars 1, n. 81.

employments are also forbidden to priests *a fortiori*. In part the letter reads:

The Holy See, ever solicitous to nurture and preserve the proper spirit of their vocation in the students for the priesthood, strongly favors the summer-villa, where the students pass their summer holidays, removed from endangering outside influences ...a precaution of paramount importance during the formative years of their ecclesiastical training.

Since the circumstances of these times do not permit the opening of villas where they do not already exist, it is most necessary that the proper safeguards be placed about the seminarians who return to their homes for the summer months and who, in many instances, are obliged to obtain employment in order to meet the expenses of the scholastic year....The Holy See knows this condition exists, and for the present, *tolerates* the employment of seminarians, except in positions which are not in keeping with the dignity of the spirit of their holy vocation.

1) Among the employments forbidden to seminarians the following must be listed:

a– positions in hotels, cafés, theatres, moving picture houses, places of amusement, such as dance-halls, bathing-beaches, billiard and pool parlors, etc.

b– positions in shops and offices in which persons of the other sex are employed;

c– positions of a political character;

d– the driving of taxi-cabs.

I am confident that Your Excellency's ardent desire to form priests according to the Heart of Christ will lead you to put into effect the above-mentioned regulations and suggestions which are *urgently* recommended by the Sacred Congregation for Seminaries and Universities.[47]

Article 4. The Priest and the Fine Arts

As befits a fully cultured person, the priest may rightly interest himself in all that makes for the beauty and fulness of human life. He may interest himself in the fine arts, for example, the arts of music, of painting, and of sculpture, to

---

[47] From a copy of the original obtained from the Apostolic Delegation.

mention but a few.[48] In fact, such an interest is of great advantage to a priest in his work. A knowledge and a proficiency in music will not only be an endless source of enjoyment for the priest, but will help him to avoid extremes in the matter of Church music. Proper study in painting and sculpture would acquaint him with the canons of profane and ecclesiastical art. He would thus be enabled to make liturgically correct choices in the selection of appointments for his church, in its statues and pictures. He will be able to discriminate between what is shoddy though flashy and the unpretentious austerity of true art.

To follow any of these arts as a trade or occupation would generally be out of the question for the average priest or cleric. It would require the expenditure of more time than the priest could legitimately afford. Furthermore, occasion for the emergence of serious scandal could arise from the steady practice of one or the other of the arts. There would be no reasonable objection in most cases to a priest's studying voice. To appear in public as an advertised soloist or to appear before a large group, not to mention undertaking a concert tour, seems to be contrary to the spirit of the law, if not also contrary to its letter.

He could, however, on infrequent occasions sing at such gatherings as special parish functions or extraordinary meetings of the clergy. To appear as soloist at a special liturgical function would likewise not be forbidden, unless there existed some contrary diocesan statute in this matter. This limitation would also be valid in all other cases, for the Code allows the local ordinaries to pass diocesan laws which would prohibit specific employments or occupations, whether these be exercised habitually or infrequently after the manner of a single act. The Sacred Congregation of the Council once decreed the special penalty of privation for two of the clerical chanters of the cathedral church of

[48] The fine (or finer) arts are usually spoken of as seven: sculpture, painting, drama, literature, poetry, architecture, and the dance. Of these seven, the dance seems to be the fine art which would be of little active interest to the priest.

Vercelli. These clerics had left their benefice and were employing their musical talents in the public theatres of Venice; such action was to be punished as wholly unbecoming the clerical state.[49] From the tenor of the letter it is clear that the Church wishes her clerics to avoid all unnecessary worldly publicity.

This element of publicity may also make it ill-advised for a priest to appear in the rôle of soloist whereby his proficiency in the use of a certain musical instrument would be demonstrated. In some localities priests have been known to appear as conductor or as an instrumental soloist, generally as pianist, with some Catholic symphonic or choral group. The general character of such a program, the sympathies of the audience, and the fact that it was being sponsored by Catholics may be factors which, when taken together, will justify such an appearance. The priest (or cleric) should not accept remuneration for his performance lest the people take scandal at the very thought that he has placed a money-value on his God-given talents.

Occasionally, several times a year, it would be allowed a priest to give a short concert before some Catholic group, or also before a mixed group which would not look unfavorably upon such a concert; judicious choice should be exercised in the selection of the music to be played. In all such cases the priest must not leave the impression that his concern in any way is for the financial reimbursement which may be involved. He may accept a modest offering to help him meet the incidental expenses incurred in the immediate preparation for the concert, and whatever other expenditures were entailed in his reaching the place of the concert.

A very practical case is illustrated in the periodic public recitals given by musical groups engaged in Conservatory study. These recitals are considered rightly a part of the curriculum. A priest who studies instrumental music can take a part in them if with his ordinary's permission he

---

[49] S. C. C., *Vercellen.*, 1 oct. 1720 — *Fontes*, n. 3215.

lawfully attends the institution which operates under secular auspices. Generally the audience is limited, the publicity is circumscribed, and the common reaction is favorable. Most people understand that it is a practice to which the priest as student ought to conform. Greater harm could result if he sought to be excused from appearing in the program, unless the school were run by Catholics, to whom the real reason for his not wishing to appear would be readily manifest.

In the question of painting and sculpture, there are definite limits to the extent of the cleric's activities in these fields. In large measure these limits are imposed by the moral law itself. For if theologians forbid the picture display of paintings and statues of nudes,[50] there is no question that it would be forbidden for priests to attend classes in painting or sculpture in which nude models are used. In fact, a great deal of prudence would have to be exercised in any given case for the sake of determining whether a priest may attend lectures or sessions in which members of the other sex act even as clothed models. There seems to be little if any justifying cause for a priest's attendance at such lectures or sessions, since the possible if not also probable emergence of scandal seems regularly to accompany his habitual act of attendance.

With the necessary exceptions being made when circumstances so warrant, it may be stated as a general rule that a priest may sponsor a public exhibition of his artistic work in both these fields. The subject matter must be consonant with the good taste and modesty of Christian art. This exhibition is not to be prompted by the desire of financial gain, though conceivably there could arise a case in which necessity would open the road for such an action to become

---

[50] Aertyns-Damen, *Theologia Moralis Secundum Doctrinam S. Alphonsi* (14. ed., 2 vols., Taurini: Marietti, 1944), I, n. 391 (hereafter cited *Theologia Moralis*); cf. also Tanquerey, *Synopsis Theologiæ Moralis et Pastoralis* (3 vols., Vol. II, 10. ed., 1936; Vol. III, 10. ed., 1937, Parisiis: Desclée et Socii), II, supplementum, *De Virtute Castitatis*, n. 49, note 1 (hereafter cited *Synopsis Moralis*).

legitimate. In these matters, as in the case of all employment which is not properly clerical, the cleric or priest is to remember that these occupations are tolerated under the provision that no scandal is given; that the time which should be given to his sacred ministry is not sacrificed; and that monetary considerations are only an accidental element.

If some priests have the added gift of real creative ability, could they sell the finished expression of this ability? What of a priest-composer or a priest-artist? Could such priests sell their musical compositions, or their paintings or wood carvings? There seems to be no reason why they could not, provided of course that the time originally given to the work did not take it beyond the classification of a hobby so as to make it a profession, with the result that their real life's work stood neglected. On his vacation and during other legitimate free time, a priest could work on these hobbies. If a priest may publish for public sale some literary work, as often happens, he is by the same token allowed to sell these expressions of another hobby, be it painting, music, or sculpture.

Article 5. The Priest and the Practice of Medicine

Canon 138 cautions clerics against engaging in those trades or professions which ill become their state. It refers to them as *artes indecoræ.* This expression implies a greater comprehensiveness of scope than did the expression *artes sordidæ,* which the older commentators employed. The practice of medicine is forbidden not precisely as an unbecoming occupation *(indecora),* but rather as one which by its very nature is not well suited to *(minus conveniens),* and, therefore out of harmony with, the clerical state.[51] It is to be admitted that those who dedicate their lives to the service of their fellow men in the art of healing enjoy the ready esteem of most people, and the medical practice itself

[51] Wernz-Vidal, *Ius Canonicum,* II, n. 123.

has the same commendable repute. Despite this, the practice of medicine is forbidden to clerics for the reasons stated in the earliest law on this subject.[52]

In addition to the demand that scandal be forestalled, there is the desire to protect the virtue of chastity, the continued possession of which might be endangered in the treatments to be given to persons of the other sex. Augustine stated that "...the law is aimed at the exercise of the medical profession as such, and intended to safeguard the honor of real physicians against usurpers and bunglers."[53] This may be true; at best, however, it is one of the lesser reasons for such a law. Canon 985, 6°, gives one good reason why clerics are not allowed to practice medicine; it states that clerics become irregular *ex delicto* if death follows from the exercise of the medical or surgical profession, if it was undertaken without an apostolic indult.

In the early days of the Church it appears that priests did practice medicine. It is held by some that Saint Luke practiced medicine as a priest.[54] Pope Benedict XIV (1740-1758) mentioned cases in which bishops practiced medicine.[55] For the clerics of this country the III Plenary Council of Baltimore (1884) forbade the exercise of medicine and surgery, regardless of whether this practice stemmed from the desire of financial reimbursement or from the loftier motives of pure charity.[56]

From the wording of the canon which speaks of those things which are at variance *(aliena)* with the clerical state,

---

[52] Council of Clermont (1130), canon 5 — Mansi, XXI, 428; Council of Rheims (1131), canon 6 — Mansi, XXI, 459; II General Council of the Lateran (1139), canon 9 — Mansi, XXI, 528.

[53] *Commentary,* II, 89.

[54] This point is difficult to prove. It is based on the assumption that St. Luke probably was in orders when he was with St. Paul as his physician during the latter's First Captivity in Rome in the year 61-63. In his letter to the Colossians, St. Paul wrote: "Luke, our most dear physician...sends you greetings" (4:4).

[55] *De Synodo Diœcesana* (2 vols., Romæ, 1806), lib. XIII, c. 10, n. 5 (hereafter cited *De Synodo*).

[56] *Concilii Plenarii Baltimorensis III Acta et Decreta* (Baltimoræ: Typis Joannis Murphy Sociorum, 1886), n. 82.

it stands clear that clerics require an apostolic indult for the *exercise* of medicine; hence such an indult would not be necessary for the performance of one isolated act.[57] It is the practice of medicine exercised *ex professo* which is forbidden.[58]

Since there is no express mention of its being forbidden, the study of medicine would be allowed to clerics.[59] This study should be made at some Catholic university; for clerics are not permitted to attend secular or state universities without the special permission of their ordinaries. This binds religious also.[60] This permission is given for the most part only to clerics who have been advanced to the priesthood, and even then to only those who seem likely to maintain the high standards of the priesthood, both scholastically and spiritually.

A priest properly qualified by reason of the completion of a prescribed medical course may practice this art occasionally, for, as has been indicated, the word *exercere* implies a steady frequency of repeated acts. Some authors hold that a performance of acts two or three times would be sufficient to constitute a violation of canon 139, § 2, especially in serious cases which might involve a danger of death. Although the exercise of forbidden medical and surgical practice is a grave sin,[61] a cleric would not be guilty of serious sin until he had practiced the art at least two or three times, according to the view mentioned above. In an emergency he would be free to act, one author even allowing the cleric to perform a Cæsarian section on a

---

[57] Canon 139, § 2: "Sine apostolico indulto medicinam vel chirurgiam [clerici] ne exerceant." Coronata, *Institutiones*, I, n. 201.

[58] Brys, "De exercitio medicinæ clericis prohibito" — *Collationes Brugenses*, XXXV (1935), 364.

[59] Cappello, *Summa*, I, n. 244; Chelodi, *De Personis*, p. 198.

[60] S. C. Consist., *decr.*, 30 apr. 1918 — *AAS*, X (1918), 237; Bouscaren, *The Canon Law Digest* (2 vols., Milwaukee: Bruce Publishing Co., 1934-1943), I, 115 (hereafter cited *Digest*).

[61] Davis, *Moral and Pastoral Theology* (3. ed., 4 vols., London: Sheed and Ward, 1938), IV, 302 (hereafter cited *Moral Theology*).

woman already certainly dead.[62] This is very definitely an exception, for there is danger of scandal; the provisions of the civil law should also be known. A lay person should be the one to remove the fœtus from a deceased pregnant woman.[63]

One cannot be said to practice medicine in any real sense of the term, much less in the canonical sense, if one prescribes a remedy in those cases which require no physical examination of the person who is ill. This would amount to prescribing remedies which are known to everyone.[64] Blat deems it permissible for a cleric to perform even a *minor* surgical operation in behalf of a friend or a servant. Though he does not explicitly mention the members of one's own family, it seems that his view may safely be extended to include them as well. This is in keeping with the general opinion that, if the cleric has sufficient skill, and if all danger of scandal has been removed previously, he may proceed to an infrequent act wherein that skill would be employed.[65]

Permission to practice medicine in the strict sense of a continued exercise of the medical art is given only for a just and grave cause.[66] It is given in the faculties which are granted to ordinaries in missionary areas by the Sacred Congregation for the Propagation of the Faith. Number 47 of the 1941 faculties reads:

[Facultas] Permittendi suis missionariis ut ad finem Regni Christi amplius dilatandi, medicinam et chirurgiam exercere

---

[62] Vermeersch-Creusen, *Epitome*, I, n. 257; cf. also Eschbach, *Disputationes Physiologico-Theologicæ* (ed. altera, Romæ, 1901), pp. 350 and 364.

[63] S. C. S. Off., decretum *Sutchuen.*, 15 febr. 1780 — *Fontes*, n. 839.

[64] Coronata, *Institutiones*, I, n. 201; Davis, *Moral Theology*, IV, 301.

[65] Blat, *Commentarium*, II, Pars I, n. 78; Vermeersch-Creusen, *Epitome*, I, n. 257; Beste, *Introductio*, p. 160.

[66] Santi (1830-1885) mentioned two examples from the late nineteenth century in which such a permission was granted: to a monk in Spain, and to an Italian parish priest. — *Prælectiones Iuris Canonici* (4. ed., emendata cura Martini Leitner, 5 vols., Ratisbonæ, 1903-1905), lib. III, tit. 50, n. 1 (hereafter cited *Prælectiones*).

valeant, dummodo in istis artibus periti sint, in curandis infirmis alterius sexus omnia quæ religiosum et sacerdotem dedecent, vel scandalo esse possint, diligenter vitent easque artes omnino gratis exerceant.[67]

Article 6. The Priest and Psychiatry

Since it is held that the prohibition against exercising the art of medicine is directed against a practice of medicine which looks to the preservation and restoration of the health of the body, it may well be held that a cleric or a priest may engage in a practice of medicine which looks to the treatment of disturbances of the mind. This question seems not to have been contemplated either by the post-Code or by the pre-Code authors. At least, they seem reluctant to discuss the point. This is an important aspect of the field of psychosomatic medicine, in which remarkable advances have been made of late, especially during World War II. By reason of his general training, and of the advantages of specialized study in Catholic psychology, a priest would be well qualified to handle these cases, not on a strictly professional basis, but in special instances.

It is said that two-thirds of all the illnesses that bring people to the doctor's office are caused by fear, worry, and insecurity. Until recently these emotional and spiritual upsets were treated with surgery and drugs. Now psychosomatic medicine is able to seek the root cause and to cure the illness by curing its cause. A priest trained in this work would be of great advantage to a diocese or a religious order. A recent article by a Catholic psychiatrist advocated a long range program that would aim at the training of large numbers of truly Catholic psychiatrists. An immediate start could possibly be made by having the various chancery offices keep a list of reliable psychiatrists, who could be called upon for consultation when the need pre-

---

[67] Berutti, *De Personis*, II, 145; for a commentary on this faculty confer Winslow, *A Commentary on the Apostolic Faculties* (New York: Field Afar Press, 1946), pp. 207-209.

sented itself. A better plan would entail the organization, under episcopal diocesan auspices, of what the author calls a "Bureau of Psychological Service," which would be set up to function at all three levels: pre-puberty, adolescent, and adult.[68]

It is the present writer's strong personal conviction that such a Bureau should be organized, and should be headed by a priest psychologist, properly qualified, whose appointment would be made by the bishop, to whom he would be directly responsible. By law the right and duty of the bishop has been clearly established to make adequate provision for the needs of his diocese in matters spiritual. In appointing a priest to this special and technical work the bishop would be looking to the safeguarding of the faith and morals of his subjects, for in many cases which would come to this Bureau the basic need and the ultimate meeting of this need would be in the realm of the spiritual.

The assignment to head such a department might be viewed as being similar to appointments whereby priests are placed in charge of welfare bureaus and charitable agencies, for all these are appointments to offices which are not strictly offices as the Code defines that term.[69] As head of this Bureau the actual work of the priest-psychologist should be limited to those cases in which previous prudent questioning by the staff of lay psychologists has revealed a problem whose roots are in the field of conscience. There is a great need for Catholic principles in this field. It seems a serious oversight to abandon many of our people to pagan psychologists, who little respect even the fundamental principles of natural philosophy, and respect even less the ramifications of these principles in the moral and religious spheres.

---

[68] Wauck, "On Casting out a Devil"—*America* (New York, 1909-), LXXVIII (1947), 181.

[69] Canon 145, § 1: "...stricto autem sensu est munus ordinatione sive divina sive ecclesiastica stabiliter constitutum, ad normam sacrorum canonum conferendum, aliquam saltem secumferens participationem ecclesiasticæ potestatis sive ordinis sive iurisdictionis."

The priest himself should ask no fees for whatever services he may render in the Bureau, for basically these services are but further expressions of one phase of his life's work, namely, the helping of troubled souls to a solution of their problems. Every priest who in the confessional gives advice to the scrupulous is practicing, in broad outline perhaps, some method of psychotherapy; for example, in the case of scrupulosity which is actually an obsessional neurosis situation. Just as morbid somatic conditions affect the calm and reasoned functioning of the mind, so neuroses may manifest themselves in the form of bodily ailments of one kind or another.[70]

It seems that what has been said in the matter of a cleric's practicing of medicine may, with the proper allowances, be applied also to his practicing of dentistry. Dentistry, particularly the type known as surgical dentistry, would also be forbidden to clerics as a profession. But there certainly could arise occasions on which a cleric or a priest who had been in that field before his advancement to orders or to the priesthood might make use of his ability for his associates and, if a religious, for members of his community. This is licit. In recent years several communities of women religious have sent members of their group to Catholic dental schools to become properly trained dentists. Their subsequent professional work is restricted to caring for the dental needs of their communities. This does not contravene the canon, for the things to be avoided, as is evidenced from certain decisions in these matters, are these: the possibility of scandal, the loss of time, and the desire for financial gain — all of which would happily be absent in such an arrangement.

Such work, accepted under obedience, seems not to differ from any other assignment given in the community, whether it be teaching school, working in the kitchen, or assisting in the office. The work is done solely within the

---

[70] On this and similar points, cf. Bonnar, *The Catholic Doctor* (2. ed., New York: P. J. Kennedy, 1941), pp. 119-163.

community and for the community. It seems permissible, moreover, for the proper authorities to allow a community which is in need of financial assistance to accept as patients those who live outside the community. But such a permission should be granted only for such time as the financial difficulties continue.

In the Church there exist societies of men and women whose life's work is the task of nursing God's sick. This charitable work is the expression of one's fulfillment of one of the corporal works of mercy, and is heartily approved by the Church. Special directives have been issued by various Congregations from time to time for those who labor in this field. The norms found therein are to be followed in the practice of medicine in so far as this is required.

Article 7. Preparation and Sale of Medicaments, Wines and Liquors

In the past, as far back as the seventeenth century, the confection of pharmaceutical remedies whose preparation postulates the application of scientific knowledge has been solidly forbidden to clerics. Most of the directives were issued to the superiors of religious houses wherein certain members of the institute, as designated for this purpose, had been preparing medicaments both for use in the house and for sale to the laity of the surrounding areas.[71] It is known that in rare cases permission was given for the religious to sell these drugs. One such case found Pope Innocent XIII (1721-1724) allowing the Nursing Order of Saint John of God to sell drugs to the people of Rome. This was for the greater public good. In addition, the permission of the Cardinal Vicar of the city was to be obtained. As a general rule the religious were forbidden to sell these me-

[71] Pallottini, *Collectio Omnium Conclusionum et Resolutionum quæ apud Sacram Congregationem Cardinalium S. Conc. Trid., Interpretum Prodierunt ab eius Institutione anno MDLXIV ad annum MDCCCLX* (18 vols., Romæ, 1868-1893), II, 514-519 (hereafter cited *Collectio*).

dicaments, which corresponded somewhat to the remedies which at present are called "patent medicines." Later relaxations made it possible for the monasteries to make these preparations in quantities sufficient for distribution to other houses of their Order.[72]

Vecchiotti (+1870) as a witness of the pre-Code law, showed that clerics were forbidden to engage not only in the making of drugs but also in the making and marketing of perfume.[73] This prohibition still holds, for this occupation seems unbecoming to the clerical state, not because it is of a sordid nature, but because of its close connection with a spirit of worldliness so aptly signified by the perfume itself. In this matter as in the matter of medicines, though a cleric may lawfully interest himself privately in the mechanics of prescription and perfume compounding, and even gain a commendable proficiency therein, he would under the dictates of prudence seek the permission of his ordinary if the results of his investigations were to be made marketable. To set up a business would be forbidden by reason of canon 142. As all authorities admit, a cleric could exercise these or other trades which are not in themselves illicit, if there existed real necessity for himself or for his family. Proper permission should be obtained. Ecclesiastical law yields to such necessity.

It is a well-known fact that some religious communities are engaged in the manufacture and sale of liquor and wines, especially of wine destined for use in the Holy Sacrifice of the Mass.[74] It is agreed that this is licitly done, provided that the raw materials, in this case the grapes, grain, etc., are not purchased from another source with the

---

[72] Pallottini, *Collectio*, II, 518.

[73] *Institutiones*, I, 395; decree of the Sacred Congregation of Bishops and Regulars as quoted in Bizzarri, *Collectanea in usum Secretariæ S. C. Episcoporum et Regularium* (Romæ, 1885), p. 338.

[74] Those who make this altar wine should be familiar not only with the decree *Dominus Salvator* issued by the Sacred Congregation of the Sacraments on the 26th of March, 1929 (*AAS*, XXI [1929], 631 ff.), but with earlier decrees of the Holy Office — *Fontes*, nn. 1104, 1125, 1133, 1138, and 1181.

intention of later re-sale either in their original state or as a finished product. Thus in the case at hand, in the preparation of liquors or wines the grain and grapes should come from the fields and vineyards which belong to the community. It is permissible to use the medium of paid labor to change these materials into liquor and wine, and then to sell the resulting product for profit.[75]

Not all will agree, however, on the licitness of selling these items at retail. Augustine, citing Heiner (1849-1919), definitely stated that a cleric would be forbidden to do this.[76] Ferraris (+ca. 1763) allowed it if the wine had been made from one's own products. He referred to a decision of the Sacred Congregation of Bishops and Regulars in support of this view.[77] If the retail sales were conducted through others, i.e., through servants or relatives, then Schmalzgrueber (1663-1735) found nothing reprehensible in such a practice.[78] As previously stated, Augustine's position seems a bit too severe. Perhaps he exclusively contemplated the case in which a cleric as an individual buys some land for the single and exclusive purpose of raising products for future sale for profit. Here it is presupposed that the communities manufacturing the wine own these properties from which the grapes come as part of the grounds belonging to their monastery or community, as the case may be. If the properties were purchased, the element of purpose is most important. The original purpose, in good faith, must look only to meeting the community's foreseeable needs. If, by accident, there is a superfluity, this may be sold, either changed or in its original form.

---

[75] Coronata, *Institutiones*, I, n. 200; Wernz, *Ius Decretalium*, II, n. 219; "Hinc religiosis sive ad clericalem sive ad laicalem religiosam pertinentibus licitum quoque est vendere res ex propriis prædiis comparatas sive fuerint immutatæ, sive mutatæ, etiam mercenariorum opera" — Fanfani, *De Iure Religiosorum ad Normam Codicis Iuris Canonici* (2. ed., Taurini-Romæ: Marietti, 1925), p. 357.

[76] *Commentary*, II, p. 97, note 76. The reference is to Heiner's *Katholisches Kirchenrecht* (2. ed., 2 vols., Paderborn, 1897), I, 227.

[77] *Bibliotheca*, sub v. *clericus*, art. III, n. 15.

[78] *Ius Ecclesiasticum Universum*, lib. III, tit. 50, n. 17.

In our day the matter of retail sale assumes less importance than it did many years ago. Now, for the most part, the liquor and wine are channeled to the consumer public through the agency of large distributors, usually sole distributors. This limits the dealings to one group only. It seems that religious communities engaged in such legitimate business should act with the previously granted counsel and permission of the local ordinary. This precaution should be taken if it is in any way possible for scandal to arise from such operations. In the matter of advertising there should obtain all due moderation. The advertising should normally be restricted within Catholic magazines and periodicals. If further infrequent and measured publicity were felt to be necessary, it should be restricted within the more conservative secular publications. The form of the advertising itself should be dignified, lest through high pressure promotion the public should come to associate the preparing of the product so closely with the religious group that the real work of the latter no longer commands prior attention. What is and must always remain a secondary and incidental labor should not cause the prime work of any religious group to suffer loss of esteem and recognition.

CHAPTER III

THE PROHIBITION AGAINST GAMBLING

PART I. HISTORICAL CONSPECTUS

In the early law of the Church, gambling and the various forms which it adopted were expressed in the Latin by the use of the words *aleæ, tali, taxilli,* and *tesseræ* together with the verb *ludere* or its derivative *ludus* or *lusus.*[1] While these four nouns refer to dice, there was a distinction which must here be noted. The word *alea* or *aleæ* was the generic term for the game of dice. The other terms possessed a restricted meaning in that they looked to a special type of die used in the playing of the game of dice. *Alea,* then, was the game; the other nouns referred to the instruments used in the playing. Since the element of dice was almost essential to the early types of gambling, the word *aleæ* (dice) came to represent without distinction almost all games of chance. The expressions *"ad talos ludere"* and *"ad taxillos ludere,"* whether used in conjunction with or even independently of the word *alea,* pointed to a special type of dice game peculiar to a given area. Among these variant forms may be mentioned those of oblong shape, rounded out at the edges and marked only on four sides *(tali).* Another form closely resembled our present type of dice, having markings on each of its six sides *(tesseræ).*[2] Some of these dice had no numbers at all, but carried instead pictures of Venus and of other well-known female deities. Often, while in the process of rolling the

---

[1] "Sotto il nome alea si deve intendere qualunque giuco di sorte o di dubbio pericolo." — Mercante, *Compendio di Diritto Canonico con Illustrazioni Istorico-Dogmatiche* (2. ed., 3 vols., Prato, 1832), I, 121 (hereafter cited *Compendio*).

[2] Harper's, *A New Latin Dictionary* (edited by E. A. Andrews, revised, enlarged by C. Lewis and C. Short, New York, 1907), p. 1835; Hefele-Leclercq, I, 263; Richeri, *Dictionarium Iuris Civilis, Canonici et Feudalis necnon Delectus Regum Feudalium* (Taurini, 1792), p. 45.

dice, the player would call on various ones of these pagan gods and goddesses to bring him good fortune. These pictures and the invocation of the pagan gods may well have been contributing factors which led the Christians to consider these dice games immoral, and finally led the authorities to ban them entirely.

If one accepts the date of origin which some authors assign to the composition of the *Apostolic Canons,* the earliest evidences of ecclesiastical legislative interest in the problem of gambling by clerics are to be found in this collection.[3] Canons 42 and 43 laid a rather heavy penalty upon the bishop, priest, deacon, and subdeacon who had been guilty of gambling.[4] The original Greek version speaks of these penalties as καθαρείσθω (in canon 42) and ἀφοριζέσθω (in canon 43). Fulton translates these as deposition and suspension respectively;[5] deposition for those in rank above the subdiaconate, suspension for the lower clergy. In the early days suspension was a milder penalty, deposition, a graver one.[6]

---

[3] There is some discussion relative to the time and origin of the *Apostolic Canons.* Hefele (1809-1893) and Beveridge (1637-1708) (*Codex Canonum Ecclesiæ Primitivæ Vindicatus ac Illustratus* [Londini, 1678], pp. 63-102) assign their composition to the end of the second or the beginning of the third century. Modern authorities believe that they could not have been composed before the Council of Antioch (341), v.g., Van Hove (*Commentarium Lovaniense in Codicem Iuris Canonici,* Vol. I, tome 1, *Prolegomena* [2. ed., Mechliniæ-Romæ: H. Dessain, 1945]), pp. 130-131 (hereafter cited *Prolegomena*), and that they are a part of the larger *Apostolic Constitutions* (Διατάξεις τῶν ἀποστόλων) composed in Syria after the year 400. This view is substantiated by many authors, among them Grisar, *Geschichte Roms und der Päpste in Mittelalter* (Freiburg, 1901), pars 1 (altera pars non apparuit), p. 735. The *Apostolic Canons* are properly the 47th Chapter of the eighth book of the *Apostolic Constitutions.* For a Latin text, confer F. X. Funk, *Didascalia et Constitutiones Apostolorum* (2 vols., Paderbonæ, 1905).

[4] Bruns, I, 7.

[5] Index Canonum, p. 95.

[6] Rainer, *Suspension of Clerics,* The Catholic University of America Canon Law Studies, n. 111 (Washington, D. C.: The Catholic University of America, 1937), p. 3.

The very early work *De Aleatoribus*, for a considerable time falsely ascribed to Saint Cyprian (+258), contains a vigorous denunciation of gambling.[7] The author, whom Harnack (1851-1930) identifies as Pope Saint Victor I (189-199), called gambling a *"crimen immortale,"* an act of idolatry.[8] If Saint Victor was actually the author of this homily, then the *De Aleatoribus* may well mark the first official stand against gambling.

In Spain, about the year 300, at the Council of Elvira, legislation was enacted which was aimed at extirpating the evil of gambling among clergy and laity alike.[9] The Trullan Synod (692) restated the law and also the penalty as found in the *Apostolic Canons*. If a cleric was apprehended while gambling, he was to be deposed; if he was a lay person, he was to be segregated.[10]

The civil law did not leave the field entirely to the Church in these matters. The State, through the agency of the Emperor, authored legislation on gambling. These laws also reached out to clerics. In Book III, title 43 of the Code (534), there is found a letter of Justinian, written to a certain Pretorian Prefect named John.[11] This letter was the means of instituting a general law which completely forbade gambling by anyone. Those who merely watched others indulging in this sport were to be considered in the same culpable category. The various bishops in their respective dioceses were to see to it that the law was observed. To this end, if necessary, they had the right to invoke the aid of the governors of the various provinces.

---

[7] *MPL*, IV, 827-836.

[8] Ryder, "Harnack on the 'De Aleatoribus' " — *Dublin Review* (London, 1836-), XII (1889), pp. 82-98.

[9] Bruns, II, 12; Mansi, II, 18; Hefele-Leclercq, I, 263.

[10] Bruns, II, 52; Mansi, IX, 967; Hardouin, *Acta Conciliorum et Epistolæ Decretales ac Constitutiones Summorum Pontificum* (12 vols., Parisiis, 1714-1715), III, 1682 (hereafter cited Hardouin).

[11] *Corpus Iuris Civilis* (3 vols., Berolini: Apud Weidmannos, 1928-1929), Vol. II, *Codex Iustinianus* (ed. stereotypa decima, recognovit et retractavit P. Krueger, 1929), p. 147. For an English translation, cf. S. P. Scott, *The Civil Law* (17 vols. in 6, Cincinnati, The Central Trust Co., 1932), XII, 342 (hereafter cited Scott).

In another law the Emperor went into lengthy detail over the penalty for those clerics who were guilty of gambling. The penalty was of three years' duration. During this time the cleric was suspended from his ministry and was sent to some monastery. No indication was given in the law as to just what powers were suspended. If this penalty was in keeping with the general severity of ecclesiastical (and civil) discipline of the times, then the cleric was probably forbidden every exercise of orders and jurisdiction — with the possible exception of the saying of Holy Mass. For good behavior the time was reduced to a year and a half. He could then be reinstated by his immediate superior.[12]

Emperor Leo VI (886-911) in his eighty-seventh Constitution ordered that ecclesiastics who "disgraced their sacred calling" by engaging in games of chance were to be sent to a monastery for three years of penance.[13] If after reinstatement they gambled again, they were to be expelled from the ranks of the priesthood. Unlike the laws of Justinian, this law made provision for "repeaters." It made no mention of a shorter period of penance in consequence of good behavior. Yet it was less strict than the *Apostolic Canons*, for expulsion from the clerical rank was not enforced as long as the offense had not been repeated.

The ninth century witnessed the convening of a considerable number of councils in the Western Church, where there was a striking need for such action. Important among these councils was that which was held in 813 at Mainz. In its 14th canon this council stated that whatever a cleric or a monk coveted over and above his just due was to be regarded as base gain. In clarification of this statement it pointed out that such an excessive coveting was

---

[12] *Corpus Iuris Civilis*, Vol. III, *Novellæ Constitutiones* (ed. stereotypa 5, recognovit R. Schoell et absolvit G. Kroll, 1928), p. 603; Scott, XVII, 81.

[13] *Ius Græco-Romanum*, Vol. I, *Novellæ et Aureæ Bullæ Imperatorum post Iustinianum* (ed. K. E. Zachariæ von Lingenthal, nova editio, Athenis, 1930), p. 154; Scott, XVII, 276.

manifest in the love of gambling. It was wrong for clerics and monks.[14] The Council of Augsburg (952) threatened deposition for the cleric who showed an absorbing interest in gambling.[15]

The *Decree* of Gratian incorporated canons 42 and 43 of the *Apostolic Canons.* These canons looked to certain vices undesirable in the life of anyone, particularly so in the life of a cleric.[16] While a cleric was not to take to excessive drinking *(vinolentus),* he was likewise not to give time to the playing of games of chance and to gambling in general *(aleæ deserviens).* The *glossa* in speaking of the penalty concluded that the bishops were to threaten clerics with excommunication or deposition, not indeed for every individual violation, but only for the practice in which there was a time element that indicated frequency of action. To call for a penalty the evil also had to be of some magnitude. Indiscriminate leveling of penalties could only weaken their effectiveness in rooting out the evil of gambling.[17]

With regard to the negative clerical obligations there was little legislation in the thirteenth and fourteenth centuries. The ordinance against gambling, as it had been established in the Council of Mainz (813), was accorded a universal force and application when it was incorporated in the Gregorian Decretals. The law pointed disapprovingly to a number of secular preoccupations in the illustrative list which it furnished. Tersely reproved among the

---

[14] Canon 14: "...quidquid plus justo appetit...turpe lucrum est... aleas amare...ecce talia et his similia ministris altaris Domini necnon et monachis omnino contradicimus"—*MGH, Leges in 4°,* Sectio III, *Concilia Aevi Karolini,* Tom. II, pars 1 (recensuit A. Werminghoff, 1906), p. 264; Mansi, XIV, 69.

[15] Canon 3: "...*aleis vacans*...deponendus erit" (italics inserted)—Mansi, XVIII, 437; Council of Gerona (in Spain) (1068) — Mansi, XIX, 1071.

[16] C. 1, D. XXXV.

[17] *Glossa ordinaria,* ad c. 1, D. XXXV, sub v. *aut desinat.* There is a similar thought in the *glossa* ad c. 2, D. LXVII, sub v. *solus,* and in the *glossa* ad c. 9, D. XCII, sub v. *castigatus,* where it is said that the first offense is not to be punished.

listed preoccupations was the passion for dice *(aleas amare)*.[18] Elsewhere in the Decretals clerics were warned not only against gambling, but also against being present at games of chance.[19]

In one of his letters Pope Innocent III (1198-1216) reflected the sternness of the Church toward one who stood identified as a public gambler *(aleator publicus)*.[20] The letter treated briefly of a dispute which had arisen between two canons with regard to the episcopal see of Poitiers: both had sought it. Neither acceded to the see. One was refused because of some documentary irregularities; the other was passed over *propter indignitatem personæ*. This latter cleric was the known gambler. He had attempted a defense on the plea that he had merely been following a custom prevalent among the French clergy. The point to be noted is that anyone publicly known to have gambled was barred from the obtaining of or promotion to any dignity in the Church. No defense was possible behind the thin shield of custom or habit.

Panormitanus (1386-1453) offered a brief insight into the terminology as it was accepted in his time. Gambling was indicated by two terms (not exclusively): *ludus alearum* (or *ludus tabularum*), which was played at tables, and *ludus taxillorum*, which was further identified only in that it was also known as hazard *(hazardum)*. Hazard bespoke a reference to games of chance. Both of these types of gambling were forbidden to clerics. With regard to the game of chess there was some uncertainty. In general, chess *(ludus scachorum)* seems not to have been forbidden, though some councils did place a ban on it.[21] As the com-

[18] C. 1, X, *ne clerici vel monachi sæcularibus negotiis se immisceant*, III, 50.

[19] C. 15, X, *de vita et honestate clericorum*, III, I. This law was borrowed from the IV General Council of the Lateran (1215), canon 14.

[20] C. 11, X, *de excessibus prælatorum*, V, 31; Potthast, n. 3662.

[21] Council of Béziers (now Montpellier) (1225), canon 24 — Mansi, XXIII, 882; the Council of Trier (1310), canon 44, forbade it to monks — Mansi, XXV, 260. Thomassinus (1619-1695) recorded the incident in which St. Peter Damian (1007-1072) supposedly chastised a bishop

mentator noted, the ban on gambling did not arise from anything inherently evil in gambling, but rather from the train of evils that too often flowed from it — cheating, lying, foul language, and blasphemous speech.[22]

Prior to the Council of Trent numerous councils were held in the various countries. Many enacted a bald prohibition against gambling without adding anything further in the law. Others decreed special regulations which were designed for handling the peculiar situation in the localities for which they were the lawmaking body. Notice will be given only to those councils whose rulings differed from the general law. The Council of Paris (1212) forbade gambling in the homes of clerics, in the cloisters of religious houses, and in church buildings.[23] The penalty for the violation of this law was the loss of his benefice for the offending incumbent. The cleric who did not possess a benefice was subject to excommunication, after the proper warning had been given. A fine was levied for the clerical gamblers of the diocese of Valence (1261). The statutes further determined that if the cleric did not pay the fine within ten days he was to be excommunicated.[24] A diet of bread and water for ten days, during which time the cleric was also suspended from office, was the stern penalty which the Council of Salzburg (1274) wrote into its law on gambling.[25] The Council of Trier (1310) ordained that those clerics who played games of chance or who gambled publicly were by that very fact suspended. To play out of a

---

with whom he was traveling. While putting up overnight in a public inn, the bishop had indulged in a game of chess. Upon being corrected, the bishop satisfied by doing immediate penance. — *Vetus et Nova Ecclesiæ Disciplina circa Beneficia et Beneficiarios* (10 vols., Mogontiaci, 1787), pars III, lib. III, c. xlvi, n. 1.

[22] *Commentaria* ad c. 15, X, *de vita et honestate clericorum,* III, 1, nn. 4, 11-13.

[23] Canon 16 — Mansi, XXII, 823.

[24] Mansi, XXIII, 1055.

[25] Canon 12 — Mansi, XXIV, 140. The Synod of Lucca (1308), canon 38, threatened with excommunication the cleric who gambled, either personally or through the agency of another. — Mansi, XXV, 183.

spirit of sociability or as a means of consoling oneself or others was tolerated under the provision that the playing be done in respectable places and with people of good name.[26] The diocesan synod of Florence (c. 1346) determined a fine as the penalty for violations of the law which forbade all gambling and all card games. Any person who retained or held back the evidence was liable to the same fine as the one who played. This applied also to those in the curia. Reporting and spying on others were encouraged by the fact that one-fourth of the fine went to the denouncer.[27]

In France in the thirteenth and fourteenth centuries, and again much later in the seventeenth and eighteenth centuries, official royal legislation banned all gambling places. It made those who operated such establishments as liable to penalties as those who abetted the evil by frequenting them. According to the French law of this later period, any cleric who gambled in violation of both ecclesiastical and civil law was tried first before the secular tribunal as a layman would be. Further, he was subject to added canonical penalties from his bishop.[28]

The explicit mention of money as an important consideration in these dice and card games occurred for the first time in this period in the decrees of the Council of Avignon (1509). Any gambling, publicly or privately done, *"in quibus ludis pecuniæ causa imbursandi interveniat clericus,"* would bring excommunication to the offending cleric.[29]

In a letter granting faculties to the clergy of the London District in October of 1753, Bishops Petre (1734-1758) and Challoner (1758-1781) forbade all secular mission-

---

[26] Canon 58 — Mansi, XXV, 263.

[27] Book 3 — Mansi, XXVI, 36-37.

[28] Richard, *Analysis Conciliorum Generalium et Particularium* (5 vols., Augustæ Vindelicorum, 1778-1782), IV, 253 (hereafter cited *Analysis Conciliorum*).

[29] Canon 18 — Mansi, XXXII, 543.

aries to play cards in taverns (inns) or to go to gambling houses.[30]

Here in our own country an original decree of the I Provincial Council of Baltimore (1829) had forbidden all card playing.[31] When these decrees were sent to Rome for a review before their publication, the Sacred Congregation for the Propagation of the Faith decided that this decree on card playing was too rigorous, for even Saint Charles Borromeo (+1584) had not in the I Provincial Council of Milan (1565) listed card playing among the games which he outlawed.[32] The II Plenary Council of Baltimore (1866) made a distinction between games which could not suitably be indulged in by a cleric, even when the games were played in private, and games, such as cards, which could be indulged in when the playing was sought for innocent relaxation.[33] The III Plenary Council of Baltimore (1884) confirmed the warnings and injunctions issued by the II Plenary Council.[34]

Part II. Discipline of the Code

Article 1. The Term "Gambling"

The concepts contained in the term itself are numerous. In its widest sense it is taken on occasion to signify any contract in which chance plays a rôle. Those who play the stock market may be called gamblers; the same holds true of anyone who takes out life insurance. It may be objected

---

[30] Myers, "Theatre Law of the Old Province of Westminster"—*Clergy Review* (London, 1931-), III (1932), 90. Challoner was made Bishop Petre's coadjutor in 1741.

[31] *Concilia Provincialia Baltimori Habita ab anno 1829 usque ad annum 1849* (2. ed., Baltimori: Apud Joannem Murphy et Socium, 1851), p. 69.

[32] Guilday, *A History of the Councils of Baltimore [1791-1884]* (New York: The Macmillan Company, 1932), p. 94.

[33] *Concilii Plenarii Baltimorensis II Acta et Decreta* (Baltimoræ: Typis Joannis Murphy Sociorum, 1868), n. 154.

[34] *Acta et Decreta Concilii Plenarii Baltimorensis III* (Baltimoræ: John Murphy, 1886), n. 74, Introduction.

that in this latter instance there is not present any expressed intention to win. That is correct, but the simple absence of any manifestation of such intention on the side of the contracting party does not alter the nature of the contract. In the case of insurance, the person is influenced by a conservative spirit, for he intends to avoid the risk instead of assuming it, while in betting, which is a form of gambling taken in its strict sense, the individual risks the loss of a small sum for the chance of getting a larger sum in return. It is a desire to get something for nothing.

Gambling in its strict sense includes games, betting, and lotteries. In its more strict sense gambling is gaming by way of staking money on some fortuitous event.[35] Gambling, then, is clearly a generic concept, verified in gambling or in gaming or in mere betting. Therefore, the term is not strictly the same as gaming, for gambling is more extensive in that it further may also include the element of betting. To have gambling in the strict sense of the term there must be a bet, a wager, or stakes of some kind. It may be explained that gambling is any kind of chance or game of skill in which money stakes are involved.

The word *game* is a more general term, of which gambling is a species. While in its restricted, almost special, sense the word *game* requires the element of chance and of uncertain outcome, in its root meaning it does not presuppose necessarily a wager or a stake. A game of ball, a football game, a tennis match, or some swimming event may be indulged in without gambling, though as a matter of fact a system of wagering and betting has grown up around these and other athletic contests. Games or play or even gambling (in itself) are all ordained primarily to the pleasures of the mind or as a remedy for a possibly unhealthy attitude of mind or of body often consequent on prolonged serious occupation. There is need for such rec-

---

[35] *A New English Dictionary* (10 vols., edited by J. Murray, H. Bradley and Associates, Oxford: at the Clarendon Press, 1888-1928), IV, under *G*, p. 35, col. 2.

reation. Thus bodily and mental recreation, sports, and the like, if enjoyed in moderation, serve a definite purpose.

Saint Thomas gave formal recognition to this need in his treatment of the virtue of *eutrapelia.* This is the virtue which regulates one's recreation, which seeks to prevent it from touching the extremes of too much or too little recreation. He wrote in part:

> Just as man needs bodily rest for the body's refreshment, because he cannot always be at work, since his power is finite and equal to a certain fixed amount of work, so too it is with his soul, whose power is also finite and equal to a fixed amount of work. . . . Now, sensible goods are connatural to man, and therefore, when the soul rises above sensible things through being intent on the operations of the mind, there results a certain weariness of soul. . . . Now, just as weariness of the body is dispelled by means of resting the body, so weariness of the soul is remedied by means of resting the soul: and the soul's rest is pleasure. . . . Such words or deeds in which nothing further is sought than the soul's delight are necessary at times to give rest, as it were, to the soul. This is in agreement with the Philosopher (*Ethics,* iv, 8) that "in the intercourse of this life there is a kind of rest that is associated with games"; hence it is sometimes necessary to make use of these things.
>
> . . . In this regard there are three points which stand in need of special caution. The first and foremost is that the pleasure in question should not be sought in indecent or harmful words or deeds. . . . Another thing to be observed is that one does not lose the balance of one's mind altogether. . . . Thirdly, we must be careful, as in all other human actions, to conform ourselves to persons, time, and place, and to take due account of other circumstances as well. . . .[36]

When employed as a verb the word *gaming* takes on a meaning which to most minds is synonymous with the word gambling, though this is a restricted usage. The dictionary defines the word thus: "To gamble; to play at games of chance for a prize, stake, or wager."[37] In the light of this

---

[36] *Summa Theologica,* IIa IIae, q. 168, art. 2 (the writer's translation).

[37] *A New English Dictionary,* IV, under *G,* p. 39, col. 1.

definition the term seems to bear the restricted meaning of games of chance only, but certainly common usage has made it applicable both to games of chance and to games which require skill. There is one author who seems to use the word *gaming* as having reference to games or events of skill only. In speaking of gaming and wagering, Davis places the distinction between the two in the fact that in gaming the event on which the stakes are laid is the result of skill, whereas in wagering the event or fact on which the wager is laid is presumed to be beyond the power of the contracting parties to effect.[38] In view of the easily defended multiplicity of meanings which this word enjoys, it is difficult to show that it is wrong to accept the word *gaming* in the restricted sense of games of skill. However, that is an unusual and uncommon use of the word, for gaming generally is applied to games of chance only, or to the so-called mixed games in which both skill and chance can enter as elements.

Considered in itself, gambling, with its concepts of betting and gaming, is not intrinsically evil. A game of chance in itself and exclusive of evil circumstances is licit and honest, for in moderation it can benefit man both as an individual and as a member of society.[39] While it is difficult to defend gambling from the moral viewpoint in all its aspects, yet it is inaccurate and bordering on puritanism to subject it to a wholesale condemnation, as is frequently done in our own day. What was put on paper in a particular article on the evils of gambling over fifty years ago may be taken even now as typical of the argumentation of many who would wrap a blanket of condemnation around gambling. One reads:

> ...Let them (ministers) present as forcibly as lies in their power the *inherent wrong* there is in it (gambling). Gambling is only another name for stealing, whether it be gambling on the sidewalk...or over the athletic contests between our college

---

[38] Davis, *Moral Theology*, II, 403.

[39] O'Brien, "The Morality of Gambling" — *The Ecclesiastical Review*, CIX (1943), 406.

institutions, or in the poolrooms, or on the race-track....Every attempt to get something for nothing, to take from a neighbor, whether money or article of greater or less value, without rendering the equivalent, is on a par with putting one's hand into the neighbor's pocket and removing what belongs to him without his knowledge or consent. From a moral standpoint, there is no difference in the transactions. *Betting is wrong; because it is wrong to take your neighbor's money without giving him anything in return.*[40]

It is not easy to appreciate the worth of the contention that it is morally evil to take anything from one's neighbor without giving him something in return. The best answer is to point to the conditions upon which gambling rests for its morality; it will be seen then that such argumentation is utterly false. All things being equal, every one who owns anything which is properly his own can give it away absolutely. He may also give it away under some condition, whether that condition depend on chance, on industry, or on a combination of both.

Article 2. Conditions for Licit Gambling

This topic is treated in the textbooks of moral theology under the general consideration given to the virtue of justice, for gambling, like buying and selling, is a contract. It is a bilateral, onerous contract in which persons engaged in a certain game or project agree that a reward or prize shall go to the winner.[41] In this definition no mention is

---

[40] Article, "The Gambling Evil" — *The Homiletic Review* (New York, 1877-), XXIII (1892), 382.

[41] Noldin, *Summa Theologiæ Moralis iuxta Codicem Iuris Canonici* (22. ed., 3 vols., Oeniponte: Typis et Sumptibus Fel. Rausch, 1934), II, n. 622 (hereafter cited *Summa*); Ross, *Christian Ethics* (New York: Devin-Adair Co., 1924), n. 763 (hereafter cited *Ethics*); Ballerini-Palmieri, *Opus Theologicum Morale* (7 vols., Prati, 1889-1893), III, n. 572 (hereafter cited *Opus Morale*); Lehmkuhl, *Theologia Moralis* (5. ed., 2 vols., Friburgi Brisboviæ, 1888), I, n. 1139; Pighi, *Cursus Theologiæ Moralis* (4. ed., 3 vols., Veronæ, 1926), II, n. 567; Merkelbach, *Summa Theologiæ Moralis ad mentem D. Thomæ* (3. ed., 3 vols., Parisiis: Typis Desclée de Brouwer et Soc., 1938-1939), II, n. 600 (hereafter cited *Summa*); St. Alphonsus, *Theologia Moralis*, lib. III, n. 871.

made of the elements upon which the outcome of the game or the event depends; the definition looks to gambling only as a contract, and considers the question of the virtue of justice which enters into almost every contract.

The word universally used in the Latin is *ludus*. In its juridic sense it is taken to mean the contract which arises between those who gamble. From this it is by extension applied also to the act or game itself in which the contracting parties are engaged. In this latter usage the word admits of a threefold division: *ludus aleatorius*, in which the outcome depends entirely or almost entirely upon chance or luck, e.g., dice games; *ludus industrialis*, in which the outcome is determined by the skill or ability of the contestants, e.g., chess, checkers; *ludus mixtus*, in which skill and luck both play a part, in more or less equal degree, e.g., in many card games.

Each and every contract or game is licit only when the required conditions are present. In addition, care is to be exercised lest these games become a source of scandal to others; they must not be such as are justly prohibited, nor are they to occasion anything sinful for those who are actively engaged in them or for those who are only spectators. It is also to be cautioned that excesses, with regard both to the time spent and the amount wagered, are to be avoided if these games are to remain licit for those who engage in them. What are the conditions which directly determine the licitness of gambling? They are given as four:[42]

I. The players must be morally able and willing to alienate the thing staked. It must belong to the gamblers, and it must also be at their free disposal. Therefore, one cannot gamble with money that does not belong to one, or with money which should be applied to the payment of outstanding debts. Still, in abstraction from altering circumstances a person as long as he had the necessary collateral with

[42] Cf. Noldin, *Summa*, II, nn. 623-624; Merkelbach, *Summa*, II, n. 600.

which to cover a possible loss may retain what he had won in gambling with the money of another; but, in consequence of the relevant circumstance which alters the case, he could keep what he had won, if he did not have any resources with which to cover any possible loss.[43]

II. The game must be freely entered into. This is necessary, for without this freedom there can be no true consent. A contract arises or falls with consent or its absence. Thus one who emerges victor in a game with an opponent who is half competent or half drunk, for example, is not morally justified in taking or retaining what he has won. The same holds true if a person is forced to play through fear, fraud, or any other unjust means. A person is not bound to pay his losses if he has played to avert insulting talk from another, provided that otherwise he would not have played.[44]

III. There must not be any cheating, nor any use of underhanded methods. One who wins by cheating is bound to make compensation both as to the actual losses and also as to the hope of victory which the loser would otherwise have enjoyed. It is to be noted that in gambling, as in warfare, there are certain stratagems that are perfectly licit, and are understood as such by those who gamble. It is allowed to bluff one's opponents, to look at cards which are exposed as a result of another's negligence, to fail to call attention to impending mistakes in play, etc.[45] These are legitimate devices and augment the ability of him who includes them in his manner of play.

---

[43] Ballerini-Palmieri, *Opus Morale*, III, n. 566.

[44] St. Alphonsus, *op. cit.*, lib. III, n. 877.

[45] Prümmer, *Manuale Theologiæ Moralis Secundum Principia S. Thomæ Aquinatis* (10. ed., recognita a P. Dr. Engelberto Münch, O.P., 3 vols., Barcelona: Editorial Herder, 1945-1946), II, n. 318.

IV. There must be some sort of equality between the parties if the contract is to be equitable. Each party must have an equal hope of gain and an equal danger of loss. This is why cheating is wrong. It would be wrong for an expert player deceitfully to conceal his proficiency with the sole hope of drawing some unsuspecting soul into a game. Under such conditions the loser would not be morally obliged to meet his losses. The principle of "*scienti et consentienti non fit iniuria*"[46] finds application here in the case of one who is willing to play even though forewarned of his opponent's superior ability. If he is willing to assume the added risk of matching skill with one openly indicated as possessing superior ability, then he is bound to pay in the event of subsequent loss.

If any of these conditions be wanting, the gambling is by that fact illicit. Even when they are present and the lawfulness of the game has been objectively established, it is to be remembered that attendant circumstances may render gambling illicit and even sinful. The false hopes aroused by an occasional stroke of good fortune often lead men into excesses. Great expenditure of time and money may easily render such games morally evil; this for clerics and lay people alike.

Article 3. Conditions for Licit Betting

Betting may be defined as "the backing of an affirmation or a forecast by offering to forfeit, in case of an adverse issue, a sum of money or an article of value to one who, by accepting, maintains the opposite and backs his opinion by a corresponding stipulation."[47] Betting is a

---

[46] Reg. 27, R. J., in VI°; article, "*Consentienti non fit iniuria*" — *Revue Ecclésiastique de Liége* (Liége, 1908-), XXIX (1937), 285-290.

[47] Slater, "Betting" — *Catholic Encyclopedia*, II, 539.

contract in which there are two or more persons concerned, which parties are in disagreement as to the truth of some proposition or the existence of some object of which neither party is certain. They agree to give a certain sum to the one who is proved to be or to have been right. This is in substantial accord with the definition as found in various authors.[48]

One important difference between gaming and betting lies in the means by reason of which the specified objective is realized. In gaming, it is the success of the play or game that ends the contract, by indicating the winner and the loser. In betting it is the truth which ends the contract, for a bet always concerns the statement and its truth. In betting, if the contract is merely unilateral, the resulting obligation is one of fidelity or justice according as the bettor wishes to bind himself. Should the contract be bilateral, as is usually the case, the resulting obligation binds in justice, provided the elements for a valid contract be present. This distinction in reality is of practical import only in those cases wherein the obligation is one that binds in justice.

The principles on gambling apply here, with the addition of these points, namely:

I. That the thing or object about which the wager is made be understood in the same sense by both parties — otherwise there is no contract.[49]

II. That the thing be doubtful or the event be uncertain with respect to both parties — otherwise there is wanting the required equality between the hope of gain and the danger of loss. If one is certain of the truth in issue, he can neither lawfully nor validly wager. If a person has definite knowledge, there is no equality of risk, as is clear. Should the

[48] Ferraris, *Bibliotheca*, sub v. *ludus*, n. 4; Merkelbach, *Summa*, II, n. 601; Noldin, *Summa*, II, n. 619; Pighi, *op. cit.*, II, n. 558; Ross, *Ethics*, p. 371.

[49] Noldin, *Summa*, II, n. 620.

other party, although forewarned, nevertheless, wish to wager, the contract is valid.[50]

III. That the reward be equal for both, unless one of the contracting parties freely offers more. This would be verified in those cases wherein certain "odds" are offered and accepted by both parties.

IV. That the object of the wager be something morally good or at least indifferent, or something not prohibited. In the Bull *In eligendis* of Pope Pius IV (1559-1565), under date of October 9, 1562, it was forbidden to bet on the outcome of papal elections.[51] In 1591, in a letter *Cogit Nos,* Pope Gregory XIV (1590-1591) extended this ban on betting to include the election of Cardinals and the possible length of life and the date of death of the Pope. This penalty was a *latæ sententiæ* excommunication reserved to the Holy Father.[52]

Another condition specified for licitness by Saint Alphonsus (1696-1787) is that there must be a *motivum cohonestans.*[53] It is on this very point that a sharp distinction is drawn between gaming and betting. It is his opinion that mere betting cannot regularly be excused from venial sin, since the motives of licit recreation and entertainment which justify gambling (gaming) are frequently absent in betting. This would seem rather severe, for there are reasonable purposes, other than that of recreation and entertainment, which may be present to render the betting licit. Among these motives is the desire to end a dispute, to break up an evil friendship, or to teach another a much needed lesson.[54]

---

[50] Merkelbach, *Summa,* II, n. 601.

[51] Mentioned in St. Alphonsus, *op. cit.,* III, n. 869.

[52] *Bullarum Diplomatum et Privilegiorum Sacrorum Romanorum Pontificum Taurinensis Editio* (24 vols. et Index, Augustæ Taurinorum, 1857-1872), IX, 397.

[53] *Op. cit.,* III, n. 869.

[54] Koch-Preuss, *A Handbook of Moral Theology* (3. ed., 5 vols., St. Louis: B. Herder Book Co., 1925-1933), V, 340.

Article 4. The Meaning of "Ludus Aleatorius"

What is probably the most delicate aspect of the examination of the law of the Code on gambling is the determination of just what the legislator intended by the phrase "*ludus aleatorius.*" Until one takes a definite stand on this point, it is extremely rash to attempt to define just what specific forms of gambling are banned by the ruling of canon 138. The whole thing is not blessed with the simplicity which at first blush seems to be present. The canon does not define this phrase. Practically all of the moral theologians and canonists offer a definition, but they are not one in that definition. A fivefold division, by reason of the divergence in the definition, may be instituted:

Group one: this group is composed of those who hold that *ludus aleatorius* is a game whose outcome depends *entirely* on chance;

Group two: in this group it is held that this phrase refers to games whose outcome depends *almost entirely* or at least *principally* on chance;

Group three: this group comprises those who say that *ludus aleatorius* is a game in which there is found *more chance than skill;*

Group four: this group embraces those whose definition when viewed in its full context and interpreted in the light of a decretal commentator, may despite its seeming contrary import be held to refer to games whose outcome depends *entirely on chance;*

Group five: here no definition is given, i.e., Bouscaren-Ellis, Vermeersch-Creusen, Cocchi, Coronata, and Berutti.

Those in group one indicate this total dependence upon chance by the use of such expressions as "*in quo ludo 'sola fortuna' intervenit,*"[55] "*ludi qui 'totaliter a fortuna' pen-*

---

[55] Aertnys-Damen, *Theologia Moralis,* I, n. 1132; Ferraris, *Bibliotheca,* sub v. *ludus,* n. 6; D'Annibale, *Summula Theologiæ Moralis* (5. ed., 3 vols., Romæ, 1908), III, n. 160, note 30 (hereafter cited *Summula*).

dent,"[56] and *"ludus totus situs in pura sorte."*[57] This same idea is expressed by other authors of this group whose terminology varies but slightly.[58]

There are two authors within the second group whose possible inclusion even in group one is contingent upon the translation of the word *potissimum.* If it is taken in a secondary though valid sense of "above all," then these authors would be in the first group. The more usual rendition of "principally" places them in this present (second) group.[59] The others[60] hold with Merkelbach (1871-1942) that under this term comes that type of game in which the result *" 'fere omnino' a casu pendet."*[61]

The definition of a game of chance which is substantially representative of the mind of the third group is: *"(ludus qui) 'casu potius quam arte' dirigatur."* Weight is added to this opinion by the fact that many who favor it

---

[56] Genicot-Salsmans, *Institutiones Theologiæ Moralis* (10. ed., 2 vols., Bruxellis: Alb. Dewit, 1922), II, n. 42 (hereafter cited *Institutiones*); Tanquerey, *Synopsis Moralis,* III, n. 1030; Brys, *"De oblectamentis status clericalis decentiæ repugnantibus"* — *Coll. Brug.,* XXXV (1935), 284; Kinane, "Clerical Obligations" —*Irish Eccl. Record,* V. Series, XI (1918), 477.

[57] Sabetti-Barrett, *Compendium Theologiæ Moralis* (19. ed., Neo-Eboraci: F. Pustet Co., 1920), n. 587 (hereafter cited *Compendium*); De Angelis, *Prælectiones Iuris Canonici* (2. ed., 7 vols. in 5, Romæ, 1908), II, pars 1, p. 11; Crnica, *Commentarium,* I, 155; Toso, *Commentaria Minora,* II, 102; Ojetti, *Commentarium in Codicem Iuris Canonici,* Vol. II, *De Personis* (Romæ: Apud Aedes Universitatis Gregorianæ, 1928), 149 (hereafter cited *Commentarium*).

[58] Regatillo, *Institutiones Iuris Canonici,* Vol. I, *Normæ Generales-De Personis* (2. ed., Santander: Sal Terræ, 1946), p. 158; De Larranga, *Prontuario di Teologia Moral* (ed. reconocida, Romæ, 1907), p. 454; Marc, *Institutiones Morales* (6. ed., 2 vols., Romæ, 1891), II, n. 2231; Lumbreras, *De Fortitudine et Temperantia* (Romæ: "Angelicum," 1939), n. 354, note 1, quoting Cajetan; Donovan, *Compendium Theologiæ Moralis ad Mentem Ballerini* (3 vols. in 1, S. Ludovici, 1895-1898), II, 164.

[59] Beste, *Introductio,* p. 189; Chelodi, *De Personis,* p. 186.

[60] Noldin, *Summa,* II, n. 622; Koch-Preuss, *op. cit.,* III, 41; Ayrinhac, *General Legislation in the New Code of Canon Law* (New York: Benziger, 1923), n. 298 (hereafter cited *General Legislation*); Lehmkuhl, *Theologia Moralis,* I, n. 1139.

[61] *Summa,* II, 633.

are well-known canonists, the majority of them pre-Code authors.[62]

The fourth group uses the phrase "game of hazard" as a synonym for the Latin "*ludus aleatorius.*" This is virtually a literal translation of the word *aleatorius*, for the word hazard, like the word *alea*, in its root meaning has reference to a certain game of dice — a game which corresponded to our game of "craps." It was a short step to extend it then to all those games, games like hazard, which in their outcome were dependent entirely on luck. Panormitanus[63] used the term as being identical with the word *ludus taxillorum*. The word *taxilli* was used in designation of a special and smaller type of dice employed in these games. From this one may conclude that the phrase "game of hazard"[64] and its other language equivalents *giocare d'azzardo*[65] and *jeux de hasard*[66] mean the same as a "game entirely dependent on chance." In reality, then, this group becomes identifiable with group one, which offers substantially the same definition for the phrase *ludus aleatorius*.

As has been noted, the fifth and final group offers no definition. Bouscaren-Ellis say that this section of canon 138 forbids "habitual gaming for money."[67] The problem is: what do they understand by gaming? In view of the definitions here set forth, one may perhaps warrantably assume that they intend to ban games which depend entirely

---

[62] Schmalzgrueber, lib. III, tit. 1, n. 46; Reiffenstuel, lib. III, tit. 1, n. 57; Wernz, *Ius Decretalium*, II, n. 214; Blat, *Commentarium*, II, n. 77; Sipos, *Enchiridion*, p. 135; Santi, *Prælectiones*, lib. III, tit. 1, n. 19; Vermeersch, *Theologiæ Moralis Principia-Responsa-Consilia* (3. ed., 4 vols., Roma: Università Gregoriana, 1944-1947), III, 17 (hereafter cited *Theologiæ Moralis Principia*).

[63] *Commentaria*, ad c. 15, X, *de vita et honestate clericorum*, III, n. 4.

[64] Augustine, *Commentary*, II, 87.

[65] Stocchiero, *Codice del Clero secondo il Codex Iuris Canonici* (Vicenza: Società Anonima Tipografica, 1928), n. 169 (hereafter cited *Codice del Clero*); Falco, *Corso di Diritto Ecclesiastico* (Padova: Tipographia del Seminario, 1930), p. 76.

[66] Cance, *Le Code de Droit Canonique* (3 vols., Paris: Libraire LeCoffre, 1927-1929), I, 161 (hereafter cited *Le Code*).

[67] *Canon Law*, p. 115.

on chance, and indeed such games exclusively; yet, one could also defend the position that they ban games in which the outcome depends both on skill and chance. Since these authors, however, do not define their terms, the matter must remain uncertain and unsettled.

The difference in definition stems from an ability to determine just how extensive a part is to be assigned to the element of chance in any *ludus aleatorius*. Four of the groups explicitly agree that chance does enter into the picture; beyond that point their uniformity is not in evidence. The view which seems preferable is that of group one. Accordingly, then, the games which are forbidden to clerics, when played for money *(pecunia exposita)* and with frequency, are those games whose final result depends upon fortune, chance, or just plain luck. In the development of this law through the centuries one notes that the early prohibition of Church and civil authorities was aimed at games of chance, i.e., games entirely dependent on chance. Soon, however, there was added to this prohibition the phrase *"et ab aliis ludis,"* with the result that all games were banned.

It was not until the fourteenth and fifteenth centuries that distinctions were made between games based on luck alone, on skill alone, or on a varying combination of both. Concomitantly distinctions were made as to which of these games were outlawed; yet, there was no agreement as to what games were prohibited, not even in regard to those games in which some skill was exhibited.[68] Many held that chess, a game of pure skill, was not to be played by clerics. Others insisted just as strongly that this game did not fall under the prohibition of the law. The Council of Trent did little to clarify the situation, for it merely indicated that it wished to restate the laws which previous Popes and councils had already decreed in this matter.[69]

---

[68] Vide *supra*, pp. 51, 53, 56.

[69] Sess. XXII, *de ref.*, c. 1 — *Canones et Decreta*, p. 142.

The existing uncertainty as to the extent of the prohibition was mirrored in the phrase *"ab illicitis ludis abstineant [clerici],"* also found in the legislation of the same Council of Trent. By this device it was left to the individual bishops to decide just which games were forbidden.[70] In the eighteenth century Saint Alphonsus definitely stated that the law was directed against games which depended entirely on luck, his argumentation being based on the early use of the term and also on its etymology.[71] From that time on increasing numbers held to this opinion, although in the century prior to the Code many authors held the term to refer to games in which chance played more of a part than did skill. After the Code, however, the stricter definition became more commonly accepted. This strict definition rightly limits the scope of canon 138. While this canon aims rather at preserving and safeguarding clerical dignity than at restricting clerical freedom, it still has in it something of a *"res odiosa."* As such it is to be limited in its interpretational scope.

Article 5. The Elements of Time and Money

It is to be recalled that this particular section of canon 138 is composed of three phrases, separated each from the other by a comma in the actual wording of the canon, each phrase possessing a separate and important thought. The first of these is *ludus aleatorius;* the second and third respectively are *pecunia exposita* and [*clerici*] *ne vacent.* These two phrases serve to limit the prohibition against the indulging by clerics in games of chance. Are clerics now forbidden without exception to play games of chance, as they were in the very early days of the Church when no explicit mention of money was made in the law? The an-

---

[70] Sess. XXIV, *de ref.*, c. 12 — *Canones et Decreta,* p. 192; Benedictus XIV, *De Synodo,* lib. XI, c. 10, nn. III-IV.

[71] "...nam *alea* est nomen comprehendens solos ludos sortis, qui non arte, sed omnino a casu penditur...." — *Theologia Moralis,* lib. III, n. 900.

swer is no, for under the law as it exists today there is no explicit mention of the element of money and a connotation of the element of time. Clerics now are forbidden to play these games with steady frequency or habituated addiction — this is in the verb *vacare*.[72]

Coronata is alone in establishing a close relationship between the element of time and the element of scandal. He seems to say in effect that one may play any number of times provided that no occasion for scandal be offered to the laity.[73] This view seems to overlook the possibility of offending against the law by playing too often, even though the faithful have no knowledge that the cleric or priest gambles or plays at all. Fortunately, it is rare that excesses come to the ears of the faithful. The aim of the canon seems to be to limit the cleric to an occasional game, in which only small stakes are wagered; the game should serve for honest recreation, and not simply for the opportunity of gaining money. If the sum is great *and* the playing is frequent, then it is difficult to excuse the cleric from serious sin.

Some authors simply postulate the association of a protracted playing with a frequent playing for constituting the action as gravely sinful. This, they hold, would constitute a grave sin even if there were no scandal.[74] This doctrine seems rather severe, unless one is to understand that there are also substantial money stakes involved. For if money is not in question, such long and protracted playing would be forbidden by the natural law perhaps, but not by the ruling of canon 138. The same is to be said of the view which holds that a cleric sins gravely if a large sum of money is involved, even though the gambling be done

---

[72] Berardi, *Gratiani Canones Genuini ab Apocryphis Discreti* (3 vols. in 4, Venetiis, 1777), I, 13a; St. Raymond of Pennafort, *Summa*, lib. II, tit. 8, 9.

[73] "...prohibetur *vacatio*, i.e., tempus in his rebus terere cum fidelium scandalo...." — *Institutiones*, I, 230.

[74] Ojetti, *Commentarium*, II, 150; D'Annibale, *Summula*, III, n. 160; Reiffenstuel indicated that this was the common teaching of the theologians of his day. — Lib. III, tit. 1, n. 58.

infrequently.[75] The wording of the canon demands that both conditions be verified before a violation of the law sets in. If the violation of this canon is to imply the presence of a serious sin, then there must be frequent playing *and* large sums of money involved. If either the one or the other of these factors be lacking, a cleric may indeed still sin gravely, but then the violation of the natural law is what produces the grave sin. The grave sin does not result from non-compliance with what canon 138 itself demands. The same holds true of scandal. A priest could sin seriously by way of giving scandal, even though he gambled but once in his life, and then only for an insignificant sum.

While a number of authors hold that it becomes wrong for clerics to spend overmuch time in playing these games (when money is involved), no one ventures to say just how much time constitutes such an excess. This silence is proof that it is difficult to establish any hard and fast rule applicable to all priests, since the particular labors of some allow them more free time than is had by others. It stands to reason that a priest stationed in a large city parish would have less free time than another priest whose work permitted him to be free several nights a week. If a priest neglects his work because of an interest in gambling, often he is not the first to be aware of it. Moreover, the attitude of one's fellow priests may often remain relatively tolerant no matter how frequently or long the playing has been indulged in. Because of this fact, if a priest's attention is called to his excesses by another priest, the guilty party should give thought to this correction. In agreement with the view of Coronata one may say that when the faithful become genuinely scandalized at the gambling habits of a priest, then surely that priest stands dangerously close to serious sin if he continues on. It seems safe to say that

[75] Aertyns-Damen (*Theologia Moralis,* I, n. 1132), for example, present such a strict view.

once or twice a week should be sufficient occasion for any priest to engage in these games.[76]

The other condition which must be present is that the playing be for money stakes. Violence is done to the real meaning of the phrase *pecunia exposita* by those very few who believe that the money must be really visible before this condition is verified. Recently submitted for a solution in the pages of an ecclesiastical journal was the question whether it was a sin and a violation of the ruling of canon 138 for priests to gamble *with money on the table.* Apparently this translation was held too rare for comment, since no reference was made to it in the response.[77] In reply it was stated that the precept of not gambling did not in itself bind under pain of mortal sin, although a precept to an individual could make it so binding. It was likewise held that gambling, *pecunia exposita,* occurred even if there was no actual display of money. Such a case could occur even when there was question of objects invested with a money value. The phrase simply meant that money was made the object of the game.[78]

A substantial sum must be involved.[79] Some writers express the same thought by conversely stating that the cleric is free from guilt if the stakes are small.[80] It will not be out of place here to note what Ferreres (1861-1936) stated. He held that the prohibition of this canon is in itself a grave one. But it does not include any game which is not entirely dependent on chance, nor does it bind if there is no money involved. If the amount is small, it is a venial

[76] Tanquerey (1854-1932) held that a priest plays frequently when he plays "*pluries in hebdomada.*" — *Synopsis Moralis,* III, n. 1030.

[77] *The Homiletic and Pastoral Review,* XLV (1944), 58 (hereafter cited *HPR*).

[78] Aertnys-Damen render it "*cum pacto pecuniæ.*" — *Theologia Moralis,* I, n. 1132.

[79] Chelodi, *De Personis,* p. 196; Cocchi, *Commentarium,* lib. II, pars I, n. 50.

[80] Kinane, "*Clerical Obligations*" — *IER,* V. Series, XI (1918), 477; Sabetti-Barrett, *Compendium,* n. 587; Santi, *Prælectiones,* lib. III, tit. 1, n. 19; Ayrinhac, *General Legislation,* n. 292.

sin.[81] This view, then, renders the matching of pennies and nickels a venial sin. More tenable seems the view of those who maintain that the prohibition is in itself a light one. For rendering one guilty of serious sin they postulate a large sum of money plus frequent playing. The violation of the natural law, as has been seen, is an entirely different consideration.

A practical difficulty is encountered when one attempts to determine an absolute sum beyond which a cleric cannot gamble without being in danger of committing a serious sin. There are several factors which tend to complicate the problem. It is a known fact that clerics (and priests) in certain sections of this country enjoy more of this world's goods than do their co-workers. This may result from a number of reasons, all of which are invested with importance only in so far as they substantiate this fact. Therefore, a priest of relative means may be able to lose from twenty-five to fifty dollars at one sitting in a gambling game or at a gambling device, while another priest could scarcely afford to lose even half that amount over a period of time. A priest who is not burdened with outstanding financial obligations could afford, both from financial and moral considerations, to lose more than some priest who is burdened with unpaid debts, or who is conscience-bound to support needy parents or relatives. It does not seem possible to arrive at a standard sum by comparison with the amounts which moral theologians set as being necessary before one is guilty of grievous sin in the matter of theft. This absolute sum has risen with the recent increases in wages and the corresponding decrease in the purchasing power of money. For a cleric who gambled too frequently the sum would need not be so high.

Priestly salaries, with rare exception, have remained static. In some instances a proper adjustment has been made. It may be stated that for the average priest (finan-

---

[81] *Compendium Theologiæ Moralis* (14. ed., 3 vols., Barcinone: Eugenius Subirana, 1928), II, n. 113 (hereafter cited *Compendium*).

cially speaking) to lose the income of a week, and certainly the income of a month, in gambling (in playing games whose outcome is effected by pure chance) would point to a serious violation of the law as it is expressed in canon 138. It may be objected that one may dispose freely of what is his own. This is true, but he may not do so in a manner which is forbidden to him in the Code. Clerics are forbidden to engage in gambling if that involves the loss of a considerable sum of money. While it remains for moralists and canonists to indicate the amount beyond which as an absolute sum clerics cannot without mortal sin involve themselves in gambling, it may safely be said that no priest can feel free in conscience to lose large sums of money in gambling when there are pressing demands on his charity at home and abroad.

Article 6. Games Which Are Forbidden

Under the definition of *ludus aleatorius*, as previously given,[82] all forms of dice games are forbidden. The most common of these seems to be the game of craps. Despite the fact that some quite earnestly contend that there is a very definite and delicate technique which, if employed in the rolling of the dice, will produce a winner, it is the common belief that this game depends entirely upon luck.[83] Also forbidden is the "21" game. This dice game is one in which the player attempts, within a predetermined and limited number of throws, to make appear (or reappear) at least twenty-one times the number chosen by himself antecedently to the initial throw of the dice. There are many variants on the principle of the game; often the employed number of dice varies from three to five. Infrequently six dice are used. When more dice are used then the number of throws becomes accordingly reduced. Known by various

82 Vide *supra*, p. 72.

83 Levinson, *Your Chance to Win* (New York: Farrar and Rinehart, 1939), p. 172.

names in different parts of the country, e.g., by the name of "chuck-a-luck" in the Middle West, it is a favorite at bazaars, parish picnics, and charitable gatherings generally. Of a similar nature in that they are based on the use of dice and the workings of pure chance are "paddle wheels" and "squirrel cages."

The use of punchboards is also forbidden to clerics. Most of the time the possibility of losing great sums of money is remote, for the cost of an individual "punch" is quite small. There are some boards, however, as found in private clubs, with reference to which the total value runs into hundreds of dollars. The prizes given on the average punchboard are merchandise; the same holds true in many of the dice games. Does this fact bring the game under the phrase *pecunia exposita?* It does, for money is the condition upon which one makes himself eligible to play the game, and, if fortunate, to receive a prize. What if tickets and not money are given before each game? This would still come within the prohibition of the law, for there is a moral unity existing between these tickets and the money with which they were originally purchased. By law many States forbid these punchboards. Under these circumstances a cleric may easily give scandal, even though he spent but little money and time in playing a punchboard. The natural law, rather than canon 138, would prohibit such action.

Another exercise of a gambling nature, known to be habit-forming for many, is the playing of slot machines. The fatal fascination of these machines may easily lead one to waste time and money in playing them. Clerics are no exception. Playing these machines is forbidden to clerics, though infrequent playing could be countenanced; they should not play publicly, however, for scandal may arise. This is doubly true if these machines have been interdicted by civil statute.

Another game of pure chance, a game likewise forbidden, is roulette. This takes no skill; it asks for nothing more than the ability to place a bet. This is a game in which the odds are always slightly against the player.[84] The game, as the name suggests, is played with a wheel to be spun rapidly (by electrical control mostly), so that the small ball (marble) which it contains may finally come to rest in one of the thirty-seven numbered compartments or slots at the edge of the rotating wheel. The ball is caused to travel rapidly around the "track," which slopes toward the center of the concave board where the wheel is rotating. On the inner edge of the "track" are set metal "studs," whose purpose is to deflect the ball when it loses its momentum.

There are no limits to the amount which can be wagered, so that theoretically there are no limits to the amounts which may be won or lost. The odds vary with the total of numbers chosen, dropping proportionately as more possible winning numbers are chosen. The highest returns are paid for winning on a single number — the player wins thirty-six times his original bet. In November of 1947 at Reno, Nevada, two college boys turned $120.00 into $9,000 by a system of "progressive parlay," based upon a "logging" of the bias of the wheel. Big time gamblers insisted that their "system" was merely luck, pointing to the fact that before they stopped playing the boys had lost several thousand dollars, and probably would have lost all their money eventually.[85]

There would probably be little opportunity for clerics to play this type of roulette, for it is found only in public gambling establishments. No cleric would enter such a place in his clerical garb, nor would he go without his clerical dress. If such a wheel were found in a private residence, caution should be exercised in the playing, which

---

[84] For a highly technical discussion of the general theory of "odds," consult Von Neumann-Morgenstern, *The Theory of Games and Economic Behaviour* (Princeton: Princeton Univ. Press, 1944); Levinson, *op. cit.*, pp. 156-169.

[85] *Time* (New York, 1923-   ), L (1947), n. 22, 64. These same young men won $35,000 at Reno in May of 1948.

should be infrequent and for extremely modest wagers. Scandal is easily given and just as readily taken.

All forms of "matching" games are ruled out. The most simple of these is the game of "heads and tails," in which the probability of either result is the same. This game is also called "odds and evens," and may be played by two or three people. To this type of gambling would also belong the use of the roulette wheels which are manufactured for private play. These do not imply any advantage for the "banker," since half the compartments are red, the other half black. The game then, from the probability standpoint, becomes identical with "heads and tails." Under the same prohibition would also come a card game known as "high card" or "single showdown." It represents the factor of luck completely, as the game (if it can be called that) depends on the cut of a single card by each of these players. The winner is the one who turns up the highest card.

What about bingo, our social gambling? This is a very innocent game, which constitutes a source of considerable revenue for parishes in localities where it is not banned by state or municipal law. Yet, strictly considered, it also is forbidden to clerics. There seems to be no great danger, however, of any violation of the law contained in canon 138, for while clerics may sponsor these events in the interests of the parish and the community, they themselves rarely have the time or the inclination to play. This seems to be the one game in which they would not have to fear the danger of scandal, even should they play. People do not seem to regard this as gambling. The game is still banned, even though it may hide under other names. It is stretching the meaning of skill a bit too far to contend, as some do,[86] that bingo is a game of both skill and luck. About all that is required for this game is that the contestant be capable of an *actus humanus*. It simply implies the ability to hear

---

[86] O'Brien, "The Morality of Gambling" — *The Ecclesiastical Review* (Philadelphia, 1905-1943), CIX (1943), 405.

and to be able to recognize numbers and match them. But this is not skill, at least not in the sense in which skill is to be understood in canon 138.

Article 7. Games Which Are Not Forbidden

Games which are entirely dependent on skill or almost entirely so, as also those which are dependent partly on skill and partly on chance, do not come within the scope of the prohibition enacted in canon 138. By common law, therefore, all types of card games are allowed if there be in them some notable element of skill. These games should be played primarily for the sake of honest recreation. If money stakes are a consideration in these friendly games, prudence would demand that they be moderate.[87]

Card playing may also indirectly result in a serious violation of the natural law itself — if it leads priests to neglect their duties, to give scandal to others, or to fall prey to a train of evils which may possibly flow from an abuse of card playing.[88] Local legislation could under these circumstances prohibit certain types or all types of card playing. Prior to the Code at least one synod in the United States forbade clerics to play cards for money.[89] After the appearance of the Code there seems to be no specific statute on this point in the synodal laws of this country. In the Province of Bruges (in Belgium) clerics are allowed to play cards, but only privately, and then only for a short time. The stakes are to be small.[90] The Plenary Council

---

[87] Sipos, *Enchiridion*, p. 135.

[88] The Sacred Congregation for the Propagation of the Faith, in words frequently repeated by the councils both in this country and in Europe, points to some of these evils which may and often do flow from gambling: "Animadvertere ipsi (clerici) debent, hominem per ludos ad fraudes, fallacias, mendacia, furta, periuria aliaque enormia scelera incitare consuevisse." — Instr. *(ad Vic. Ap. N.)*, mense aug. 1827 — *Fontes*, n. 4739.

[89] *Synodi Diœcesanæ Grandormensis Primæ Statuta* (Grandormensi Civitate, 1903), n. 57.

[90] Brys, "De oblectamentis status clericalis decentiæ repugnantibus" — *Coll. Brug.*, XXXV (1935), 284.

of Maynooth (1927) in Ireland forbade the involvement of large sums of money in card games, and warned against the protraction of these games to a late hour.[91]

The phrase *ad multam noctem,* as it occurs in the Maynooth Council, is indefinite enough to allow considerable leeway. In the original draft of the statutes of an earlier synod in 1900 the phrase read *ad undecimam horam,* but the other phrase was substituted by the Holy See itself. From this it appears that Rome does not wish the bishops to be overstrict in the prohibitive limits which they set to card playing. The punishment should conform to the misdeed. Pope Benedict XIV (1740-1758) reviewed one such case in which an appeal was made to the Sacred Congregation of the Council from an *ipso facto* enacted excommunication as it attached to a diocesan law. This law forbade gambling in any manner whatsoever.[92] The Congregation admitted the general right of the bishop to make laws on this point, but cautioned against such a heavy censure. The enactment of such a penalty was justified, however, in certain cases which called for drastic intervention on the side of episcopal authority. As Ryan remarks, there should be a truly objective warrant and cause for a bishop when he attaches sanction to his laws. The nature and intensity of the sanction should be tempered to the gravity of the matter at issue, with consideration of all circumstances of person, place, and time.[93]

Among the card games which enjoy popularity among the clerics who seek partial recreation and relaxation in card playing, one may mention cribbage, gin rummy, skat, pinochle, and poker. The game of bridge, also a favorite,

---

[91] "...districte prohibemus ne qui sacerdos chartarum lusus *ad multam noctem* protrahat." — *Acta et Decreta Concilii Plenarii Hiberniæ* (Dublin: Typis Browne et Nolan, 1929), n. 45.

[92] *De Synodo,* lib. X, c. 2, n. 11.

[93] Ryan, *Principles of Episcopal Jurisdiction,* The Catholic University of America Canon Law Studies, n. 120 (Washington, D. C.: The Catholic University of America Press, 1939), pp. 138-139.

although it requires a large element of skill, offers some interesting examples of the working of chance, which for many provides an important part of the attraction of the game. Quite popular is the game of poker. It is distinctly American in character and association, in spite of its French origin and its popularity among many peoples, including the Chinese. In poker, skill plays a great part; in fact, it is the more skilled player who is certain to win in the long run. The one who plays solely for recreation may enjoy a beginner's luck, but in the final analysis it is skill that measures the rewards.

How often may a priest play poker? For how long a time? How much may he afford to lose? These are questions which each priest must answer for himself. Circumstances vary in each case. Poker playing is not forbidden by the common law, nor is it forbidden by diocesan statutes — if it is, that is the rare exception. However, the demands of the natural law are to be met. Priests who play poker would do well to arrange these games only with their fellow priests whenever this is possible. The danger of scandal is very real when a priest becomes a part of a lay poker group. Such associations do not remain secret for any length of time, and once they become broadcast can easily become a source of understandable scandal to others. In certain predominantly Catholic areas a long standing custom has removed the element of scandal from poker playing with the laity. This is the exception. Women should never be part of the group in which a cleric plays poker, nor is it prudent to play with a lay group within one's parish. The playing of poker is in itself a legitimate recreation. If played too often, however, without limit on the stakes and the betting, it may bring sudden and often permanent embarrassment and even sin to the clerics and priests who play. Prudence and common sense must be exercised at all times.

Article 8. Betting on Horses

The term gambling also includes betting. One very popular form of betting is that of betting on horse races.[94] This is legal in those States which allow and recognize pari-mutuel betting.[95] Pari-mutuel means that the odds which are paid by the track to the winner are figured on the basis of the total amount bet on each horse to win, to place, and to show, less a small per cent which goes to the management. It is not necessary that machines be used in order to have pari-mutuel betting. As a matter of fact they are in operation at most tracks, as they afford a quicker and more accurate means for the needed calculations.

Bookmaking (the taking of bets at or away from the track by non-licensed agencies) is generally forbidden by statute even in those States where pari-mutuel betting is legal.[96] Bookmaking is a flourishing business. Despite police attempts to close in on these "bookies," they are still active all over the country, by their activities serving only to complicate further the problem of professional gambling. The highest odds paid by these "bookies" are customarily 20 to 1 to win, 8 to 1 to place, and 4 to 1 to show. This prevails no matter how favorable the actual track odds were. A few large scale gamblers are the exception and will offer the exact track odds.

As has been noted, this bookmaking is almost everywhere forbidden by law. This very fact constitutes an added reason why clerics who use this means of betting on horse races stand in danger of giving real scandal. While

---

[94] In 1946 some $1,800,000,000 was expended in "at-the-track" betting. In addition it is estimated that illegal bookmakers outside the tracks handled about $4,500,000,000 in bets.

[95] For a brief history of bookmaking and pari-mutuel betting in this country, cf. O'Hare, *The Socio-Economic Aspects of Horse-Racing*, The Catholic University of America Studies in Sociology, n. XII (Washington, D. C.: The Catholic University of America Press, 1945), pp. 19-40.

[96] As recently as 1946 bookmaking was outlawed in those states which permitted horse racing, with the exception of New York and Louisiana.

"bookies" themselves have no scruples over breaking the law, they are genuinely "surprised" when they are contacted by a priest who desires to place a bet. For a priest who frequently places bets in this manner there is reason to balance the just causes which may induce him to bet, on the one hand against the evils of the system, and his part in maintaining an enterprise which exists outside the law on the other hand. It is to be admitted that in the over-all picture the outsider's share in maintaining the "bookie" system is small, but in proportion to the amount that he bets, he is responsible for the violation of legitimate statutes set forth by authorized public authority.

This method of placing bets was expressly forbidden in several pre-Code synods in this country.[97] Unless revoked, these laws still bind, as they are *præter Codicem*. If this betting is not forbidden by diocesan law, then it is allowed, for the common law does not extend to this. It is dangerous business, however, and therefore one in which priests should have no part. The words of Kinane, in his comment on the decrees in the Maynooth National Synod which forbid this type of betting, either personally or through another, are much to the point:

> Clearly, what the Fathers of the Council wished to eliminate was, not so much betting, as betting with the bookmakers, on account of the danger which such a practice involves for priests themselves and the scandal which it is calculated to give the laity; and these evils are present in a notable degree even when the bets are small.[98]

---

[97] *Statuta Diœceseos Trentonensis* (Trentonii, 1897), n. 301; *Acta Synodi Roffensis Tertiæ* (Rochester, 1914), n. 136.

[98] Kinane, "Notes and Queries"—*IER*, V. Series, XXXVI (1930), 414; also Kinane, "Notes and Queries"—*IER*, V. Series, XXXIX (1932), 540.

CHAPTER IV

THE PROHIBITION AGAINST CARRYING WEAPONS

PART I. HISTORICAL CONSPECTUS

The hallmark of Christianity even from the days of its struggling infancy has been charity — a love of peace. Violence and all that it represents stand as alien to the Christian concept. The weapons and the implements of force are foreign to the clerical state. It is understandable then that the laws of the Church should forbid clerics to carry weapons, even privately.

Without making any distinction, the I Council of Arles (314) forbade all Christians to carry weapons in time of peace.[1] Since nothing further was added, it may reasonably be inferred that it was, on the contrary, permissible to bear arms in time of war. This, indeed, could be lawful for the laity, but it remained unlawful for clerics. In the sixth century a new penalty was added to a law which forbade clerics both to dress in clothes unbecoming the sobriety of the clerical state, and to carry weapons. At the Synod of Auxerre (ca. 581) the bishops ordered a diet of bread and water for the violators of this law.[2]

Only water and little bread for thirty days was hard punishment, truly, for such a misdeed. This leads one to believe that the custom of carrying arms was in all likelihood strongly entrenched in that particular diocese, at least. From the wording of the canon the penalty is seen to encompass only those who were *de facto* apprehended with weapons on their person. Of importance also was the 19th

[1] Canon 3 — Mansi, II, 471; Hefele-Leclercq, I, 209; Hardouin, I, 265.

[2] Canon 5: "...quodsi...clericus aut cum indecenti veste aut cum armis inventus fuerit...detentus *aqua tantum et modico pane* diebus singulis sustentur (italics inserted)" — *MGH, Leges in 4°*, Sectio III, *Concilia Aevi Merovingici*, Tom. I, (recensuit F. Maassen, 1893), p. 156; Bruns, II, 243.

canon of the IV Provincial Council of Toledo (633). While the large number of archbishops and bishops who came from Spain and Gaul dealt primarily with the question of military service, the tenor of the canon reflected the desire of the Church that clerics have nothing to do with any weapons, save those of the spirit.[3] The main purpose of the canon was to restate and reformulate an earlier law, which had enacted that no one given to military service was to be advanced to the priesthood. The general practice of bearing arms was branded a *"perniciosa consuetudo nequaquam retinenda."* In this same Council canon 45 spoke of performing penance in a monastery. This was the penalty for those clerics who willingly took part in any uprising or internal struggle.[4]

The Council of Bordeaux (663-675) ordered that clerics were not to carry or to retain in their possession spears or any other type of weapon.[5] This law seems to have had a further purpose, aiming as it did at the reduction of large scale clerical hunting. With clerics coming more and more from the ranks of the converted barbarian nations, there arose a special need to set proper bounds to this type of recreation. One efficient method was to forbid clerics to carry weapons.

Saint Boniface (+754), representative of Pope Zachary (741-752) in Germany, presided over the German Plenary Council of 742. This council was convoked at the order of the Frankish authorities. In its second canon it forbade clerics to bear arms. It also forbade them to join the army.[6] It did, however, make provision for a prince to have a bishop or two in the company, together with the chaplains of the latter. Other priests could be joined with the group

---

[3] Bruns, II, 229; Mansi, X, 624.

[4] Bruns, II, 235; Mansi, X, 630.

[5] Canon 1: "...clerici...nec lanceas nec alia arma habere nec portare debeant...."—*MGH, Leges in 4°*, Sectio III, *Concilia Aevi Merovingici*, Tom. I, p. 215; Council of Laudun (673-675), canon 2—*MGH, ibid.*, p. 218.

[6] *MGH, Leges in 4°*, Sectio III, *Concilia Aevi Karolini*, Tom. II, pars I, p. 3; Mansi, XII, 365; Hardouin, III, 1919.

for the restricted purpose of hearing confessions, of saying Mass, and of ministering to the spiritual needs of those concerned. This was very definitely the extent of their labors. Under no condition were they to bear arms. This seems to be the first formal recognition which a particular church gave to the idea of having priests serving as chaplains with the armed forces.

In England, Archbishop Egbert of York (+766) drew up a long list of canons for the clergy of his diocese. In the 155th of this long series of directives and canonical precepts (attributed to him), Egbert forbade his clerics to bear arms, reminding them that a cleric killed while bearing weapons was to be denied any offerings or prayers. He was not to be deprived of Christian burial, however.[7]

Toward the close of the eighth century there was much unrest in Italy. The Eternal City witnessed turbulent days in connection with the papal elections. In 769 a council was held in the city of Rome itself under the headship of Pope Stephen IV (768-772).[8] Here special directives were issued with the aim of eliminating the turmoil and intrigue which had become identified with these elections. In a special section on this point, legislation was passed relative

---

[7] "Clericis quoque non debet armis uti...quicumque clericus in... rixa mortuus fuerat, neque oblatione neque oratione postuletur pro eo; sepultura tamen non privetur...." — Wilkins, *Concilia Magnæ Britanniæ et Hiberniæ a Synodo Verolamiensi (A. D. CDXLVI) ad Londinense (A. D. MDCCXVII)* (4 vols., Londini, 1737), I, 112 (hereafter cited *Concilia*). These canons of Egbert are in the majority taken from the Penitential of Halitgar, Bishop of Cambrai (817-830). This is true of Books 1-3, while the 4th Book may be the work of Egbert, though some authorities question this. For a detailed treatment of this point, cf. Haddan and Stubbs, *Councils and Ecclesiastical Documents relating to Great Britain and Ireland* (3 vols., Oxford, 1869-1873), III, 413-416. Also Le Bras, "Penitentiels" — *Dictionnaire de Théologie Catholique* (14 vols., Paris: Libraire Letouzey et Ané, 1903-1939), XII, 1160-1178 (1168).

[8] Some historians and canonists identify this Pope as Pope Stephen III. The identification as here given is found in the *Annuario Pontificio per l'anno 1947* (Città del Vaticano, 1947), p. 12. Pope Stephen II, elected as the successor of Pope St. Zachary (741-752), died within three days of his election. Cf. *ibid.*, p. 11.

to those who attended papal elections with weapons in their possession.[9] The law had been occasioned immediately in that a layman, Constantine, had been set up as Pope a short time previously; and that by force of arms. In the matter of a few days he had received in rapid succession tonsure, minor and major orders, and consecration as Bishop of Rome. This pseudo-Pope fared badly, for he ended his mortal days blind, in a monastery under sentence of life imprisonment.[10] It was at this council that it was enacted that for the future only cardinal-priests or cardinal-deacons should be eligible for the papacy, and that in the election none but clerics should take active part. The laity's share was reduced to the opportunity of cheering the newly elected Pope and of signing the *acta* of the election in sign of agreement. The penalty enacted for those who carried weapons was that of major excommunication.[11]

A number of less important councils of the eleventh century adhered closely to a restatement of the general prohibition.[12] In the wording of the law it was the term *clericus* which was most frequently used, though one finds *presbyter* on rare occasions. On these occasions it seems that the law referred exclusively to priests. The Council of Naples (1120) in its 20th *capitulum* gave the first express recognition to a cause which justified the bearing of arms

[9] "Si quis cum armis in electione pontificis...inventus fuerit, anathema sit." — *MGH*, *Leges in 4°*, Sectio III, *Concilia Aevi Karolini*, Tom. II, pars I, p. 88.

[10] For the unusual story of the cruelty and intrigue surrounding this papal election, with special reference to the person of the unfortunate Constantine, cf. Mann, *The Lives of the Popes in the Early Middle Ages* (18 vols., London: Herder, 1902-1932), I, 362-376.

[11] The division of excommunication into major and minor was abolished by the Constitution *Apostolicæ Sedis* (Oct. 12, 1869) of Pope Pius IX, and was not revived by the Code. Excommunication as it existed before 1869 corresponded to the major excommunication of the earlier law. — S. C. C. Off. *(Petrocaricen.)*, 5 dec. 1883, ad 1 — *Fontes*, n. 1084.

[12] Canon 30 of the *Canons of Aelfricus* (1049) — Mansi, XIX, 701; Council of Rome (1059), canon 10 — Mansi, XIX, 915; Council of Gerona (1068), canon 1 — Mansi, XIX, 1071; Council of the Province of Narbonne (1068) — Mansi, XIX, 1073; Council of Clermont (1095), canon 4 — Mansi, XX, 817.

by clerics. A cleric could carry a weapon for the purpose of defense. The right itself was a natural law right, namely, the right of self-defense. The Council spoke rather of the instruments to be used in the exercise of that right.[13] Other excusing causes were mentioned in the councils of the period of the decretists and the decretalists.

Following the Decree of Gratian, the Decretals of Pope Gregory IX (1227-1241) make reference to earlier rulings on the subject of bearing weapons. The canon was taken from the Council of Poitiers (1079) : here it was stated that clerics who carried arms were to be excommunicated.[14] In commenting upon this decretal, Panormitanus was of the opinion that a cleric who carried a weapon without just cause was guilty of mortal sin. His conclusion was based on the serious nature of the penalty which was attached to any violation of the law forbidding it.[15]

There were three cases in which a cleric was allowed to bear arms. The first case considered the situation in which a cleric would thus be able to save his own life only by taking the life of the aggressor. By this action he did not incur any irregularity.[16] The second case was one in which the cleric could use arms in defense of his own personal possessions. Here he became irregular if he struck with a weapon the one who intended to rob him. The same irregularity befell the cleric who struck with a weapon an aggressor, even though the action was occasioned by an attempt to defend the life or the property of another; this was the third case. Defense of one's homeland was also given as a cause for bearing arms. This seemed to look more to the

---

[13] "Si clericus causa defensionis arma detulerit, culpa non teneatur." — Mansi, XXI, 265.

[14] C. 2, X, *de vita et honestate clericorum,* III, 1; canon 10 — Mansi, XX, 299.

[15] *Commentaria,* ad c. 2, X, *de vita et honestate clericorum,* III, 1, nn. 1-6.

[16] Fagnanus, *Commentaria super Quinque Libros Decretalium* (5 vols. in 3, Venetiis, 1709-1729), lib. V, tit. *de homicidio,* c. 10, n. 28 (hereafter cited *Commentaria*).

element of formal military service, and thus appears out of place with the other reasons given.[17]

The general term *arma* included those instruments which according to their natural use were intended for offense or defense. The emphasis primarily was on the so-called "offensive" weapons, such as lances, spears, machines for throwing stones, broad and short swords, etc. In a wider and somewhat less proper sense the word was used for including all those instruments which men employed to inflict injury on another. Some of the Pontifical Statutes forbade even the carrying of small knives *(cultelli minores)*.[18]

Shortly after the Decretal period many of the councils mentioned causes which justified at least a temporary bearing of weapons on the part of the clergy.[19] A synod held at Valence in 1261 felt that the abuses in this regard had become a scandal in the diocese. Clerics definitely were not to carry weapons, although they were allowed to carry a short sword while they were traveling. When they reached their destination, or also when they had to put up along the way, the sword was to be removed. There was a monetary penalty for all violations of this statute.[20] In other places for the carrying of weapons it was demanded that the special permission of the bishop be had. He alone was to pass on the acceptability of the reason adduced.[21]

---

[17] Panormitanus, *Commentaria,* ad c. 2, X, *de vita et honestate clericorum,* III, 1, nn. 8-9.

[18] Gonzalez-Tellez, *Commentaria,* lib. III, tit. 1, c. 2, nn. 3-5.

[19] Council of London (1175), canon 11 — Mansi, XXII, 150; Council of Trier (1277), canon 10 — Mansi, XXIV, 200; Council of Buda (1279), canon 11 — Mansi, XXIV, 276; Council of Prague (1346) — Mansi, XXVI, 83. The Council of Buda allowed the carrying of weapons in consideration of a manifest cause for fear.

[20] Mansi, XXIII, 1056.

[21] Provincial Council of Ravenna (1286), canon 3 — Mansi, XXIV, 617; Council of Lucca (1308), canons 40, 60, 69 — Mansi, XXV, 184, 190, 194; Council of Avignon (1326), canon 39 — Mansi, XXV, 765. In these cases the penalty was generally a fine. The I Council of Ravenna (1286) enacted an excommunication instead.

The Council of Trent did not exact any specific decree on this point.

Pope Innocent XIII (1721-1724) in a letter to certain bishops called for a greater stress on ecclesiastical discipline.[22] It was important that no one be allowed to join the clerical army if he was not sufficiently qualified. It was most important that those who already were part of this army follow a praiseworthy way of life, positively by exhibiting a moral integrity consonant with their status, negatively by avoiding those things which were forbidden to them. To carry weapons was forbidden them. The bishops were urged to press for an observance of this law by giving proper warning. If this warning went unheeded, the recalcitrant clerics were to be declared deprived of their *privilegium fori* and of their benefices.

In the United States the II Plenary Council of Baltimore (1866) stated that by the law of the Church those clerics who carried weapons were excommunicated.[23]

Part II. Discipline of the Code

Article 1. The Carrying of Weapons and the "Iusta Causa Timendi"

Canon 138 seeks to prevent clerics from doing anything or from engaging in anything which would prove unbecoming to their state in life. Unless there be a just cause for fear, clerics are forbidden to carry arms or weapons. The basic reason, as given in the *Decretum Gratiani,* is that the confidence and trust of the cleric is to be in God rather than in weapons.[24] One is less inclined to display Christian meekness when armed and able to revenge himself on his adversaries than when armed only with the proper weapons of clerics, patience and Christian forgiveness.

---

[22] Const. *Apostolici ministerii,* 23 maii, 1723, § 8 — *Fontes,* n. 280.

[23] "Clerici arma ferentes ecclesiæ lege excommunicantur" — *Conc. Plen. Balt. II Acta et Decreta,* n. 153.

[24] Cf. c. 3, D. XXXVI.

Canon 138, which looks to the private carrying of arms, is not to be confused with canon 141 of the Code which forbids clerics to join without permission the military forces of a country, or to take part in any way in civil strife or in disturbances of the public order. Likewise, canon 138 does not prohibit the use of a gun, for example, in that type of legitimate hunting which is not forbidden in virtue of canon 138. Reference here is principally to the *aperta delatio armorum*,[25] occasioned in ordinary life by the existence of a just cause for fear on the part of the cleric. It also refers to the carrying of hidden weapons. Merely to carry a weapon for purposes of dress or display is not held a sufficient cause to excuse one from acting contrary to the provisions of this canon. For clerics (i.e., seminarians) to wear side arms or to carry swords while acting in a play would not constitute a violation of this law.

The law originally simply forbade clerics to carry weapons. Many of the clergy had come from wealthy families among whom there existed the practice of carrying weapons. This custom had not been laid aside when the clerical state was entered upon, and it was not uncommon for some clerics to look upon the wearing of arms as almost a part of the clerical garb. Legislation was necessary to change this misconception. Later on, a just cause was recognized and clerics while on a journey were allowed to carry weapons. The law when first set forth had a more practical application than it enjoys now. As the law now stands, it is not allowed a cleric to carry arms unless there be a just cause for him to fear. If he is allowed to carry arms, then he may also retain them in his possession. Permission under the law to do both these things is a recognition of the natural law right of self-defense.

If a cleric has reasonable cause to feel that his life is in danger, he may carry a weapon for purposes of self-defense. Accordingly it also seems lawful for a cleric to

---

[25] Vermeersch-Creusen, *Epitome*, I, n. 255, 2.

carry a weapon in times of great local or national unrest.[26] In this regard, however, one should exercise special prudence, for there seems to be present the danger of scandal and of possible unhappy repercussions, should it become known that a priest was carrying a gun on his person. If this can reasonably be foreseen, the cause for carrying the weapon would have to be proportionately more urgent, according to the natural law. Augustine pointed to the agitation against the clergy in Italy, especially in Rome, toward the turn of the century, and showed that to have been cause for carrying arms.[27] Many priests received licenses from the Pretor to carry a revolver at that time.

What is to be said for the priest who has to venture into a dangerous neighborhood in response to a sick call? Such a consideration seems to offer a justifying cause for carrying some sort of weapon. Each individual case calls for a decision truly based on the known circumstances. The better procedure would call for an attempt to make arrangements with the local law enforcement agency for the needed protection. In some communities this service is given to priests whose work takes them into dangerous areas. Unless it were an absolute necessity, a priest ought not to carry a gun when the Blessed Sacrament is on his person; but such a necessity might arise from the need to protect the Blessed Sacrament Itself. In this country the likelihood of an attack, either on the person of the priest or on the Blessed Sacrament, seems sufficiently remote to demand that the priest have a well-founded suspicion of imminent foul play before he can take a gun with him. In times of actual persecution of the Church one can see reason for keeping arms for defense only — for use when needed. To seize upon the mere possibility of persecution as a reason for carrying arms is extreme. In missionary countries there can more easily be envisioned a case in

---

[26] Crnica, *Commentarium*, I, 155.
[27] *Commentary*, II, 87.

which the priest (or cleric) would be allowed under the law to carry a gun as protection against wild animals, or against unfriendly natives who might be incited to active resentment through false stories spread by enemies of the Church.

Article 2. Irregularity Arising from Voluntary Homicide

It is clear that a cleric may carry (and use if necessary) a weapon, e.g., a revolver or a knife as a means of legitimate defense for his own life and his possessions of value; such a weapon may also be employed in the defense of the life of an innocent neighbor. Would a priest become irregular if in self-defense he killed some person? According to canon 985, n. 4, anyone who commits voluntary homicide (or abortion) becomes irregular *ex delicto.*

Such an irregularity forbids the conferral and the reception of orders. Since whoever is excluded from one thing is likewise barred from everything connected with it, it follows that a cleric who is irregular cannot exercise the orders already received. Homicide in general signifies the killing of a human being. It includes both intentional and unintentional killing. In a restricted sense it means the unjust taking of the life of another.

As a solution for the problem here raised, one may note that necessary homicide does not render one guilty of sin, nor does the person (if a cleric) contract an irregularity as a result of this action. In the *Decree* of Gratian it was stated: *"Idem [id est, nullam irregularitatem incurrere] de illo censemus quo mortem aliter vitare non valens suum occidit vel mutilat invasorem."*[28] The same passage indicated that for the further advancement to higher Orders in such a case a dispensation was required. This was not required, however, for the exercise of Orders already received. The

---

[28] C. 6, D. L.

phrase "*qui mortem aliter vitare non valens*" was important, for it pointed to the notion of the *moderamen inculpatæ tutelæ.*

In taking the life of another the killing is willed, not as the simple taking of the life of another, but as a defense of one's own life or of that of an innocent third party. The irregularity is escaped only if the killing of an unjust aggressor was necessary in the sense that there were no other effective means at hand for affording the desired self-protection. If one could have taken to flight, called or shouted for help, or protected oneself by merely wounding the attacker, then one would have become guilty of serious sin if instead one had resorted to killing the attacker. If in such circumstances the killing were perpetrated by a cleric, he would contract the irregularity.[29]

It is to be remembered that one is not justified morally in killing another while protecting personal property of small or relatively small value.[30] Thus, while a priest might act within the bounds of the civil law were he to kill a person who attempted to steal a jug of altar wine, it is highly debatable if objectively he could be excused from all sin. He would be using extreme measures to retain an item of minor importance. It would be an entirely different matter if the act of killing were occasioned while a priest is making an effort to save the ciboria and their Contents from profanation.

---

[29] Coronata, *Tractatus Canonicus de Sacramentis* (3 vols., Taurini: Marietti, 1943-1946), II, 163; Gaspari, *Tractatus de Sacra Ordinatione* (2 vols., Parisiis, 1893), I, n. 433. This view is not shared by all. Some demand the positive will of killing the aggressor precisely as a non-necessary means of defense; the *fact alone* of the killing does not suffice for the contracting of the irregularity. In practice it is left to the ordinary to determine *in foro externo* whether or not there was due moderation. In the internal forum it would be within the province of the confessor to judge. — Cappello, *Tractatus Canonico-Moralis de Sacramentis* (3 vols. in 6, Vol. II, pars III, Taurinorum Augustæ: Marietti, 1935), Vol. II, pars III, p. 474 (hereafter cited *De Sacramentis*).

[30] Aertyns-Damen, *Theologia Moralis,* I, n. 581, II.

Article 3. Dispensation from the Irregularity

If a cleric has incurred an irregularity as the result of voluntary homicide, how is it to be removed? The most common method is by way of dispensation. The Roman Pontiff *iure proprio* dispenses from all irregularities. The dispensation is valid even though a just cause may have been lacking. In the case of one who intends to go on to further Orders, the Holy See is never accustomed to grant the dispensation if the irregularity has arisen from *public* homicide. And only with difficulty does it dispense even in cases wherein the delict remains occult.[31] But it more readily grants a dispensation when there is question of permission for the further exercise of Orders already received.

Ordinaries by law enjoy a limited power of dispensing. They themselves *(per se vel per alium)* can dispense their subjects only from those irregularities which arise from an occult delict, with the exception of irregularities stemming from voluntary homicide and abortion.[32] Therefore, the ordinary cannot absolve from an irregularity arising from homicide regardless of whether the delict be occult or public. Further, he could not dispense in virtue of the power which is his from canon 81 in order that a candidate be allowed to go on to higher Orders.[33] Even the Holy See is not accustomed to grant a dispensation under these conditions. If the delict were occult and the Holy See could not be approached, then in the presence of all the other conditions postulated in canon 81, the ordinary could dispense *priests*.[34]

---

[31] "Delictum est *publicum* si iam divulgatum est aut talibus contigit seu versatur in adiunctis ut prudenter indicari possit et debeat facile divulgatum iri; *occultum, quod non est publicum.*" — Canon 2197, 1° and 4°.

[32] Canon 990, § 1.

[33] "A generalibus legibus Ecclesiæ Ordinarii infra Romanum Pontificem dispensare nequeunt, ne in casu quidem peculiari...nisi difficilis sit recursus ad Sanctam Sedem et simul in mora sit periculum gravis damni et de dispensatione agatur quæ a Sede Apostolica concedi solet."

[34] Cappello, *De Sacramentis*, II, pars III, p. 483. A response was given recently by the Code Commission relative to canon 81. This re-

It is not easy to visualize a case in which those who are in minor Orders, or even those who are in any of the major Orders, would stand in immediate need of this dispensation, since it looks only to the exercise of Orders already received. If there were real need, however, and the demands of canon 81 were met, then it seems that the ordinary could also validly dispense these clerics.

Article 4. The Civil Law and the Carrying of Weapons

A priest who feels that he has a valid and just cause which canonically warrants his keeping in his possession (or on his person) a concealed weapon should give careful consideration to the rulings of the civil law. It is an offense in practically all communities to carry a concealed weapon without express or written permission of the police authorities. Special permits are granted upon the presentation of a sufficient cause. In recent years, in consequence, no doubt, of the alarming increases in armed robberies and burglaries, these permissions have been harder to obtain. However, it is rarely that a priest is denied such a permission. This is due to the generally understood fact that the average priest has no desire to carry a gun unless there be a real cause for such unusual action.

Priests in sparsely settled areas, or priests encharged with the banking of considerable sums of money, have been known in the past to have obtained the necessary legal recognition entitling them to carry a gun. These are also reasons recognized under the *iusta causa timendi* as mentioned in canon 138. As far as the banking of money is concerned, it is certainly more fitting and more dignified for a priest to take out insurance against theft or to engage the services of companies whose work it is to bank large

---

sponse pointed out that the clause "*nisi difficilis sit recursus ad Sanctam Sedem*" does not obtain in those cases where the ordinaries enjoy easy recourse (facile recurrere possunt) to the Papal Legate in their region, which Legate communicates with the Holy See. — *AAS*, XXXIX (1947), 374; *The Jurist*, VIII (1948), 105.

sums of money. Such procedure is preferable to carrying a gun. An equally satisfactory arrangement may suggest the requesting of police protection for these excursions to the bank. To ask for a permit to carry a gun when police assistance is easily obtainable seems to violate at least the spirit of the canon.

To keep or carry a concealed weapon without the specific authorization of the law would upon apprehension render the culpable bearer subject to a fine or jail sentence on the charge of carrying "concealed weapons."[35] The law is violated when this permission is lacking and the weapon is on the person, whether it be actually visible or whether it be hidden. Stilettos, daggers, bayonets, swords, along with firearms, come under the term weapons. A penknife may also be considered a concealed weapon, especially if actual injury has been inflicted with it. Most police officials (especially in localities with a large colored element) look upon the "switch-blade" knife (one in which the blade shoots out rapidly upon application of pressure to a certain portion of the handle) as a concealed weapon. This is a type of knife meant to serve for quick action. It is similar to the penknife in which a piece of wood has been inserted be-

---

[35] "Any person who shall within the District of Columbia have concealed about his person any deadly or dangerous weapon, or who shall carry openly any such weapon, with intent to unlawfully use the same, shall be fined not less than fifty dollars nor more than five hundred dollars, or be imprisoned not exceeding one year, or both: *provided further*, That nothing contained in this section shall be so construed as to apply to any person who shall have been granted a written permit to carry such weapon or weapons by any judge of the police court of the District of Columbia; and authority is given...to grant such a permit for a period of not more than one month at any one time...." — *The Code of the District of Columbia* (Washington, D. C.: Government Printing Office, 1930), tit. 6, ch. 4, section 114.

"No person shall within the District of Columbia carry either openly or concealed on or about his person, except in his dwelling, home or place of business or on other land possessed by him, a pistol, without the license therefor issued as hereinafter provided, or any deadly or dangerous weapon capable of being so concealed." (As amended November 4, 1943, 57 Stat. 586, ch. 296). — *The Code of the District of Columbia 1940 Edition,* Supplement IV, Vol. I, tit. 22, ch. 32, § 22-3204.

tween the blade and the handle. A lead pipe, loaded gloves or socks, brass knuckles when used for purposes of defense — all these would come under the term *"arma"* as employed in canon 138. When used for reasons other than that of defense the civil law classifies them as concealed weapons. In canon law the phrase *arma gestare* includes what the civil law understands by the carrying of "concealed" and "dangerous" weapons. Canonically such an action is legitimate when there is a just cause for fear.

It is entirely possible for a cleric who knowingly violates the civil statute to be freed without fine or jail sentence. This favor would come to him out of deference, in most cases, to his being a minister of organized religion. It could also be granted upon his having furnished proof of his ignorance regarding what the civil law demanded on this point. Certainly, whatever be the reason for his being excused, the cleric should not attempt to violate the law with the hope of his being able upon apprehension to fall back upon his professional status as a reason for special immunity. All clerics and all priests should be the very first to exhibit a conscientious observance of all civil laws, unless these be manifestly unjust. That a law is unjust is to be proved, and not readily to be presumed. The law against carrying "concealed weapons" is a just law made for the good of society.

CHAPTER V

THE PROHIBITION AGAINST HUNTING

Part I. Historical Conspectus

Among the various kinds of amusement and recreation in which clerics in the early days interested themselves with becoming moderation was hunting. Generally it was done in such wise that it was not a source of scandal to the faithful, or wasteful of any precious clerical time. It is not until the sixth century that one finds any reference to hunting as a sport forbidden to clerics. Here again was evidenced the influence of the customs of the barbaric nations. These peoples, by reason of their very way of life, devoted much time to hunting. It was for them a means of procuring the necessities of life, as well as a means of sport and relaxation. But eventually, because of abuses, it became necessary to forbid hunting, clamorous hunting, to clerics.

> Degenerando pero negli ecclesiastici il divertimento della caccia in prejudizio dei poveri, ed in iscandalo, poiché si trascurava il servizio divino, fu duopo vietare alle persone sacre, di nutrire i cani ed i falconi per lo cacchio, perché in questo sollazzo e nel piacere, che vi si prendere, era impossibile conservare quello spirito d'orazione et quella decenza et gravita che sono il carattere de' chierici.[1]

The Council of Agde (506) in its 55th canon forbade bishops, priests, and deacons to have hounds and hawks to be used in hunting, and this under severe penalty.[2] This same legislation was incorporated almost verbatim into one of the disciplinary canons of the Council of Epaon (517).[3]

---

[1] Moroni, *Dizionario di Erudizione Storico-Ecclesiastica* (103 vols. in 52, Venezia, 1840-1861), VI, 189 (hereafter cited *Dizionario*).

[2] Bruns, II, 157.

[3] Canon 4 — Bruns, II, 167; Mansi, VIII, 559.

In 742 the famous Council of Germany determined that no cleric was to own hunting dogs, hawks, or falcons. In the same canon there seemed to be an identification of *venatio* with *vagatio*.[4] Since the latter term connotes an element of leisure and the absence of haste, it may be assumed that the hunting of those days was protracted over a period of long hours, perhaps over a period of days. If clerics remained "in the field" for this length of time it is not difficult to see how their priestly work was ignored.

A special rule for abbots was drawn up by the Council of Paris (829). Some of the abbots of the area who had discovered that their limited duties afforded them almost unlimited free time had formed the habit of spending too much of that time in the chase. These men were reminded of their obligation at all times to give an example of holy living to their subjects. To that end they were to give up their hunting.[5]

The first papal letter which treated of the problem of hunting as it was related to clerics was one from the pen of Pope Nicholas I (858-867). The exact date of its composition is unknown; it was addressed to a certain archbishop named Alduin.[6] Several of the faithful had complained to the Holy See that a young bishop named Lanfred had been spending a great deal of time in hunting *(venationi deditus)*. This was a vice at that time affecting many of the German and Frankish clergy. The archbishop was ordered to convoke a provincial synod. Lanfred was to be summoned to appear before this gathering, and there in the presence of the suffragan bishops he was to be warned of the evil of his ways. Should he ignore this admonition,

---

[4] Canon 2 — *MGH, Leges in 4°*, Sectio III, *Concilia Aevi Karolini*, Tom. II, pars I, p. 1903; Mansi, XII, 365; Hardouin, III, 1919.

[5] Canon 37 — *MGH, ibidem*, p. 636.

[6] Jaffé, *Regesta Pontificum Romanorum ab condita Ecclesia ad annum MCXCVIII* (2. ed. [by Kaltenbrunner (to the year 590), Ewald (from 590 to 882), and Löwenfeld (from 882 to 1198), and so referred to as JK, JE, and JL], 2 vols. in 1, Lipsiæ, 1885-1888), n. 2847 (2153). This letter is incorporated in Gratian, c. 1, D. XXXIV.

showing his contempt through continued disobedience, he was then to be excommunicated. His further perduring in his contumacy would bring deposition.

Some of the bishops retained hunting dogs right at the episcopal residence. They defended their action by saying that such dogs were needed for protection. The bishops assembled at the II Council of Mâcon (585), a national synod of the Frankish kingdom, felt that hymns and good works would be of more value than the barking of dogs when it came to the matter of protection.[7]

King Edgar (959-975) was the author of a set of "Ecclesiastical Laws" which he drew up to insure proper clerical discipline in the dioceses of his Anglo-Saxon Kingdom. This was in 967. In canon 64 he expressed the desire that none of the clergy should give themselves to hunting. Instead of merely banning one thing without offering something in its place, the King suggested that the clerics spend more time with their books.[8]

The law on hunting which Gratian took from previously existing legislation was the ninth century letter of Pope Nicholas — the letter just considered.[9] In the *glossa* mention was made of three types of hunting: *oppressiva, arenaria,* and *saltuosa.*[10] The first type, not further explained, seemed (from c. 3, D. VI) to be that in which animals and human beings were killed merely for the sake of killing; this type, as expected, was illicit.[11] *Arenaria* was the type which took place in the arena, where a hunter engaged a wild beast. While illicit, this type was relatively safe, for often the teeth of the animal had been previously removed.

---

[7] "Custodienda est igitur espiscopalis habitatio hymnis, non latratibus, operibus bonis, non morsibus venenosis." — Mansi, IX, 955.

[8] "...sacerdos non sit venator...sed incumbat libris suis...." — Mansi, XVII, 437.

[9] C. 1, D. XXXIV; JE, n. 2847 (2153).

[10] *Glossa ordinaria,* ad c. 1, D. XXXIV sub v. *bestiarum.*

[11] Gonzalez-Tellez (*Commentaria,* lib. V, tit. 24, c. 1, n. 5) thought that this referred only to the killing of humans. He points to Genesis, 10, and Psalm 143.

The third and final type was in itself perfectly legitimate. It was the type which took place in the forests and wooded areas; it corresponded to hunting as this sport is known today.

For various reasons this type of hunting could also become illicit: *ratione temporis* — it was forbidden to hunt during Lent; *ratione personæ* — it was illicit for clerics to hunt. Of importance was the distinction introduced at that time, a distinction which was honored in the law, namely, the differentiation of clamorous from non-clamorous hunting. The former was forbidden to cleric and lay person alike, while the latter type was allowed. The law as interpreted implied that a cleric could prepare a trap or set nets, provided that it was done *"sine strepitu et clamore."* [12]

The Gregorian Decretals contained a special title: "On the Cleric Hunter." Two of the laws in that title were taken from the Council of Agde (506).[13] The penalty was decreed for those (bishops, priests, and deacons) who were *often* found engaged in this sport for the pleasure it afforded. In case of necessity, if it were a single case, the cleric was allowed to hunt. But it was never to be clamorous hunting. Never was it to become habitual. Even with these limitations, it was not made allowable for a bishop to hunt.[14] The ruling of Pope Clement V (1305-1314), given at the Council of Vienne (1311-1312), was later incorporated in the Clementine Decretals.[15] In that passage the Pope spoke out against several abuses that needed to be remedied immediately. One of these concerned the recitation of the canonical hours in the cathedral churches. The bishops were instructed to see to it that the clerics did not leave church early to go hunting; nor were they to bring their dogs and falcons to church with them.

---

[12] *Glossa ordinaria,* ad c. 1, X, *de clerico venatore,* V, 24.

[13] Canons 1, 2, X, *de clerico venatore,* V, 24.

[14] *Glossa ordinaria,* ad c. 1, X, *de clerico venatore,* V, 24, *casus,* et sub v. *voluptate.*

[15] C. 1, *de celebratione missarum,* III, 14, in Clem.

In the Clementine Constitutions (1314-1317), in a special section on the status of monks and canons regular, there are found some references to hunting.[16] Monks and their habitual associates *(familiares secum morantes)* were not to hunt, nor were they to keep animals for that purpose. It appears that one of the purposes of the law was to keep the monks at home, for they were allowed to hunt only in the wooded properties, reserves, and such areas as belonged to the monastery.

The Council of Trent mirrored the fact that not all hunting was forbidden. Clerics were commanded to shun all *illicit* hunting.[17]

The law on hunting, as well as almost all the other laws on clerical obligations, underwent its greatest development in the period of the late Middle Ages. This resulted in great measure from the development of the theological science, especially in the field of moral theology. The raising of questions and the offered solutions of many problems of a practical nature helped to clear up some of the uncertainty relative to the extent and application of the law. This together with conciliar legislation and papal decrees helped to shape the law. What is contained in the present Code of Canon Law is the result, with minor exceptions, of these influences.

For clerics in the United States the law of the Council of Trent found restatement in the II Plenary Council of Baltimore (1866), whose decree required clerics to refrain from all types of forbidden hunting.[18]

---

[16] Cc. 1, 2, *De statu monachorum vel canonicorum regularium,* III, 10, in Clem.

[17] Sess. XXIV, *de ref.*, c. 12 — *Canones et Decreta,* p. 192. At least one Pope of this period spent a great deal of time in hunting. "Egli (Pope Leo X [1513-1521]), pertanto occupava nell cacchia tutto il tempo che poteva, specialmente nei mesi di settembre e ottobre d'ogni anno, non potendosene distaccare, se non che per far concistoro, o cappella Papale." — Moroni, *Dizionario,* V-VI, 193. In this same reference the author mentions by name some twelve Cardinals of this time — all great hunters. One of them was killed in 1562 while he was hunting.

[18] *Conc. Plen. Balt. II Acta et Decreta,* n. 153.

PART II. DISCIPLINE OF THE CODE

Article 1. Distinction Between Clamorous and Non-clamorous Hunting

For many clerics, especially for those who live in areas where wooded sections and farm lands are in abundance, hunting has long been a source of honest and satisfying recreation. The vast majority of authors agree, and the text of the law supports this view, that it is perfectly lawful for clerics to hunt, provided that it is not clamorous hunting. They are not to spend an undue amount of time even in non-clamorous hunting. Pope Benedict XIV (1740-1758) seemed to stand alone in his contention that *all* hunting was forbidden to clerics.[19] His opinion was based on the 55th canon of the Council of Agde (506), whose text was the classical text of the law against hunting.[20]

This view is no longer tenable in the light of the wording of the present law; even at an earlier time this view was not popular. It is true that the particular canon which was incorporated in the Decretals seemed to forbid hunting which was in no sense *clamorosa.* However, it may be argued that the Council of Agde primarily, though implicitly, dealt with clamorous hunting, since the very things which it mentioned were all part of the apparatus connected with that type of hunting. It made no distinction between clamorous and non-clamorous hunting for the simple reason that it may not have known any type other than that which we call clamorous. It may be held that the interpretation of the law, then as now, allowed clerics to engage infrequently in moderate or quiet hunting, although

---

[19] *De Synodo,* lib. XI, c. 10, n. viii. It is not clear whether Phillips (1804-1872) similarly considered all hunting forbidden to clerics. — *Kirchenrecht* (7 vols., Regensburg, 1845-1872), I, 703.

[20] "Episcopis, presbyteris atque diaconibus canes ad venandum et accipitres habere non licet. Quod si quis talium personarum in hac voluptate sæpius detectus fuerit, si episcopus est, tribus mensibus se a communione suspendeat, presbyter duobus mensibus se abstineat, diaconus uno ab officio vel communione cessabit." — Bruns, II, 157.

this latter type was little known or little engaged in. What was to become the customary distinction between clamorous and non-clamorous hunting came from the canonists of the Middle Ages, probably from the time of the *glossæ* on the Gregorian Decretals, where this distinction was found for the first time.

One could defend the view that the original legislation of the early Church forbade all hunting, but it is difficult for one to see how Pope Benedict XIV, writing in the eighteenth century, could say that all hunting was forbidden in his day. Such a proposition stands in patent disagreement with the general interpretation of this law. If it be questioned whether *de facto* ecclesiastical law now forbids all hunting, the answer is no. It is all but unanimously held that clamorous hunting or riding to hounds is forbidden; that non-clamorous, quiet or moderate hunting is not forbidden. By reason of the natural law, the latter may become unlawful if overindulgence in it results in scandal, neglect of duty, or some other evil of a similar nature.[21] This view conforms well to the canons which order that clerics shall not *indulge* in hunting (which is allowed); they further order that they are never to *exercise* that form of hunting which is called clamorous.[22]

All will admit that whatever type of hunting is condemned is not so condemned on intrinsic grounds, for as Saint Thomas pointed out, in itself hunting is lawful.[23] By the natural law the right to hunt was given to all. Yet it would be wrong to question how the Church can take away this right from her clerics. In reality the Church does not remove this right. It merely exercises its power to limit

---

[21] S. C. de Prop. Fide., instr. *(ad Vic. Ap. N.)*, mense aug. 1827 — *Fontes*, n. 4739.

[22] "*Exercitium* etiam singulos actus afficit, *indulgere* e contra implicat protractum exercitium et consuetum." — Coronata, *Institutiones*, I, p. 232, note 1; Wernz-Vidal, *Ius Canonicum*, n. 122; Cocchi, *Commentarium*, lib. II, pars I, n. 50; Toso, *Commentaria Minora*, II, 103; Chelodi, *De Personis*, p. 197; Berutti, *De Personis*, II, 142; Blat, *Commentarium*, II, n. 77; Vermeersch-Creusen, *Epitome*, I, n. 255.

[23] *Summa Theologica*, IIa IIae, q. 64, art 1.

the use of it and to set bounds to the full exercise of a right whose existence it recognizes and defends. The State does the very same thing when it draws up penalties for those who hunt during those seasons which it has declared to be closed to hunting. The natural liberty of one to hunt is restricted for the common good in civil society; for the good of a particular group in the Church.[24]

Moderate, quiet hunting for purposes of relaxation, necessary recreation, utility and the like is legal and licit. By reason of the natural law, quiet hunting too frequently engaged in, with possible loss of time, disregard of priestly work, and even the occasioning of scandal is wrong. Clamorous hunting under all conditions is forbidden to clerics as the one type unbecoming to their state in life. The prohibition is in itself not a grave one. Frequent violations are necessary for grave fault; while to take part in such hunting even on one occasion may be unlawful, it is not gravely so — unless it gives rise to grave scandal.[25]

In order that a cleric may know whether the type of hunting in which he desires to engage is licit or whether it is forbidden, he must first know whether it comes under the heading of clamorous or non-clamorous hunting. The distinction comes from the time of the Decretal law. It is from that law that its meaning must also be sought.[26] Pope Benedict XIV, borrowing freely from the decretalists and commentators of the sixteenth and seventeenth centuries, offered a definition of these two kinds of hunting:

Alia siquidem est clamorosa, alia quieta; illa magno armorum, canum, accipitrum apparatu et tumultu exercetur, ut apri, cervi et majores feræ capiantur; altera solis laqueis et retibus, aut

---

[24] Gonzalez-Tellez, *Commentaria,* lib. V, tit. 24, c. 1, nn. 8-10; Schmalzgrueber, lib. III, tit. 24, n. 4; Reiffenstuel, lib. V, tit. 24, n. 1.

[25] St. Alphonsus, *Theologia Moralis,* lib. IV, n. 606; Ferreres, *Compendium,* II, n. 115; Kinane, "Clerical Obligations" — *IER,* V. Series, XI (1918), 479.

[26] "Canones qui ius vetus ex integro referunt, ex veteris iuris auctoritate...sunt æstimandi." — Canon 6, 2°.

etiam armis, sed paucis adhibitis canibus, ad occidendum lepores, vulpes, aliasve minores feras, sine ullo strepitu instituitur.[27]

From studying this definition one may wonder if it is necessary in order that hunting be clamorous, that there be a combination of dogs, falcons, arms, etc., and these in large numbers. If it were necessary then there would be certain forms of hunting which come under neither division. Such a combination does not seem to be required. To the writer, the keynote of the definition seems to be contained in the very words themselves, *quieta et clamorosa*. Whenever hunting is attended with great noise and tumult, whether this arises from a large collection of animals or arms or people, or from a combination of all, it is clamorous. If, on the other hand, it is engaged in or carried on quietly, no matter how large the numbers, it is quiet hunting. Forbidden to clerics would be fox hunting, still popular in certain parts of the country. Very few clerics would have any association with fox hunts, or with riding to hounds as it is also known. On rare occasions they may be asked to bless the group before the hunt begins. There is nothing in the law which would forbid a cleric to be present in a more or less passive rôle, as spectator. The canon has active participation in mind and it is this which it forbids.

Those moralists who seek to place the difference in these types of hunting in the presence or absence of one dog more or less seem to be forgetting the background of the law. Thus they do violence to its true meaning and purpose. Lehmkuhl (1834-1918) defined quiet hunting as that which is carried on with traps, snares, and nets (or even a gun), but with only *one* or *two* dogs.[28] May one infer then that three dogs will turn it into clamorous hunting? It is not being facetious to point out the possibility that a cleric who goes rabbit hunting with as many as four dogs may nevertheless engage only in non-clamorous hunting. And this

---

[27] *De Synodo*, lib. XI, c. 10, n. viii.
[28] *Theologia Moralis*, II, n. 615.

simply because it is unattended with any din, commotion, or uproar. To argue from the number of dogs to the type of hunting cannot be adopted as a consistent or satisfactory method of determining just what is or is not allowed. A safer norm looks to the actual amount of noise and confusion which from experience is known generally to accompany the particular type of hunting in which the cleric wishes to engage. Lehmkuhl, however, considered the use of arms permissible. It is interesting to recall that at the Vatican Council (1870-) one of the protests, when the *schema de vita et honestate clericorum* came up for discussion, was directed against the use of guns while hunting.[29]

Another author noted that "hunting with a gun and *a* dog does not seem to be prohibited of itself."[30] Even this, he claimed, was not free from a certain amount of scandal unless it took place rarely. This is probably not true at the present time — at least in this country. Such hunting would offend neither canon law by being clamorous or the natural law by being an occasion of scandal. The extent of the prohibition of canon 138 is independent of the element of scandal, for canon 138 is not merely an extension of the natural law. Did the author hold that hunting with *two* dogs was prohibited? His opinion seems entirely too rigorous. It was apparently based on the supposition that the barking of one extra dog was *always* of itself sufficient to change quiet hunting into clamorous hunting. When this word was first applied to hunting, it was applied to a type which involved great numbers of men, of animals, and of equipment — conditions which would be verified today only on the rarest of occasions. The priest who goes out for a day of hunting with his guns and his dogs need not fear that he is engaging in clamorous hunting.

The law says nothing about fishing, a sport which is popular with the American clergy. From early times it has been agreed that it is lawful for clerics to fish, for it is a

[29] Mahoney, "The Vatican Council and Priestly Sanctity" — *The Ecclesiastical Review,* LXXXIV (1931), 114 (hereafter cited *ER*).

[30] Sabetti-Barrett, *Compendium,* n. 588.

quiet, dignified pastime.[31] All likewise recognize the right of the local ordinary to forbid it, by way of an individual precept, if in a rare case too much fishing should be detrimental to one's labors. The same penalty could also be leveled by the local ordinary upon a cleric who would continue, after being warned, to fish in open violation of the State ordinances; violations of this nature bring disfavor to the whole body of clerical fishermen.

Article 2. Hunting and the Wearing of the Clerical Garb

It is the belief of at least one canonist that according to the law of the Church, even in those cases in which a cleric is allowed to hunt, it would not be allowed him to lay aside his ecclesiastical garb. To do so in public would require the special permission of the local ordinary. This permission is granted only for a reasonable cause.[32] There may be others who hold this same view; the writer has been unable to find any who make explicit mention of this fact. Vito reasons that there are two distinct laws; the satisfactory observance of the one does not bring with it a dispensation from the observance of the other. This is true. It is proper to recall, at the same time, the wording of canon 136 which speaks of clerical dress.

Canon 136, § 1, calls for the wearing of a becoming clerical dress according to the lawful customs of the locality and the prescriptions of the local ordinaries. The matter is left in great measure to them. When the authors speak of the "laying aside of the clerical garb in public" they contemplate the situation in which a cleric removes his clerical dress with the hope of thereby concealing the fact that he is a cleric. There is no question of this at all when clerics go out hunting dressed in a garb that is not strictly clerical. In this country, though perhaps not in Italy and

[31] *Glossa ordinaria,* ad c. 11, D. LXXXVII, sub v. *piscatores.*

[32] Vito, *Quistioni Canoniche* (4 vols., Napoli: Tipografia Raffæle Picone, 1926-1930), IV, 68.

in other sections of Europe, it would be extremely rare and not a little unusual to see a clerical group set out on a hunting excursion dressed in their clerical attire. Certainly amazement and possibly mild scandal would arise from such a sight.

In view of the particular conditions which prevail in America, where Catholics are a minority, more unfavorable comment would arise from a priest's wearing his priestly attire when hunting than would arise if he appeared, as is our present custom, dressed in somber civilian attire. It has long been the custom for American priests who hunt to dress in conservative non-clerical garb, just as they dress in civilian attire when playing golf or when engaging in other legitimate recreational pastimes. This practice seems commonly to have been accepted by the local ordinaries to whom the Code has entrusted the duty of vigilance in clerical dress.

Shortly after the Code appeared, a letter from the Sacred Congregation of the Council gave ordinaries the power to threaten with suspension all clerics (even not their own) who would lay aside the clerical garb.[33] The Congregation mentioned the specific evil which it would root out — the practice, namely, of some clerics to change into civilian attire that they might more easily pursue forms of entertainment forbidden to them. There is no question of an evil, however, in the recreation of a group of clerics who hunt on their day of leisure or during a part of their vacation.

The same Sacred Congregation issued another decree on ecclesiastical dress in 1931.[34] Clerics are to wear becoming ecclesiastical dress in public, even during the summer months. Important is the fact that the respective ordinaries (in each country) are given the right to regulate that dress so that it will be proper to the clerics. It is safe to say that the bishops of the United States have exercised

[33] S. C. Conc., litt. circ., 1 iul. 1926 — *AAS*, XVIII (1926), 312; Bouscaren, *Digest*, I, 138-140.

[34] S. C. Conc., *decr.*, 28 iul. 1931 — *AAS*, XXIII (1931), 336; Bouscaren, *Digest*, I, 123-125.

this power. They have sanctioned, perhaps only tacitly, conservative and modest non-clerical attire for priests while (and only when) engaging in hunting or in some other form of honest recreation. While this may not be clerical dress in a strict sense, it may be said to have become the accepted dress for clerics under these special circumstances. As far as investigation has revealed it, no synod in this country had demanded expressly that clerics wear clerical garb while in the act of hunting. Such a demand was made in the Council of Latin America.[35]

Article 3. The Right of Local Ordinaries to Prohibit Hunting

The Council of Trent in using the words *"ab illicitis venationibus* [*clerici abstineant*]" and in failing to fortify them with penal sanctions, gave the individual local ordinaries great freedom in determining both the extent of the prohibition and the nature of the penalties.[36] Because of this freedom as given to the bishops it was often difficult to judge in any given case whether the penal sanctions enacted in diocesan statutes were or were not too severe. The ancient rigorous prescriptions had by that time fallen into desuetude. Shortly after the Council of Trent, in 1596, an appeal was directed to Rome against a censure of excommunication. In a certain diocese this had been legislated as the penalty for violations of the law on hunting. The Sacred Congregation of Bishops and Regulars adjudged the penalty unwise under the circumstances as set forth in the case.[37]

Ferraris (+ca. 1763) referred to a decision given by the Sacred Congregation of the Council. In this particular instance the Council lifted a suspension inflicted for hunting, and substituted in its place a monetary fine.[38] In both

---

[35] *Acta et Decreta Concilii Plenarii Americæ Latinæ* (Romæ: Typis Vaticanis, 1900), n. 651.

[36] Sess. XXIV, *de ref.*, c. 12 — *Canones et Decreta*, p. 192.

[37] S. C. Ep. et Reg., *Eugubina*, 16 ian. 1596 — *Fontes*, n. 1546.

[38] *Bibliotheca*, sub v. *venatio*, n. 1.

of these cases the Holy See had not quarreled with the right of the ordinaries to determine these penalties, but in the *particular cases* they were adjudged as too severe.

By the law of the Code all clamorous hunting is outlawed, as is non-clamorous hunting under certain conditions. By their own precept, particular or common, or by diocesan statute, local ordinaries can prohibit, for example, all hunting with a gun, or all hunting at a certain time of the year, or on certain feast days — provided that there be a just cause for such action.[39] In the diocese of New Orleans, by way of example, clerics may not hunt on feast days and on days of fast and penance.[40] A just cause for such action would be the need of eradicating certain abuses. Local ordinaries could also fortify their statutes with penalties according to canon 2221, but these penalties should be proportionate to the offense, as is required by canon 2218.[41]

Should scandal arise, the bishop could forbid all quiet hunting, too. Though the *venatio non-clamorosa* is not absolutely prohibited by canon 138, neither is it declared to be a right of the clergy, even when practiced in moderation. However, there are limits to the severity of the penalty which the bishop may impose. In view of the well-known decision given in reply to an appeal by the priests of the Archdiocese of Gniezno-Poznán in Poland,[42] a local ordinary cannot, without *grave* and *special reasons*, punish a violation of his law with a *latæ sententiæ* suspension. What the decision intended to set forth was not that the local ordinary lacked power to bar all hunting when these special reasons were present, but that he should keep in mind the principle of the "*æqua proportio cum delicto*" when it came to establishing the penalty for non-observance of his statute.

---

[39] In Ireland clerics may not hunt if dogs or horses are used. — *Acta et Decreta Conc. Plen. Hiberniæ*, n. 48, 2.

[40] *Constitutiones Diœceseos Novæ-Aureliæ in Synodo Diœcesana Sexta Lata* (New Orleans: Sam Taylor Press, 1922), n. 23.

[41] Vermeersch, "Quæstiones" — *Jus Pontificium*, I (1921), 11.

[42] S. C. C., resol., *Gnesnen, et Posnanien.*, 2 iun. 1921 — *AAS*, XIII (1921), 498; Bouscaren, *Digest*, I, 125.

CHAPTER VI

THE PROHIBITION AGAINST FREQUENTING TAVERNS

PART I. HISTORICAL CONSPECTUS

Ecclesiastical authorities have not been unaware of the universal truth of the words of Saint Paul: "...nor will drunkards possess the kingdom of heaven" (I Cor. 6:11). The Church knows that clerical decorum and all priestly endeavor will suffer if clerics are allowed to frequent taverns. To prevent this the Church has always demanded in its laws that clerics refrain from lingering in such places. This general topic has been given considerable attention in the writings of several of the Fathers of the Church and in the legislation of many of the councils. His present purpose will limit the writer to a consideration of those canons in which clerics are urged to stay away from these taverns. A gradual minor development occurred in the law and this will be noted. The fundamental prohibition remained, though the later introduction of extenuating circumstances modified its extent. Moreover, the prohibition was affected by the fact that the nature of the *taberna* has changed in recent times, and that today it is a place which serves almost exclusively for drinking.

By way of introduction to the actual official legislation of the Church which imposed this prohibition, one may point out several passages taken from the writings of Saint Jerome (+420). These excerpts form three of the canons in the *Decree* of Gratian.[1] They point out the general truth that drinking exposes clerics to great evils, and that excesses in food and drink ill become those who are to preach mortification and penance to God's poor. They serve, by

[1] Cc. 3, 4, 6, D. XXXV.

their condemnation of excessive drinking, as a background for the later prohibitions of the Church. Their importance is seen in the fact of their incorporation into the *Decree* of Gratian. There was yet another motive behind this law. This was the Church's desire that her clergy spend as little time as possible, aside from the consideration of spiritual matters, mingling with the laity. In ecclesiastical councils one finds rulings to the effect that clerics, even when abroad in the exercise of their ministry, were not to stand idly in the streets or in the market places talking with the people. Their presence likewise was not expected at the fairs and other public gatherings.

If one accepts an early date for the composition of the *Apostolic Canons*,[2] then it is there that the earliest evidence of the prohibition affecting the entrance of clerics into taverns in strictly nonconciliar law is found.[3] It states that if a cleric is discovered eating in a tavern or an inn he was to be suspended. This punishment, however, was not incurred if the cleric had been compelled to lodge there for reasons of travel, or because of some unforeseen contingency. Mention may also be made of the passages in the *Apostolic Constitutions* wherein are indicated the qualities which a bishop of the Church should possess. High in priority are sobriety and temperance. But these virtues would not be nurtured by those who frequented taverns. Thus, indirectly this constitution forbade clerics to enter such places.[4]

The Council of Laodicea (343-381) in its 24th canon used the words *"non oportet tabernas intrare."* It made a careful enumeration of the various classes of clerics in both minor and major Orders, and then stated that all alike were not to enter taverns. The Greek word which this Council used for tavern was καπηλεῖον, a word found in the Greek

---

[2] Vide *supra*, p. 52, footnote 3.

[3] Bruns, I, 8.

[4] Funk, *Didascalia et Constitutiones Apostolorum*, I (Bk. 2), 32.

Councils and also in the *Apostolic Canons* above considered.[5] The III Council of Carthage (397) pointed out that clerics were not to enter taverns, either to eat or to drink, unless compelled to do so when traveling.[6] Reference should again be made to the Synod in Trullo (692). Canon 9 has already been cited in the treatment of unbecoming arts and professions.[7] In the present connection this canon forbade clerics to act as inn-keepers. For this reason it appealed *a fortiori* to the fact that clerics were forbidden to enter taverns.

Some of the Penitential Books of the Frankish Church in the period from 725 to 750 enacted rather stringent sanctions against those who were guilty of going into taverns. For drunkenness there was specified the rather sobering penance of a three months' period of fast on bread and water.[8]

---

[5] This word is derived from another noun καπηλεία, which means *any retail trade*. Hence καπηλεῖον becomes the *shop* of anyone engaged in retail trade. Used with the proper qualifying adjective it indicates the specific type of trade. It is often used for tavern or inn, as in Church legislation, for example. — Liddell-Scott, *A Greek-English Lexicon* (new edition revised and augmented by Jones, 2 vols., Oxford: at the Clarendon Press, 1940), I, 875.

[6] Canon 27 — Bruns, I, 125. This canon found its way into the *Decretum Gratiani* (c. 4, D. XLIV) and into the laws of at least one other council: the Council of Africa (425[?]) — Mansi, IV, 483. In a marginal note Mansi (1692-1769) indicated that this Council reflected merely a compilation of the enactments of various other African councils. Cf. also Van Hove, *Prolegomena*, p. 180.

[7] Bruns, II, 40; Mansi, XI, 946.

[8] Mansi, XII, 460-480-496. These Books of the Frankish Kingdom, as well as those of Celtic and Anglo-Saxon origin, weakened rather than strengthened the desired observance of the law in general. By them false doctrines were spread. Private teaching took on the aspect of official pronouncement, as it was set forth in the form of canons. The over-all result was one of unhappy and deep confusion: *"Certi errores, incerti auctores."* In the twelfth century a rational and systematic attempt was made at organizing this vast wealth of matter. The work enjoyed only limited success. The Penitential Books had made their mark on canon law. On the general subject of the decline of Canon Law in this period one may confer Fournier-Le Bras, *Histoire de Collections Canoniques en Occident depuis les Fausses Décrétales jusqu 'au Décret de Gratian* (2 vols., Paris: Recueil Sirey, 1931-1932), I, 79-107 (hereafter cited Fournier-Le Bras).

From the tenth century up until the appearance of the *Decretum Gratiani* (ca. 1140) there is evidenced little legislative activity affecting the entrance of clerics into taverns. Immediately preceding this, in the eighth and ninth centuries, the legislation on this point originated almost exclusively in the Frankish kingdom. It repeated earlier conciliar rulings and is striking for its absence of any new element.[9] Bishop Theodulphus of Orleans (797) issued a capitulary in which he forbade his priests not only to go to taverns (either to eat or drink) but also to go to the homes of the laity. The reason for this was the well-grounded fear that after eating and drinking, the cleric might not as effectively refresh his host *"epulis spiritualibus,"* as his host had dined him *"epulis carnalibus."*[10]

The *Decree* of Gratian carried two canons which bore directly on this topic.[11] This merely passing treatment of a point so frequently the subject of legislation in earlier councils may be taken as evidence of an improvement in the observance of the law. It possibly may also be explained in the fact that one-half of Distinction XXXV is composed of canons which treat of the closely allied topic of drinking.[12] If clerics came to a realization of the dangers which awaited them and others as a result of excess in drink, there would be proportionately less need for a restatement of this law. Drunkenness was the source and feeder of all other vices.[13]

In the various Decretal collections there was incorporated but a single decree which restated the law that for-

---

[9] Council of Frankfort (794), canon 19 — Mansi, XII, 908; III Council of Tours (813), canon 21 — Mansi, XIV, 86; II Council of Rheims (813), canon 10 — *MGH, Leges in 4°*, Sectio III, *Concilia Aevi Karolini*, Tom. II, pars I, 289.

[10] Canon 13 — Mansi, XII, 997. This same Capitulary appeared in 994 as the *Book of Ecclesiastical Laws.* Wilkins (*Concilia*, I, 265, note 1) attributed it to Theodolphus, as does Van Hove (*Prolegomena*, p. 184).

[11] Cc. 2, 4, D. XLIV. Canon 2 repeats canon 24 of the Council of Laodicea, while canon 4 repeats canon 27 of the III Council of Carthage.

[12] Cc. 3, 4, 6, 9, D. XXXV.

[13] C. 9, D. XXXV; Singer, *Die Summa*, p. 84.

bade clerics to enter taverns. This was in the Gregorian Decretals. Its author was Pope Innocent III (1198-1216), and it was given at the IV General Council of the Lateran (1215).[14] The necessities of travel were recognized as a sufficient cause for a cleric to seek help, shelter, food, and lodging in one of these taverns or inns. The definition of a *taberna* offered by Grannieto in the seventeenth century had been applicable from the fourth and fifth centuries, and continued applicable for some time. It has been in recent times that the concept of a *taberna,* translated as tavern, has undergone considerable change. Grannieto defined it as a place in which wine and things of a similar nature were for sale.[15]

The early law had been content with stating the prohibition. Many of the later councils included in their restatement of the law a particular reason for which the presence of clerics was undesirable in these *tabernæ.* The Council of Westminster (1173), for example, warned its clerics against going to taverns because they were not to take part in public drinking bouts.[16] The Council of Salzburg (1274) was possibly the first provincial council to give recognition within its law to the fact that a cause which was evidently reasonable and just would excuse the entrance of a cleric into a tavern or a place adjoining a tavern.[17] This sounds very much like the law of the Code in canon 138, except that the Code requires the judgment of the local ordinary on the *iusta causa.* The mention of "a place adjoining a tavern" also seems to have a definite relation to the phrase of the Code, "*aliaque similia loca.*" The Council of Salzburg instituted the penalty of suspension for any cleric found loitering in such a place. This suspension was to last

[14] C. 15, X, *de vita et honestate clericorum,* III, 1.

[15] "Taberna accipiatur pro ea in qua vinum et similes res venduntur" — Grannieto (Grana-Nieto), *Catena Iurium sive in Decretalium Gregorii IX Librum II et III Commentarium* (nova ed., Lugduni, 1678), lib. III, tit. 1, c. 15, n. 6.

[16] Canon 10: "Clerici non eant...ad potationes publicas." — Mansi, XXII, 143; Council of York (1195), canon 12 — Mansi, XXII, 655.

[17] Canon 12 — Mansi, XXV, 140.

only until the offending cleric had done one day's penance by fasting on bread and water.

A ruling of the Council of Constance (1300) intimated the existence of occasional turmoil and disorder in taverns. It provided that any cleric who suffered any injury or injustice during his unlawful presence in a tavern was not to seek redress from the ecclesiastical authorities.[18]

For the most part reasons of travel were the only expressed cause in consideration of which a cleric could stop at a tavern or an inn. A later Council of Salzburg (1310) listed other causes: (1) the honoring of a friend or a distinguished personage; (2) the cleric's mental inadvertence with reference to the law; and (3) the presence of some necessity — but never the seeking of pleasure.[19]

What of clerics who went into taverns while they were dressed in their ecclesiastical garb? Apparently there were some who were guilty of such a practice. Perhaps it was an offense proper to Paris alone. At any rate a Council of Paris (1429) felt compelled to enact a statute against the practice. Clerics were not to enter taverns in their clerical dress, for they were not to frequent these places at all. Regardless of garb, they were not to enter taverns.[20]

By the time of the Council of Trent the law was fairly constant, and the Council merely gave added weight to the prohibition by means of its restatement.[21]

For the United States the II (1866) and the III (1884) Plenary Councils of Baltimore applied the law. Exception, however, was made for that necessity which might arise from reasons of travel.[22]

There are several things crystal clear from the history of the law. It is first of all an old law. It was absolute in

---

[18] Canon 4 — Mansi, XXV, 30.

[19] Canon 1 — Mansi, XXV, 226-227.

[20] Canon 20 — Mansi, XXVIII, 1429.

[21] Sess. XXIV, *de ref.*, c. 12: "... (clerici) ab illicitisque venationibus, aucupiis, choreis, tabernis... abstineant." — *Canones et Decreta*, p. 192.

[22] *Conc. Plen. Balt. II Acta et Decreta*, n. 162; *Conc. Plen. Balt. III Acta et Decreta*, n. 80.

its prohibition. It referred to places which were a combination hotel, restaurant, and tavern, the latter in the sense in which now the term "tavern" is accepted generally. Gradually the extent of the law was modified and provision was made for exceptions — mostly incidental to travel. The present law presented the factor of necessity and the presence of a just cause as allowing a cleric to enter a tavern without fear of violating the law through the fact of his entrance.

Part II. Discipline of the Code

Article 1. Definition of the Word "Taberna"

For the American clergy the universal law against entering taverns had been antedated by the particular law of the III Plenary Council of Baltimore.[23] This decree indicated one of the purposes of the law, namely that clerics abstain from anything that would discredit them as individuals or their fellow clerics as a group. Clerics are not to be a stumbling block to themselves or to others. The presence of a cleric or a priest who is drinking in a tavern or some similar place is often a source of genuine scandal. Many things which stand as perfectly legitimate for others are forbidden to clerics. This is not due to some intrinsically evil element. It is rather that these things are repugnant to true clerical dignity. The cleric by first tonsure has solemnly signified his desire to put away the things of the world. The full expression of that desire

---

[23] "Ut flagitii occasionem, quæ in cauponis et tabernis deesse non solet, clericis adimamus, cauponarum aditu et usu eis omnino interdicimus, nisi in itinere necessitatis causa." — *Conc. Plen. Balt. III Acta et Decreta*, n. 80. This law is found also in the II Plenary Council, *Acta et Decreta*, n. 162. The word *caupona* designates a place which provides lodging, food, and drink. It not infrequently was found in a context together with the word *popina*, which word refers to a place which specializes in food, although it also serves drinks (It. *bettola;* Fr. *restaurant;* Angl. *eating-house*). — Forcellini-Corradini-Perin, *Lexicon*, Tom. I, pars 2, p. 560; Tom. III, pars 2, p. 759.

necessitates abstention from certain secular activities, e.g., going into taverns.

What precisely is to be understood by the word *taberna* (which is rendered in the English by the word inn or tavern) is not set forth in the general law. Nor did the Decretal commentators as a group give any definition. As has been indicated in the historical conspectus, Grannieto in the seventeenth century defined a *taberna* as a place in which wine and similar items were for sale.[24] This definition, unfortunately, was valid only for a relatively short time after it was given, for with the changes in social conditions the concept of tavern also changed. The variety of definitions offered by commentators and authors since the Code, while fairly consistent, reflects various nationalistic concepts of this word. While it is true that this law is a product of the earlier legislation of the Church, its real meaning must also be gathered from viewing it in the framework of a changing social pattern. In practice the definition is best left to particular law. Such a ruling, together with local practice, will be the safest and most accurate norm of determining what places are forbidden to clerics. This same thought was expressed by the bishops of the Province of Malines in 1920 when they prefaced their law on taverns with a definition beginning with these words: *"Habita ratione nostri moris patrii."*[25]

To arrive at a general definition of tavern is no easy task. This definition must be flexible enough to include elements which will enable it to be applied to conditions which may exist in one country and not in another. Some help may be derived from studying some of the definitions already offered. The great sin here is either one of excess or of defect. The definition is either too strict or it is so lenient as to defeat its own purpose by carrying within

---

[24] Ferraris less than a century later defined a *taberna* as a place in which bread, wine, and cooked foods were for sale. — *Bibliotheca*, sub. v. *clericus*, art. V, n. 14.

[25] *Acta et Decreta Concilii Provincialis Mechliniensis Quarti anno MCMXX Mechliniæ Habiti* (Mechliniæ: H. Dessain, 1923), n. 133.

itself the seeds of the law's future non-observance. From a study of the word *taberna*, of the etymology of this word, and its early usage in literature, it is seen that the word may be applied to any place used for the sale of merchandise. One might call it a stall, or, with dignity, a shop. To indicate the specific type of shop and the merchandise sold therein, a qualifying adjective would be joined to the word, e.g., *vinariæ tabernæ, librariæ tabernæ.*[26]

The history of the law reveals that the earliest absolute prohibitions were directed against the entering of clerics into these *tabernæ vinariæ.* Later on in the Middle Ages simply the word *taberna* was used. It then meant an inn or tavern. This is the period which framed the law as it is found today. Clerics were not to enter these taverns or inns unless the necessities of travel so compelled them. The reason for this was clear. The taverns of that day, as seen in the literature of the times, were not high-class establishments. Entrance into such places was the cause of immediate wonderment, ridicule, and unfounded suspicion. That little scandal was taken resulted from the fact that the people who frequented these places were almost immune to scandal — highwaymen, fugitives from justice, and women of questionable virtue. In these places one could obtain lodging, food, and drink. For this reason one cannot dismiss as inaccurate any definition of *taberna* which includes such places as serve both food and drink. From the historical approach that notion is definitely verified.

One author so defined *taberna,* but hastened to add that *tabernæ* were not to be included under the notion of a place which clerics were forbidden to enter.[27] To deter-

[26] Ojetti, *Commentarium,* II, 152; Crnica, *Commentarium,* I, 155; Toso, *Commentaria Minora,* II, 103; Beste, *Introductio,* p. 139.

[27] Vermeersch, "De significatione vocis tabernæ in c. 138" — *Periodica de Re Canonica et Morali Utili præsertim Religiosis et Missionariis* (*Periodica de Religiosis et Missionariis,* Brugis, 1905-1919; *Periodica de Re Canonica et Morali Utili præsertim Religiosis et Missionariis,* Brugis, 1920-1927; *Periodica de Re Morali, Canonica, Liturgica,* Brugis, 1927-1936, et Romæ, 1937-) XI (1922), 19 (hereafter cited *Periodica*).

mine what type of *taberna* would be included in the prohibition of canon 138, he required that attention be given rather to the social conditions of the persons who frequent such places than to the things offered for sale. This looks back to the history of the word in the Middle Ages; it is also realistic enough to accept the fact that not all such places which serve food and drink in our time are filled with unsavory characters. Yet, it seems to the writer that, when an attempt is made at a definition of the word *taberna,* the most important element is the clear inclusion of the product sold there. It is precisely on this element that the definition hinges. Even if an establishment were not forbidden to clerics as a *taberna* and it were frequented by undesirables, the cleric and the priest would shun it independently of any positive law to that effect.

Beste offers a definition which seems to be too inclusive.[28] According to this definition *taberna* in its more extensive sense includes hotels, restaurants, and cafés frequented by people of respectable character who seek food and lodging; it also refers to those establishments where at all time of the day (and part of the night) intoxicating drinks and liquors are publicly sold and consumed — these are saloons,[29] bars, poolrooms, and cabarets, places which are most commonly visited by a lower class of people. The interpretation of the statutes of the II and III Plenary

---

[28] *Introductio,* p. 139; other authors similarly offer an extensive definition. They apply *taberna* without distinction to hotels, restaurants, and places which serve only drinks. — Ayrinhac, *General Legislation* p. 301; Blat, *Commentarium,* II, n. 77; Crnica, *Commentarium,* I, 155; Coronata, *Institutiones,* I, 232. Mothon implicitly offers the same definition when he notes that in most of the dioceses of France the clergy cannot eat, drink, or stay "dans les hôtels, auberges, cafés, restaurants et autres lieux publics." — *Institutions Canoniques* (3 vols., Vol. I, *Des Personnes,* Paris: Societé Saint Augustin, Desclée, De Brower, 1922), I, art. 243 (hereafter cited *Institutions Canoniques*).

[29] Augustine (*Commentary,* II, 87) also used this word saloon as a synonym for *taberna.* A saloon "in the United States (is) a shop where intoxicating liquors are sold and drunk, commonly without meals." — *Webster's New International Dictionary* (2. ed., unabridged, Springfield, Mass.: G. & C. Merriam Co., 1944), p. 2206.

Councils of Baltimore, in which entrance into any *popina* or *caupona* was forbidden to clerics, exempts from the prohibition of the law those places whose single or chief purpose is to provide *("quæ unice inserviunt")* food and lodging.[30]

This is a law which through its prohibitory character restricts the exercise of clerical rights. In keeping with the principles of canon 19, the interpretation of this law should be a strict interpretation. The word *taberna* should be so defined as to safeguard and guarantee liberty within the law. However, it seems to be both a violation of the spirit of the law and an unfair disregarding of the evident evolution in the meaning that attached to the term, to define tavern, as some authors do, as a place where wine alone is sold.[31] However, if the author intended "wine only" to mean that no food was served or that it was not served primarily, but only as an accommodation, then he would be close to another current definition. This definition, in this country and in other English-speaking countries, has been canonized by local practice. In these countries a tavern is a place to which the general public may go to drink wine, beer, and other intoxicating beverages.[32] This does not include in these countries places whose main purpose is to provide food and lodging. Thus entrance into hotels and restaurants is not forbidden, even though drinks may be served with the meals. In these countries, the law is against entering all places whose principal or sole pur-

---

[30] Beste, *Introductio*, p. 139.

[31] Aichner, *Compendium Juris Ecclesiastici* (6. ed., Brixinæ, 1887), p. 252; Ojetti, *Commentarium*, II, 152. The latter takes exception with Toso (*Commentaria Minora*, II, 10) for including those places where beer is also sold.

[32] Genicot-Salsmans, *Institutiones*, II, n. 43; Davis, *Moral Theology*, III, 301; Vermeersch-Creusen (*Epitome*, I, n. 255) hold that when this definition is given, "ex usu satis liquet in lege ecclesiastica agi tantum de tabernis *in quibus omne genus potus omnibus promiscue et minutim propinatur*"; Cance, *Le Code*, I, 162. In his *Theologiæ Moralis Principia*, III, 16, Vermeersch reshaped a definition which he had given earlier in 1922 (*Periodica*, XI [1922], 19).

pose is to sell intoxicating liquors. Here in our country, therefore, if diocesan statute indicates nothing to the contrary, one may hold that the word tavern does not apply to those places whose prime purpose is to dispense food.

Borrowing from what has gone before in this discussion a tavern may be defined as: any establishment which is licensed exclusively or primarily for the sale of wine, beer, and other intoxicating (alcoholic) liquors, or for the sale of any single item of these commodities. Mainly it serves drinks; secondarily, it may also serve food. This definition finds valid application everywhere.

The provisions of synodal law in this matter, regardless of whether the law was made prior to or subsequent upon the promulgation of the new Code of Canon Law, retain their force. Clerics then are bound to the statutes of their respective dioceses in this matter. One synod (1913) forbade priests to enter saloons *"sumendi potus causa,"* under the threat of an *ipso facto* contracted general suspension reserved to the ordinary.[33] One may wonder if the penalty would be incurred if the priest entered a tavern but did not take anything to drink, or, if he drank only soft drinks. This would be a violation of the prohibition which in canon 138 demands that a cleric is not to enter taverns. That prohibition says nothing about drinking, although it is naturally supposed that it is for this reason that one enters a tavern. The III Plenary Council of Baltimore speaks of the *aditus et usus cauponarum,* which inclines one to the belief that a priest would have to enter and drink before he would contract the penalty. However, it may be objected that the Council was not talking about taverns in the sense in which that word is now understood. It was speaking of a place where food was served.

Not infrequently in diocesan statutes one finds the phrase *"tabernæ et similia loca vendendis emendisque li-*

---

[33] *Statuta Diœcesana Lata in Synodo Prima Cheyenniensi* (Omahæ: Swartz Printing Co.), n. 30. The word saloon is used also in the *Statutes of the Diocese of Crookston* (St. Louis: Herder, 1923), n. 13.

quoribus destinata."[34] Thus worded, such a statute is extensive enough to include liquor stores and "beer depots," whose purpose it is to sell beer, wine, and liquor to "carry out." The objection that the customer does not drink his purchase then and there, as he does in a tavern, is not valid. In many cases the customer in a tavern does not drink whatever he buys right there in the tavern or even on the premises. Even if a liquor store did not come under the term *taberna* in such statutes, it would fall within the extensive grasp of the phrase *"aliaque similia loca."* It seems to be the practice, *Ordinario non reclamante,* for clerics to enter such places, but only rarely. The custom in the diocese is to be considered, though it could hardly be justified if it allowed contravention of the statute to become habitual.

At least two dioceses have the added prohibition in their laws that clerics are not to enter taverns within the physical confines of their own parish,[35] or of neighboring parishes as well.[36]

Article 2. The Phrase "Aliaque Similia Loca"

A. Private Clubs

In setting forth a definition of tavern many give an exaggerated importance to the element of public and indiscriminate sale. A tavern is conducted by its owner in such a way that everyone is free to enter it, there to order something to drink. This, however, does not necessarily make the factor of public sale of the essence in the defini-

---

[34] *Synodus Diœcesis Omahensis Quarta* (Omaha: Typis Burkley Printing, 1934), n. 25; *Statuta Archidiœcesis Sancti Francisci in Synodo Diocesana Secunda Lata* (San Francisco: The Monitor Publishing Co., 1936), n. 35; *Acta et Decreta Synodi Diœcesanæ Toletanæ Primæ* (Toleti: Apud Cancellariam Curiæ, 1941), n. 25.

[35] *Synodus Diocesana Fargensis Prima* (Milwaukiæ: Bruce, 1941), n. 39, 1°.

[36] *Constitutiones Dioceseos Novæ-Aureliæ in Synodo Diœcesana Sexta Latæ,* n. 21.

tion of the word tavern. A cocktail lounge or bar in a private club is in reality a tavern, despite a change in name and a change of setting. That it has the policy of offering its services only to members of the club and their guests brings about no real change in its nature — it remains a place for the serving of drinks. Nor does a place which serves drinks need to exist as a separate entity, i.e., in a building apart, in order to be called a tavern. It may well be part of another establishment, as in the case of private clubs and hotels. Even if one could validly demonstrate that a bar or a cocktail lounge in a private club is not a tavern, it would not be possible to hold that it does not come under the phrase *alia similia loca.* Nor is it to be contended that a cleric may drink at the bar of a private club for the reason simply that such drinking is not public drinking. In the writer's judgment such a practice does constitute public drinking. The difference in publicity between drinking in a tavern and in a private club is one of degree only. Custom in many dioceses has sanctioned the moderate use of wine (and other alcoholic beverages) with one's meals when dining in public — in a public restaurant or in the dining room of a private club. This is especially true in those countries where the use of wine is traditional, although one recalls the prohibition existing in France as given by Mothon.[37]

B. Cocktail Lounges and Hotel Bars

Among the *alia similia loca* must be listed the cocktail bar or the cocktail lounge, which is almost properly an American convention. These places are really taverns; despite soft lights, music, and expensive decorations, they are of the same stock, catering to the thirst of the public. Although they serve food on a minor scale for the further convenience of their patrons, their main business, as their very name indicates, is in drinks. Priests are to avoid these

[37] *Institutions Canoniques,* I, art. 243.

places, for they are forbidden to them by law. The same is to be said of hotel bars which do not differ fundamentally from the cocktail lounge.

C. Supper Clubs and Night Clubs

There can be no doubt that dance halls (especially those which maintain bars), roadhouses, and night clubs come within the scope of the phrase, *aliaque similia loca,* and hence of the prohibition of canon 138. If priests with cause urge young Catholics to avoid such places, there can be little question of their own responsibility and strict obligation not to patronize such places, in or out of the clerical garb. Not all supper clubs are forbidden. A distinction is to be made. There are some supper clubs which are in reality the main dining rooms of leading respectable hotels. With sufficient reason, on rare occasions, and preferably with fellow priests or a group of laymen, a priest or a cleric may dine in such a place. This is true almost exclusively in the United States and other English-speaking countries. As a general rule it is safe to follow the prudent practice of any given locality with regard to clerics or priests and their presence at such places. There are other supper clubs which differ little from night clubs, where the emphasis is on drink, and entertainment which is often vulgar and risque.[38] It goes without saying that no cleric or priest would enter a night club or a supper club of this type without grave and serious cause, proportionate to the possible evil which might arise.

D. Bars in Places of Recreation

There seems to be no objection to a priest's going to a roller-skating or ice-skating rink for lawful recreation — if he is not prohibited from doing so by diocesan statute. He

[38] Recently a leading American weekly carried an article on night clubs and night club entertainment in America. One of the illustrations bore the illuminating and discouragingly accurate caption: "N. . . . N. . . . singing his dirty songs."

is not to drink at the bar in any of these places. In some dioceses parish priests (pastor and assistants) bowl in regular league competition. In many of these bowling establishments there is a bar. The presence of such a bar on the premises of an establishment which is dedicated primarily to legitimate recreation does not prevent the cleric from going there for his recreation. However, he should not join with the others at the bar. It is more important to preserve clerical dignity than to seek favor and standing with the laity. This is doubly true if such favor be measured by the priest's ability to be a regular fellow and to take a drink with them at the bar.

If all the men were Catholic and if a lunch were served after the bowling has been completed, there is no reason why a priest may not have a glass of beer or some other drink with his lunch. Since this is not a situation envisioned by the Code, and further since it is deemed quite proper in the United States, a priest is safe in following the accepted practice of the locality. The presumption is that the local ordinary knows of such conditions. If he says nothing to the contrary, he may be presumed to tolerate, at least, the existing practice. The same may be said of priests who belong to (or who have access to) private country clubs. Their activities after they have finished golfing may well be regulated by what the majority of prudent priests do under these same circumstances.

Article 3. Excusing Causes

One of the causes — in fact, *the* cause recognized by way of explicit mention in the Code — which releases clerics from the observance of the ban on not entering taverns is necessity. This lasts as long as the necessity lasts. Necessity knows no law. The definition of tavern must be recalled. If one looks to the word tavern in its widest sense (hotels, restaurants, and bars), then an obvious example of necessity would be the need of food or the need to seek lodging while one is on travel. Again, a case of sudden illness would be a justifying cause, as would also the transaction of an important business.[39] A cleric may also enter a tavern even when this term is understood in its narrow sense if it were necessary for him to make an important telephone call, or to seek directions on a trip. Again, a matter of illness would also be sufficient cause to allow him to enter a tavern. There are other extenuating circumstances; common sense is to be used at all times.

If the ordinary grants his permission for a just cause, clerics may enter taverns. This is a provision of the Code. Actually, it is difficult to envision many cases in which the ordinary would approve of a cleric's entering a tavern when understood in its narrow sense. One *iusta causa* would be had in the need of ministering to the sick and the dying; also in the need of a visit on matters of a strictly spiritual or properly parochial nature. When one author speaks of the ordinary allowing clerics to go into *tabernæ* on the occasion of banquets and gatherings of religious associations, study groups, etc., it is clear that he means a restaurant or hall. Drinking places would scarcely be used for such gatherings, except in extreme necessity.[40]

There is some question as to the type of approbation which will suffice as regards this just cause. At least a tacit approbation is needed if it is to prove sufficient.[41] In many cases an explicit consent is held to be given, inasmuch as the reasons are not infrequently listed in the diocesan statutes. In a single case, if it were of significant importance, a presumed approbation would suffice.[42] Even when this permission is granted, the priest or cleric is to

---

[39] Regatillo, *Normæ Generales-De Personis*, p. 157.

[40] Claeys Bouuaert-Simenon, *Manuale Juris Canonici* (3 vols., Gandæ et Lœdii: Dessain, Vol. I, 3. ed., 1930; Vol. II, 1931; Vol. III, 3. ed., 1931), I, n. 295.

[41] Vermeersch, *Theologiæ Moralis Principia*, III, 16; Cocchi, *Commentarium*, lib. II, pars I, n. 50; Sipos, *Enchiridion*, p. 135; Berutti, *De Personis*, p. 143.

[42] Blat, *Commentarium*, II, n. 77; Wernz-Vidal, *Ius Canonicum*, II, n. 122.

remain in the tavern only as long as the precise nature of his business will demand.

Article 4. Clerical "Peregrini" and Local Diocesan Statutes

In canon 14, §§ 1 and 2, a definite statement is given regarding the extent of the jurisdiction of a local ordinary over those who are not legally bound to him by ties of domicile or quasi-domicile. Travelers, with the specific exceptions embodied in this canon, remain outside the jurisdiction of any local ordinary other than their own. Clerics who come into a particular diocese in which they have neither a domicile nor a quasi-domicile, without the intention to establish either one, are not generally held to observe the statutes which bind the clerics of that diocese. If they are bound, then it is by reason of explicit mention, or by way of exception to the normally expected application of law. This exception is the fact that they are bound by any and all laws whose purpose is to secure the public order *("consulere ordini publico")*.

It is admitted by canonists and civil jurists that there is obscurity in the term *public order*. This obscurity is mirrored in the divergence of opinion evidenced in the attempt to define just what laws are said to look to the public order. This much is to be held as certain: that the public order is not synonymous with the public or common good. It is on this point that much confusion can and does arise. All laws, by a postulate of their very nature, are ordained to the common good. The concept of public order is less extensive. It seems to be constituted of two elements: public necessity and a strict uniformity of conduct on the part of everyone in that territory. As constituting public order, this latter element is conceived as necessary to provide for that public necessity.[43] In its special use of the

---

[43] Hammill, *The Obligations of the Traveler According to Canon 14*, The Catholic University of America Canon Law Studies, n. 160 (Washington, D. C.: The Catholic University of America Press, 1942), p. 146.

word *ordo* the Code emphasizes the element of strict uniformity. The very *consulere* when followed by the dative case means: to look to, to regard, to secure.[44] Laws which secure public order must be restricted to those laws which aim completely and definitely at that uniformity of conduct which is to the interest of the whole community.

A practical difficulty may arise for the clerical traveler who enters another diocese there to meet with laws which do not *clearly* look to the public order. In some instances, precisely because the law is not clearly related to the public order, the legislator will have taken pains to point out in the law itself that it does aim at securing the public order. It then binds all, including strangers. If it were not for this explicit explanation, the traveler would be justified in maintaining his freedom of action. The presumption which is instituted by law is that the traveler is free; his freedom remains until his subjection to the local law has been determined. There is no problem in the case of those diocesan statutes which further delineate the provisions of the Code relative to the desired interior holiness of clerics or to their perseverance in ecclesiastical studies.[45] These laws are designed to foster the good of individuals, and hence do not pertain to public order. Therefore, they are not binding on the traveler.[46]

Less evident is the exemption of the visiting cleric in regard to the obligation to obey the local statutes which forbid occupations or recreations which are unbecoming to the clerical state. And the difficulty is heightened and grows more perplexing with the specific prohibitions. How may one determine, when the statute restrains clerics from this or that recreation or place, whether it be with a desire to strengthen their virtue, or whether it be with an aim at securing the public order, or perhaps both? To say

---

[44] Forcellini-Corradini-Perin, *Lexicon*, Tom. I, pars I, p. 823.

[45] Canons 124-126; 129-131.

[46] Van Hove, "Leges quæ ordini publico consulunt." — *Ephemerides Theologicæ Lovanienses* (Brugis, 1924-), I (1924), 161 (henceforth cited *ETL.*)

that statutes in these matters can be ordained for the public good, but that they are not necessarily so ordained, seems to offer little help.[47] Yet the statement is accurate, for it is not easy to establish the precise nature of public order. In seeking to establish it, one has to keep in mind the conditions which prevail in any community.

A statute enacted upon identical subject matter may in one diocese look to the public good, while in the second it may not. Public necessity and uniformity of conduct may be required in the one and not in the other diocese. In a predominantly Catholic community the law may have as its objective the preservation of clerical prestige. It would thus involve a matter of public order. In a non-Catholic community the same law might have as its primary object the personal sanctification of the individual priest or cleric.[48] It is a problem further complicated by the fact that the obvious purpose of the law is not always clear. The cleric must honestly and sincerely attempt to resolve his doubts, and only then proceed to act.

There is another element which may well require of a traveler the full observance of a particular diocesan statute independently of the demands of positive law. This is the reasonable fear of scandal. A law which must be obeyed for fear that non-observance would create scandal is not by that fact a law which looks to the public order. The obligation to avoid the giving of scandal has its roots in the natural law. Whenever it is prudently foreseen that scandal would result from the violation of a law, the traveler must follow the law. This is a matter for the individual conscience; it is a decision that is to be reached

---

[47] "Les statuts en ces matières peuvent ètre, croyous-nous, d'ordre public, mais ils ne le sont pars nécessairement." — Van Hove, "Leges quæ ordini publico consulunt," — *ETL*, I (1924), 161.

[48] Kinane, " 'Peregrini' and the laws which take care of public order," — *IER*, V. Series, XLII (1934), 124; cf. also Canestri, "De lege cum sanctione pœneli lata in peregrinos" — *Apollinaris* (Romæ, 1928-), VII (1934), 97.

once the circumstances of time, of person, and of place have all been carefully weighed.

Actually scandal does not arise as often as some are inclined to believe. People may be shocked or surprised, or they may even express amazement at the actions of another, but this is not scandal.[49] Scandal is an act or a deed which leads another into a sin which he would not otherwise commit — an act or a deed which is immoral in itself or immoral by reason of circumstances.[50] Scandal is mentioned in this consideration simply for the purpose of showing that the obligation of avoiding scandal is a factor which generally exists apart from the securing of the public order. This is opposed to the teachings of one canonist, who held that any law whose violation results in scandal is meant to secure public order.[51] If the violation of a certain law consistently and directly, in all cases, led others to sin, then the obligation of avoiding scandal would pertain to the public order. But such an assumption is verified only by way of exception. It cannot be regarded as reflecting what exists by way of general occurrence.

The traveling cleric or priest must make an honest effort to discover the purpose of the law. Conscientious clerics will make that effort. But it is not always easy to discover that purpose. There is no hard and fast rule by whose application one may arrive at the knowledge of whether or not a certain diocesan statute is enacted for the securing of the public order. The ultimate decision as to the law's purpose rests with the local ordinary, who should state this purpose in the law. The law should also be suf-

---

[49] Roelker, "The Traveler and Local Statutes," — *The Jurist,* II (1942), 109.

[50] "...dictum vel factum minus rectum præbens occasionem ruinæ (spiritualis)" — St. Thomas Aquinas, *Summa Theologica,* IIa IIae, q. 43, art. 1.

[51] Michiels, *Normæ Generales,* I, 320. This view of Michiels is shared also by Lumbreras, "On Episcopal Censures," — *HPR,* XLVIII (1948), 845.

ficiently promulgated.[52] The traveler is to keep in mind that, if his obligation is not clearly established, he is not bound by the law. The presumption is for his freedom. He becomes subject to the local ordinary only when that subjection has been clearly shown.

According to canon 2226, § 1, anyone who is bound by a law is liable to the penalty which is attached to its violation, unless express exemption is established. Some of the many local diocesan statutes, especially those which look to clerical comportment, carry with them a penalty. Sometimes this penalty is as severe as a suspension which is incurred *ipso facto*. If a visiting priest is bound by the law, then he is subject also to the penalty. The local ordinary may punish him if the law binds the traveler. These particular laws are not infrequently restatements of the universal law of the Code, to which restatement there has been added a specific penalty. The fact that the traveler is bound by the provisions of the universal law does not make him subject to this particular penal sanction. He is subject to this law and liable to its enacted penalty only if in its nature of a legal ordinance it means to secure the public order or otherwise concerns those matters which render the stranger subject to the local legislator.[53]

---

[52] "Leges instituuntur, cum promulgantur." — Canon 8, § 1. "Leges episcopales statim a promulgatione obligare incipiunt, nisi aliud in ipsis caveatur; modus autem promulgationis ab ipsomet Episcopo determinatur." — Canon 335, § 2.

[53] Van Hove, "Leges quæ ordini publico consulunt," — *ETL*, I (1924), 165-166.

CHAPTER VII

THE PROHIBITION AGAINST ATTENDANCE AT UNBECOMING SPECTACLES, DANCES, AND OTHER GATHERINGS

PART I. HISTORICAL CONSPECTUS

One of the remnants of paganism which caused great concern to the Church was the acceptance still accorded to theatrical productions and other public spectacles of a questionable character. There were some which were not immoral, yet clerics were not to attend them because of their public nature, or because of the possibility of scandal. The early Church had for a time allowed clerics to attend wedding banquets, after the example of our Lord who attended the wedding feast at Cana.[1] But this practice was soon changed. The Council of Laodicea (343-381) pointed out that it was not fitting for ministers of the altar to be present at the entertainment which was offered at these wedding celebrations. In order that they might not embarrass both themselves and their hosts, the clerics were to take their leave when the musicians arrived.[2]

The III Council of Carthage (397) went a step further. It forbade not only the clergy to attend spectacles and public entertainments, but also the children of the clerics

[1] St. John, 2:1-12.

[2] Bruns, I, 79. In the Capitularies collected by Martin of Braga this same canon is found listed as chapter 40 — Mansi, IX, 856. Bruns (II, 55) listed it as canon 60. This collection of Martin was one of the most important of the Spanish Church (*MPL*, LXXXIV), and was composed or compiled sometime after 563. The work was compiled for the use of the clergy of his diocese. It is really a summary and short systematic outline of canon law. The material is from former councils, especially those of Greece and Spain. — Van Hove, *Prolegomena*, pp. 278-279.

as well.[3] At that particular time the obligation of clerical celibacy had not been definitely imposed. The Council wished to forestall all unnecessary censure of the clergy, thus also obviating possible scandal. In a Synod falsely attributed to the city of Carthage another law with regard to the attendance of clerics at spectacles was passed. This law, supposedly of the so-called IV Council of Carthage (398), was found in the *Statuta Ecclesiæ Antiqua*.[4] This canon forbade clerics to make a spectacle of themselves: it forbade them to sing at banquets.[5] The first offense brought a severe reproof, and if the cleric continued to sing at banquets he was to be excommunicated.

Clerics in the fifth century, by the law of the Council of Vannes (465), were prohibited from attending wedding banquets.[6] Previously they had been allowed to attend, but were to leave when the musicians made their entrance. The Synod of Auxerre (ca. 581) inveighed against a practice which was not consonant with the sacredness of God's house. This was the practice of having dances performed within the church building by young girls. The preparation of any entertainment in church was also forbidden.[7]

---

[3] Canon 15: "Filii clericorum ad spectacula non accedant." — Bruns, I, 125.

[4] Mansi, XII, 956; Bruns, I, 140-151. This collection of 104 canons was the work of a private individual, who took the canons from many sources. The work probably originated after the controversies of the Pelagian and Monophysite heresies, but before the end of the sixth century. Despite the fact that Hardouin and Mansi attribute these canons to a IV Council of Carthage, no such Council was ever held. — Hefele-Leclercq, II, pars 1, pp. 102-105, footnote 2.

[5] "Clericum *inter epulas cantantem* supradictæ sententiæ severitate coercendum." — Mansi, III, 956. The Council of Sens (578) forbade clerics to *dance* at banquets. — Mansi, IX, 915 (italics inserted).

[6] Canon 11 — Bruns, II, 144; Mansi, VII, 954. This is reproduced in the Council of Agde (506), canon 39 — Bruns, II, 154; Mansi, VIII, 331; and also in the *Decree* of Gratian, c. 19, D. XXXIV.

[7] Canon 9: "Non licet in Ecclesiis *choreas et puellarum cantica exercere*... (italics inserted)" — Mansi, IX, 913. The *canticum* was a dramatized poem. This prohibition is repeated in canon 9 of the Council of Sens (573-603) — *MGH, Leges in 4°*, Sectio III, *Concilia Aevi Merovingici*, Tom. I, 180.

Clerics were touched by this canon in that they were held responsible for maintaining proper decorum in church.

The responsibility of the priest (and other clerics) in these matters was also touched upon by the III Provincial Council of Toledo (589), known for its condemnation of Arianism in the Spanish Church. The Council noted that on some of the feast days there were celebrations which little honored the memory of the saints. It therefore ordered that in the future these dances and indecent songs were not to be tolerated by the clergy.[8] The Council was speaking of a custom, also prevalent elsewhere in Europe, of adding extra celebration to the strictly liturgical honor paid the saints. Very definitely an abuse had arisen and the Council was solicitous about its correction.[9]

The single important addition of the seventh century is found in the Trullan Synod (692), in canons 24 and 51. The first of these canons looked directly to priests and monks, and forbade them to attend horse races and theatrical productions.[10] The second of these canons condemned

---

[8] The title of the 23rd canon reads: "...ballimachiæ et turpes cantici prohibendi sunt a Sanctorum solemnitatibus" — Mansi, IX, 999; the full text of the canon is in Bruns, I, 219.

[9] Today on the feasts of the Immaculate Conception and of Corpus Christi, and on the last three days before the Carnival, a dance takes place in the Cathedral of Madrid. Called the *Los Seises*, it is performed by sixteen altar boys. — Goadby, "Dancing in Church" — *The Catholic Digest* (St. Paul, 1936-), III (1939), No. 3, January, 31-33. Another traditional dance, dating back to the eighth century is the penitential dance of Echternach in the Duchy of Luxemburg. It is performed each year on Whit Tuesday. — Sheehan, "Dancing before the Lord" — *The Catholic Digest*, X (1946), No. 9, July, 22-24.

[10] "Ne cui liceat eorum qui in sacerdotali ordine enumerantur vel monachorum in equorum curriculis subsistere vel scenicos ludos sustinere." — Mansi, XI, 954; Hardouin, III, 1670; Bruns, II, 44. "There can be no doubt that in the last decades of the seventh century at Constantinople there was a fully developed and popular mimic drama presented in public and at private houses, which had ramifications into the fields of the vulgar festivals...." — Nicoll, *Masks, Mimes and Miracles*, p. 145.

all actors and their plays. This was a rather sad commentary on the state of the Greek theater of the period, and an even sadder one on the failure of the Christians to rise above it.[11]

The ninth century was rich in legislation, but most of it was merely a restatement of previous conciliar law.[12] This activity was mostly in the Frankish kingdom, where the personal interest of Charlemagne (+814) had done much to remedy an unfortunate situation which had arisen out of the social and political turmoil of the previous century. The Council of Mainz (813) used the word *pompa,* for the first time; this word eventually made its way into canon 140 of the Code of Canon Law.[13] Clerics were to remain away from all public shows and spectacles; they were to flee, literally, from banquets which exhibited any evil or improper element.

It is to be recalled and kept in mind that these laws of the first ten centuries were made against a background of paganism, immorality, cruelty, and violence. This may explain the lack of any discrimination in the canons between legitimate theatrical entertainment and the admittedly bad elements in the amusements of the time. Ecclesiastics of those times feared, possibly, to provide such distinctions, lest they be regarded as a compromise. It was in this period that one finds the introduction of the word *spectaculum,* a word which would be used through later centuries to embody the threefold condemnation of the pagan theater, circus, and amphitheater.

The *Decree* of Gratian introduced a new element in canon 3, Distinction XXIII. It was a rather lengthy section which Friedberg (1837-1910) identified as being from the

---

[11] Mansi, XI, 967; Bruns, II, 52.

[12] Council of Tours (813), canon 8—*MGH, Leges in 4°*, Sectio III, *Concilia Aevi Karolini,* Tom. II, pars I, p. 289; II Council of Rheims (819), canon 19—*MGH, ibid.,* p. 256; Mansi, XIV, 80.

[13] Canon 10—*MGH, Leges in 4°*, Sectio III, *Concilia Aevi Karolini,* Tom. II, pars I, p. 263.

work of Isidore of Seville (560-636), *De Vita Clericorum.*[14] The over-all theme of the canon was that clerics were to lead exemplary lives. To that end they were to remain aloof from the pleasures of the world. They were not to attend spectacles, dances, parties, or public displays and gatherings.[15] By public spectacles, Rufinus (+ca. 1190) understood generally those worldly entertainments which brought harm to those who viewed them, not so much because of the entertainments themselves, but because of what took place at them. They were called *spectacula* inasmuch as they were staged for the public at large. Another name for them was *ludicra,* so called because many of them took place in connection with games *(in ludis geruntur).*[16] The gloss gave somewhat the same idea, basing the prohibition against public spectacles on the fact that often immoral games and practices took place there.[17]

There was also repeated in the *Decree* of Gratian a canon which forbade clerics to be present at the dances which often accompanied wedding banquets.[18] At these banquets there were songs, dances, and obscene bodily movements in the plays and skits. These contaminated the sight and hearing of those who were given to God's service. It was simply a law aimed at reminding clerics that the occasions of sin and of scandal were to be avoided just as readily as sin itself.

In the early times the people not infrequently used to gather for some refreshment after the anniversary Masses for their deceased. As in the case of the Agape of even earlier times, abuses had crept in, and this to such an extent that clerics were warned against going to these gatherings.

---

[14] Friedberg, I, p. 80, footnote 140.

[15] "...a mundi voluptatibus sese abstineant; non spectaculis, non pompis intersint." — c. 3, D. XXIII.

[16] Singer, *Die Summa,* pp. 52-53.

[17] *Glossa ordinaria,* c. 3, D. XXIII, sub v. *non spectaculis.*

[18] C. 37, D. V, *de cons.*

They had turned into banquets with excesses in eating and drinking, with entertainments that were unchristian.[19]

In the Decretal period there were abundant references to an abuse that had grown out of the laudable custom of using theatrical performances to honor the memory of some saint, or to present some religious truth. Pope Innocent III (1198-1216) attempted to correct this evil, which had been defended on the score of its existence by way of customary usage. In a letter addressed to the Archbishop of Gniezno (in Poland) and to his suffragan bishops, the Pope urged that immediate countermeasures be taken. The evil had proximately arisen from the practice of staging theatricals in the church buildings themselves.

Originally the custom had grown up around certain religious feasts. It had gone astray, in one respect or another, and a correction was to be made. It would be hasty to conclude, however, that there were any immoralities involved. It was rather a question of propriety.[20] It was felt that the church was not the place for such productions, and that clerics were not to take part in them. Subdeacons, deacons, and even priests had taken active part in these festivities, which were connected with the feasts of Saint Stephen, Saint John, and the Holy Innocents, all within the Christmas cycle of feasts.[21]

---

[19] C. 7, D. XLIV. Gratian gave the source as the Council of Nantes. Friedberg (I, 158) noted correctly that it is not from this Council, but from the Capitulary of Hincmar of Rheims. Fournier-Le Bras (I, 259) held that, while there was no such council, the canons attributed to it are genuine, having been, for the most part, taken from various of the Penitential Books.

[20] C. 12, X, *de vita et honestate clericorum*, III, 1 — Potthast, n. 2967.

[21] The development of the religious drama was given impetus by certain features of the Church's liturgy. It seems that its first beginnings were in connection with the mimic doll group of Christmas time representing the Nativity. Another group was found at Easter time, when actors representing the three Marys and the Angel dramatized the Resurrection. This was in the tenth century. — Nicoll, *op. cit.*, pp. 176-177; Dubech, *Histoiré Genérale illustrée du Theâtre* (6 vols., Paris: Libraire du France, 1931-1934), II, 38-51; also De Robeck, "Nativity Plays in Italy" — *Dublin Review*, CXCVI (1935), 85-99.

In the late Middle Ages the miracle or mystery plays enjoyed great popularity. These plays were a great aid to the devotion of the people, and helped to counteract the paganism of the purely secular stage. Yet there were abuses. Because of these abuses there was some ecclesiastical objection to them. This is seen in the following excerpt from a late fourteenth century homily:

No man may hear at once...effectively the voice of the Master Christ and of his own lusts. And since miracle playing is of the lust of the flesh and the mirth of the body, no man may effectively hear them and the voice of Christ....[22]

From what has gone before in this discussion and from what is to follow, one notes that a great deal of influence had been exerted by conciliar legislation in the formation of the prohibition affecting the attendance of the clergy at shows. In the twelfth century a general prohibition was enacted against the clerics' attending or conducting dances or choral groups. This was never to take place, especially not in churches, in cemeteries, or in processions. To do so would be a mortal sin.[23] From the IV General Council of the Lateran (1215) came the law that clerics were not to be present at (literally, give their services to) theatricals of any type whatsoever.[24] The Council of Florence (1346) forbade clerics to attend the dances and choral work performed by women. In fact, under no condition was a cleric to be a spectator at any entertainment which was staged by women.[25]

---

[22] Coyle, "The Church and the Theatre"—*ER*, XCII (1935), 139; Dubech, *Histoiré Genérale illustrée du Theâtre*, II, 38-51.

[23] Diocesan Statutes of Odo, Bishop of Paris (c. 1198)—Mansi, XXII, 683; Council of Paris (1212), canon 4—Mansi, XXII, 843; Synod of Bayeux (1300), canon 31—Mansi, XXV, 68; Council of Pont-Audemer (1305), canon 7—Mansi, XXV, 129.

[24] Canon 16—Mansi, XXVI, 1050.

[25] Book 3—Mansi, XXVI, 36; the Council of Sens (1528), in canon 25 (Mansi, XXIII, 1194), warned clerics against going to public dances; they likewise were not to sing the love ballads of the day and other ditties which were then popular.

The Council of Salzburg (1274) took action against the practice of dressing groups of young boys as canons to sing the Office in church on certain of the more solemn feasts. One of the boys, attired in episcopal robes, intoned the opening antiphons at Vespers. More harm than good had come from this practice, and the Council urged that it be stopped.[26] No cleric was to dance, especially in public, nor was he to incorporate melodies of secular songs into his Masses. No matter how commendable his talent, his voice was not to be heard in song at wedding banquets. These were rulings enacted by the Council of Seville (1512).[27] In the same Council the national sport of bull-fighting was forbidden to clerics. They were to be neither active participants nor even spectators.

One of the more popular features of the social life of medieval times was the tournament or joust. These tournaments achieved great popularity at the close of the eleventh and in the beginning of the twelfth century, and continued on until after the fifteenth century. In Italy they enjoyed particular favor in the larger cities of Milan, Sienna, Ravenna, and Naples.[28] The word as a general term included mock battles, displays of horsemanship, fighting, and contests whose aim was the proof of physical prowess. Very often they resulted in bloodshed, not infrequently in death itself. In an attempt to end these bloody and useless contests, the Church denied Christian burial to anyone who died as the result of injuries sustained in them.[29] Even previous to the law of the Council of Würzburg (1287),[30]

---

[26] Canon 17 — Mansi, XXIV, 142; Nicoll (*op. cit.*, p. 19) called it the Feast of the Boy Bishop.

[27] Canon 23 — Mansi, XXXII, 603.

[28] Some say that the *torneamentum* came from the Trojans, who moved over into Italy after the destruction of their cities by the Greeks. But it seems more probable that the tournament originated during the eleventh century in France. From France then it spread to England. Later it became popular in continental Europe.

[29] Pope Innocent II (1130-1143) at the Council of Rheims (1131), canon 2 — Mansi, XX, 460.

[30] Canon 4 — Mansi, XXIV, 852.

several Popes had outlawed the participation of the clergy, actively or passively, in these events, notable among them being Pope Alexander III (1159-1181) at the III General Council of the Lateran.[31] Later, Pope Clement V (1305-1314) solemnly forbade these tournaments under pain of excommunication and interdict reserved to the Holy Father himself. For some unknown reason, Pope John XXII (1316-1334) recalled this law, and absolved all who had been under censure for their participation in these tournaments.[32]

All the anathemas of councils and of Popes availed little to lessen the favor which these games enjoyed in France. It took the tragic death of King Henry II (1547-1559) to do that. He was killed in such a tournament in 1559.[33] Gradually the tournament and the popularity which it had died out, and one finds no further mention of it in ecclesiastical legislation.

For the preservation of ecclesiastical honor and dignity the bishops of the United States, gathered in solemn session at the III Plenary Council of Baltimore (1884), ordered that priests were not to attend public horse races, theaters, and public spectacles.[34]

---

[31] Canon 20: "Following the example of our predecessors Innocent and Eugene [Eugene III (1145-1153)], we forbid these detestable jousts or fairs, commonly known as tournaments, in which soldiers generally come together by agreement, and, to make a show of their strength and boldness, rashly engage in contests, which are frequently the cause of death to men and danger to souls. If anyone taking part in them should meet his death, though forgiveness (through the Sacrament of Penance) shall not be denied him, he shall, however, be deprived of Christian burial." — Schroeder, *Disciplinary Decrees of the General Councils* (St. Louis: Herder, 1937), p. 231. The initial legislation [in the Synod of Clermont (1130), canon 9] was incorporated in canon 14 of the II General Council of the Lateran (1139). The IV General Council of the Lateran (1215) also enacted a prohibition regarding tournaments. — Schroeder, *op. cit.*, p. 295.

[32] Moroni, *Dizionario*, Vols. LXXVII-LXXVIII, 238-239.

[33] Richard, *Analysis Conciliorum*, IV, 945.

[34] *Conc. Plen. Balt. III Acta et Decreta*, n. 79.

Part II. Discipline of the Code

Article 1. The Attendance of Clerics at Public Spectacles

A. Preliminary Notions

It is to be kept clearly in mind that it is not the object of canon 140 to launch an indiscriminate prohibition against the attendance of clerics at all entertainments and recreations of a public or a private nature. Such false rigorism is not the aim of this canon. It would be both unwise and misleading to interpret canon 140 exclusively in the light of its early history. There was a certain consistency in the conciliar legislation before and after the Council of Trent, for it condemned the attendance of clerics at the theater, at dances, and the like. What must be understood is that the condemnation, although severely stated, was directed against entertainments which were of a highly questionable morality. These existed in abundance, in fact, to such an extent that Pope Benedict XIV held that a cleric or lay person could scarcely view the comedies of his day without committing serious sin.[35] The Holy Father condemned the view of Ferrari (1576-1669), who had held that, while it was wrong for clerics to take part in these theatricals, it was permissible for them to attend such shows no matter what their morality or manner of presentation, provided that they felt there was no probable danger of sinning, and provided that scandal was not given.

The general law as it stands today, positively phrased, does not prohibit clerics to attend public entertainments, etc., with two exceptions. They are not to be in attendance: (1) if these plays, sporting events, dances, and the like (particularly those held in public theaters) are unbecoming to clerics; and (2) if their presence would give rise to scandal.[36]

---

[35] *De Synodo*, lib. XI, c. 10, nn. XI-XIII.

[36] Toso (*Commentaria Minora*, II, 107) refers to these as the subjective and objective reasons for the prohibition.

This is the extent of the law. In many cases the issue will be clear. In borderline cases the cleric will follow the dictates of a well-formed conscience, after he has carefully weighed the pertinent factors of place, person, and circumstance. If there is a diocesan statute covering the matter, that is to be followed. Before he will allow himself full freedom of action, the cleric will have made sure, in so far as he can reasonably do so, that no scandal will follow from his course of action. Clerics cannot attend those entertainments which, though in themselves not censurable, are considered as such by the people as far as clerics are concerned.[37] It seems that this is more readily the case if these events are in a public theater or auditorium — not necessarily, however, nor exclusively.[38] In the law of the Code the prohibition is conditioned by two factors, namely, the unbecoming nature of the entertainment (*in se* or in the judgment of reasonable people) and the danger of scandal.[39]

B. The Word "Spectaculum"

From the Greek verb σκέπτω, and the Latin verb *spectare,* meaning "to look at, to be a spectator at," the word *spectaculum* has the very broad meaning of "anything to be looked at." In ecclesiastical terminology it was applied to theatrical productions. Later, by extension, it came to include the productions of the pagan theater and the activities of the circus and the amphitheater. With the passing centuries there arose a variety of public events to which the word was equally applicable.

Thus, today, under the term *spectaculum* come all forms of theatrical presentations and all sporting events, par-

---

[37] Ramstein, *A Manual of Canon Law* (Hoboken: Terminal Publishing Co., 1947), p. 181.

[38] Ayrinhac, *General Legislation,* p. 307.

[39] These conditions need not be present simultaneously, though generally that is the case. Thus a priest who would go to a night club or stage show, attired in a civilian garb, in a city where he was unknown, would probably not be guilty of giving scandal.

ticularly those intended for public consumption. Under theatrical events would come plays, concerts, moving picture shows, etc., while under sporting events would be included a host of activities, such as football, baseball, races of all sorts, bullfights, soccer, and the like.

C. Attendance of Clerics at Sporting Events

When one speaks of clerics and priests going to public sporting events, one speaks of a practice which is limited for the most part to English-speaking countries. The greatest liberty within the law is enjoyed by the American clergy. As far as the writer could ascertain from conversation with European priests and from a limited stay abroad, it may be said that it is not customary for the European clergy to attend these public sporting events. There may be exceptions; the actual practice is determined by the general reaction of the people. This varies with the different nations and is generally unfavorable. Then, too, diocesan statutes are severe on these points.

The common law itself does not forbid *all* spectacles. Only those are forbidden which are unbecoming or which occasion scandal. Apparently the people of this country (with the possible exception of those areas in which the number of Catholics is small and the priests are few) do not think it improper for clerics to be seen at the majority of these sporting events. One may say that in the United States the only events forbidden by the general law are those which in any way detract from the honor and respect due to clerics.[40] The American people are not in this matter easily scandalized. With rare exception does the presence of priests at sporting events cause anyone to think less of them or of the priesthood. The advent of television now enables priests to witness their favorite sporting events in the security of their rectory.

---

[40] Beste, *Introductio*, p. 140.

1. Professional Prize Fights:

This is a matter upon which there is some disagreement. Lack of unanimity flows from a failure of some to distinguish between boxing, where the emphasis is on sportsmanship, skill, and exercise, and professional prize fighting, with its emphasis on commercialism and brutal bodily punishment. A priest may feel free to attend those amateur boxing cards which are arranged by private clubs, gyms, and schools — perhaps even by his own Catholic Youth Organization (CYO). These are generally meant to be exhibitions of boxing skill. Despite the fact that this skill is often not noticeable to any appreciable degree, these bouts are kept well in hand by reason of interested supervision. There is happily lacking that bruising punishment which is part of professional prize fighting.

There are some who hold that professional prize fighting may easily become morally wrong. They appeal to the principle that it is a sin to deprive another of the use of his reason without sufficient cause. If this is true, then priests could not attend these fights — this independently of the demands of canon 140, where the presumption maintains that the events not prohibited by it are morally non-objectionable. Whatever one may hold for or against this view,[41] it seems unbecoming for clerics to attend these highly publicized ring encounters.[42]

Theoretically there is the hope that these will prove to be exhibitions of skill; practically it is a question of brute force, of two men with the intention of knocking each other out or of rendering each other so physically unfit as to

---

[41] "Nihilominus hujusmodi certamen facile illicitum fieri potest... graviter...si certamen eo tendat ut unus ex certantibus...sensibus destituatur." — Aertyns-Damen, *Theologia Moralis*, I, n. 586, 5°.

[42] *Acta et Decreta Synodi Diœcesana Quebecensis Secundæ Anno 1940 Quebeci Celebratæ* (Quebeci: Apud Cancellariam, 1940), decretum 54, § 1. This decree forbids clerics to attend not only prize fights, but also all public athletic events.

make the continuation of the fight an impossibility.[43] The presence of a priest at such a fight is judged on the basis of what actually transpires at most of these fights. When the crowd roars at the sight of a fighter in trouble, it is not so much the stamp of their approval on skill as it is the expression of their desire to see more punishment administered. It seems incongruous for clerics to be present at such spectacles. People make no saving distinctions. To their minds the priest is there for the same reason that accounts for their presence. He is held to approve the things that they approve. With rare exception, clerics and priests will do well to seek their pleasure elsewhere.

2. Baseball and Football Games:

The presence of priests at these games (and one may also include basketball) causes no unfavorable comment. Certainly, there is no scandal in the act of attending. Priests act wisely if they attend these games in the company of fellow priests or of laymen, for uncharitable minds and sharp tongues always work overtime when a cleric appears at a public function accompanied by persons of the other sex. Many diocesan statutes speak of this very point.

The attendance of priests at some of these athletic events has become a part of their duties. This is true in those colleges and high schools where a cleric or a priest has been appointed as athletic director, or even as coach. The functioning of a complete athletic program within the

[43] Recently the validity of boxing as a sport was seriously questioned in a response given in the *Journal of the American Medical Association*. It was stated that in boxing the primary target is the head, while the goal is to injure or physically punish the opponent. This is at variance with sports in which injury is incidental, as for example in football where the touchdown is the goal and the injury only a possible by-product. The doctors point out that "every knockout causes definite and irreparable damage." This is substantiated by the statement that the incidence of mental injury among those who stay in boxing for any length of time is nearly fifty per cent. Sharp emphasis is given to the fact that boxing exerts a brutalizing influence on spectators and appeals to the lowest human instincts. — *Journal of the American Medical Association* (Chicago, 1883-), CXXXVI (1948), No. 13, 907.

framework of the CYO has brought many priests into closer contact with sporting events. In our country it is not unheard of for a member of the hierarchy to attend an occasional athletic contest. In Europe, one of the Cardinals of the Church threw in the first ball at a championship soccer match. This may be taken as an indication that people take no reasonable offense from the attendance of clerics at all types of sporting events.

Back some twenty-five years ago at least two diocesan synods forbade priests to go to baseball or football games.[44] Sometimes the faithful think it unusual when they see priests at sporting events at times when confessions customarily are heard in the parishes. The Archdiocese of Omaha forbids its parochial clergy to attend baseball, football, and basketball games on those days and at those hours when confessions are to be heard.[45]

Although canon 140 does not treat of this point as such, a priest does well to remember that while in attendance at these sporting events he does not enjoy the same freedom of expression that belongs to others. He must exhibit a manly dignity at all times. At no time should he give way to a violent voicing of his displeasure with those who are officiating at these events. Nor does it appear in good taste to take public exception to others who may not share his personal views on the relative merits of the teams or of the individual athletes. The presumption is that the priest attends these events for legitimate relaxation and enjoyment. If he cannot relax, or if his enjoyment involves the embarrassment or discomfort of others, it is preferable that he remain at home. Other means of relaxing should then be sought instead.

---

[44] *Statuta Diœceseos Pittsburghensis in Synodo Decima Quarta Lata* (Pittsburgh: St. Joseph's Protectory Press, 1920), n. 8, 2. This has been reënacted in Pittsburgh in 1929 and 1939. Cf. also *Statutes of the Diocese of Crookston*, n. 17.

[45] *Synodus Diœcesana Omahensis Quarta*, n. 19 (c). In St. Louis, priests are forbidden to attend public games on Sundays and holydays of obligation — *Synodus Diœcesana Sancti Ludovici Septima* (Sancti Ludovici, 1929), n. 28.

3. Horse and Dog Racing:

Horse racing has a long and eventual history which reaches back as far as Thotmes III (1501-1447 B. C.) of the XVIII Egyptian Dynasty. Its popularity has grown over the centuries in almost all parts of the world. Today in Europe, England, and the United States (to mention but a few places) it yearly attracts millions of enthusiasts. It is a year-round sport in our country, where in some twenty States many tracks are in operation. The clerics of this country have only somewhat of a theoretical knowledge of horse racing, since they are bound by the decree of the III Plenary Council of Baltimore (1884), which forbids them to attend public race tracks.[46] Horse races do not seem to have in themselves anything unbecoming for the clergy to see. For whatever the reason may be, some diocesan synods have repeated the ruling of the III Plenary Council.[47]

The question whether or not horse races are included among the *forbidden spectacula* of the Code, or whether or not custom may have tempered the law of the III Plenary Council of Baltimore, is no longer debatable. As Barrett has noted: "Though there has been no official publication of them, it is a matter of common knowledge that our Bishops have received documents from the Holy See urging the punishment of clerics who attend the races."[48]

4. Bullfights:

Bullfighting is to Spain and the Latin American countries what baseball is to the United States — it is the na-

---

[46] "...mandamus ut sacerdotes a publicis equorum prorsus abstineant cursibus." — *Conc. Plen. Balt. III Acta et Decreta*, n. 79.

[47] *Synodus Diœcesana Sancti Ludovici Septima*, n. 28; *Statuta Diœcesana in Synodo Prima Cheyennensi Lata*, n. 13. Any priest having a domicile or a quasi-domicile in the Archdiocese of Baltimore who attends horse races at public tracks incurs *ipso facto* a non-reserved suspension *a divinis*. The penalty does not apply to horse races at county fairs. — *Letter of the Ordinary*, March 28, 1947.

[48] *A Comparative Study of the Councils of Baltimore and the Code of Canon Law*, The Catholic University of America Canon Law Studies, n. 83 (Washington, D. C.: The Catholic University of America, 1932), p. 53 (hereafter cited *A Comparative Study*).

tional sport. Without attempting a description of the mechanics of this fascinating sport, it may be noted that bullfighting was introduced into Andalusia by the Moors when they conquered that province. Originally it was a sport of the aristocracy. They sponsored the bullfights as entertainment in which they themselves participated. In the seventeenth century its nature changed somewhat when the nobility began hiring professional substitutes to do the fighting for them.

Known in Spain as *corridas de toros* or simply as *toros*, bullfighting has been condemned by the authorities of the Church. Pope Saint Pius V (1566-1572), after having forbidden this sport under penalty of death in the city of Rome, also forbade it everywhere in the Spanish Kingdom in his Bull, *De salute*, of November 1, 1567.[49] For all secular princes and civil authorities who sponsored these affairs the penalty was an *ipso facto* incurred excommunication. The same penalty, and in addition the deprivation of ecclesiastical burial, fell upon all seculars and religious who attended these fights. In deference to the appeals of the Spanish King,[50] Pope Gregory XIII (1572-1585) in his Bull *Exponi nobis*, of August 23, 1575, so mitigated this earlier prohibition that the penalty of excommunication remained only for clerics *in sacris*. Still another change brought it about that excommunication remained only *"pro monachis et Fratribus Mendicantibus, cæterisque cuiuscumque ordinis et instituti regularibus."* This was effected through the Bull *Suscepti muneris* (January 12, 1597) of Pope Clement VIII (1592-1605). The secular clergy were forbidden to attend, but the prohibition did not carry the penal sanction of excommunication. One of the reasons which the Pope gave as having prompted him to reduce the

---

[49] This and other papal documents here cited are found in Santi, *Prælectiones*, lib. V, tit. 13, nn. 3-6; Moroni, *Dizionario*, LXXVII-LXXVIII, 239.

[50] Pereda, "La Iglesia y los Toros" — *Razón y Fe* (Madrid, 1901-), CXXX (1944), 509.

penalty was the natural propensity of the Spanish people to view such events.[51]

The whole problem was much discussed by the Spanish theologians of the seventeenth century. The final conclusion was that it was not a mortal sin for a cleric to watch a bullfight. In the seventeenth and eighteenth centuries many of the Spanish cardinals and bishops, and even the papal nuncio, attended the bullfights. Several of the bishops had publicly stated that there was no scandal involved. The present practice in Spain is fluid. Although theory and practice are at variance, this circumstance does not connote any rebellion against pontifical decrees. It is rather that in the Spanish mind there exist reasons to believe that time and circumstances have conditioned these decrees for a milder application. Many dioceses have special regulations which forbid clerics to attend these bullfights. These regulations are conscientiously observed.

In 1893 the Spanish Bishop of Ciudad Rodrigo received from the Sacred Penitentiary a reply to a doubt which he had proposed.[52] The bishop had inquired as to the validity of a custom prevailing in some dioceses of Spain whereby a priest would attend a bullfight with the Sacred Oils in his possession — to be used in a case of necessity. The reply indicated that such a practice was out of order, and therefore was not to be tolerated. The Holy Oils could be kept in a decent and becoming place nearby, but there was not to be anything which could positively encourage the thought that official approval was given for this type of entertainment.

5. Other Athletic Events:

There are a great many other events, such as hockey matches, tennis matches, track and field events, which clerics may attend if this is not forbidden by diocesan statute. Clerics should not attend women's swimming meets

[51] Pereda, "La Moral y los Toros," — *Razón y Fe*, CXXXII (1945), 301.

[52] *Fontes*, n. 6441.

or gymnastic exhibitions or other athletic events. In reality there seems little likelihood of that. What is to be said of the ice-show, a fairly recent and popular addition to the American recreational and amusement scene? While not entirely a sporting event, it may here be treated as such. It seems generally accepted that clerics may attend ice-shows. The cleric would do well to consider the possible reaction which his presence may have on the people of the community in which he views the show. This reaction may well differ from that of his own community. There are some good-intentioned faithful who think that the abbreviated costuming of the female performers is an objectionable element. This view is not without merit, and if it prevailed in any community the cleric could not attend the ice-show.[53] As a general rule, if clerics are allowed to seek recreation by skating at indoor rinks where such costumes are also in evidence, he would also be allowed to attend these ice-shows. He would be forbidden to take an active part as a performer in such shows, however.

D. Participation of Clerics in Sporting Events

If the cleric cannot do the lesser thing, then he cannot do the greater. The phrase *ne intersint* forbids passive attendance at, and, *a fortiori,* active participation in forbidden *spectacula.* In many cases he could not actively participate in *spectacula* which he would be allowed passively to attend, e.g., big league baseball or football, ice-shows, etc. One of the popular sports now is softball or kittenball. Unless the bishop has forbidden his clergy to participate actively in this sport, a priest could play with a parish team or with a team of Catholic young men, in a league under Catholic auspices. He should not play with great frequency, however; if there were much publicity at-

[53] On this point *Time* magazine reproduced an item taken from the official paper of the Archdiocese of Quebec, *L'Action Catholique.* It read in part: " 'To do figure-skating, is it really necessary for girls to uncover their legs completely?. . .The costumes generally worn by most girl skaters are frankly indecent.' " — *Time,* LI (1948), n. 16, 42.

tached to his playing it would be better that he discontinued such activity. It has been known in the past that local ordinaries have given special permission which allowed certain priests in small towns to play hardball with a local team.

Priest golfers can take part in competition confined to their own club or in open competition with other clubs. From the spirit of the law public competition would be forbidden. Interpreting the law strictly, however, one may say that in the town where he is stationed a cleric may participate in a public tournament and exhibition, provided that there is no occasion of scandal or any great loss of time.[54]

E. Attendance of Clerics at Theatrical Presentations

1. Theatrical Plays:

Clerics are not to attend presentations of the legitimate stage if these productions themselves or the presence of clerics thereat would be unbecoming to the clerical state. Especially is this true if the event takes place in a public theater. The word *public* is frequently used in the Code of Canon Law, but it has not the same shade of meaning in every context. In fact, there are five different definitions of it in the Code for as many different subjects, i.e., impediments,[55] delicts,[56] documents,[57] worship,[58] and oratories.[59] The closest analogy to the public theater is provided by the *public oratory*, but it remains only an analogy. In the absence of a legal definition, one must fall back on common usage as the test of the *propria verborum signifi-*

---

[54] Kinane, "The Priest and Golf Competition"—*IER*, V. Series, XXV (1930), 646.

[55] Canon 1037.

[56] Canon 2197, 1°.

[57] Canons 1812-1814.

[58] Canon 1256.

[59] Canon 1188, § 2, 1°.

catio. A *public* theater, then, may be defined as a theater which is generally and habitually open to the public.[60]

It makes no difference whether the play or the dramatic exhibition be produced by a professional company or by a group of amateur players. The definition remains the same. If this event is objectionable, in part or in whole, clerics are forbidden to attend. One cannot overstress the point that what is unbecoming and what is scandalous depends not only on the nature of the play but also on the ideas and customs prevalent in any given locality. The final judgment as to what is unbecoming or scandalous rests with the local ordinaries. Whatever decrees are made, these must be obeyed. The absence of any specific statute allows the cleric full liberty within the restraint imposed by the common law.

The law of the Code is more lenient than the law of the III Plenary Council of Baltimore, which forbade clerics to be present at *all* plays and public spectacles.[61] This prohibition is not to be understood, it appears, as in the Code, by reason of customary interpretation. This particular part of the law on plays is abrogated.[62] An attitude which forbids practically all entertainments, plays, and the like seems too rigorous — unless, of course, serious abuses demand the application of such severity. It is out of keeping with the norms according to which these things are to be judged. No priest nor any conscientious layman finds anything wrong in a priest who attends a decent theatrical performance. As a rule, people in this country regard theatergoing as a proper amusement and recreation. They take no offense at the clergy's going to respectable places of amusement to view respectable entertainment.[63]

---

[60] Browne, "Notes and Queries" — *IER*, V. Series, XLIV (1934), 526.

[61] *Conc. Plen. Balt. III Acta et Decreta*, n. 79.

[62] Barrett, *A Comparative Study*, Appendix I, p. 207; Bouscaren-Ellis claim the law still to be in effect throughout the United States. — *Canon Law*, p. 117.

[63] Woywod, *A Practical Commentary on the Code of Canon Law* (9. ed., revised by C. Smith, 2 vols., New York: J. F. Wagner, 1945), I, 58.

The severity of the III Plenary Council of Baltimore may have been occasioned by the discussions at the Vatican Council (1870-) upon the subject of *spectacula.* No doubt many of our bishops were present at these particular discussions. One of the addresses was delivered by Archbishop Simór of Gran (in Hungary). His Excellency said in part:

I do not speak to you from my own experience, Reverend Fathers, for I am not accustomed to frequent theater and spectacles, but, nevertheless, I know from descriptions that the theater and present day spectacles do not differ much in baseness from those early affairs of the pagan nations. Is it permissible for our priests to frequent theatrical spectacles of this kind? Not at all. Therefore this should be forbidden in graver terms, and prohibited not only for this cause, namely, lest the eyes and ears of these (priests) be scandalized. . . but because the priests give great scandal to the faithful by frequenting such productions. They are stumbling blocks, rocks of scandal to the faithful.[64]

There can be no quarrel with the evident truth that clerics are never free to attend immoral productions. To say that all productions are immoral, however, and thus to level an indiscriminate ban on all theatergoing is to cast unmerited disrepute upon the whole theater, which is potentially (and in some cases actually) a medium for good. The presence of clerics at worth-while theatrical productions causes no adverse criticism in this country. The priest who knows that he is not free to attend just any show or play will choose those which are unquestionably of a high caliber.

2. Musical Comedies and Stage Shows:

Musical comedies or revues are very much a part of the menu of the American theater. There are many which are well-written, possessed of decent dialogue and catchy music. There are others which are to be shunned by all, cleric and lay alike. That priest displays a strictly worldly mentality if he reasons that if a show is not immoral he is free to

---

[64] Mansi, L, 532 (the writer's translation).

attend. The law is also opposed to those shows which are in any way unbecoming. The unbecoming nature would not of necessity mean that it was an immoral nature. Any show which depends for its popularity on innuendo, off-color jokes, suggestive lyrics, or immoral costuming is absolutely forbidden to clerics. A priest should make diligent inquiry as to the precise nature of the show before he goes to any musical comedy. If it has any of the elements mentioned above he cannot attend.

In our larger cities there is usually at least one show house which offers a stage show or vaudeville performance together with its cinema attraction. Some of these shows feature second-rate talent with third-rate routines, many of the songs and jokes being openly suggestive. A priest must know what entertainment is offered before he can attend a show. The mere desire to see a certain worth-while movie is not cause sufficient to justify his taking other "poor" entertainment along with it. Very definitely such entertainment is forbidden to clerics and priests. The priest is to be a man of culture. He exhibits that culture in his prudent choice of uplifting entertainment. He always chooses the best of the best. No priest should patronize any musical comedy or stage show which he knows to possess any objectionable element. It need not be sinful to be objectionable. People find it hard to resolve the contradiction between the approval which his presence bespeaks and his clerical garb which represents a set of values which cannot countenance such entertainment.

3. Operas and Concerts:

Prior to the Code, operas were held to be included under the term *spectacula*. Clerics were forbidden to attend.[65] In this country clerics attend operas just as they attend other musical events of a cultural nature, such as concerts by symphonic and choral groups, and recitals by individual artists, vocal and instrumental. Some few operas are

[65] Kinane, "Notes and Queries"—*IER*, V. Series, XXIV (1910), 297.

based upon objectionable themes. One may reasonably presume that a priest who is familiar with opera will have sufficient knowledge upon which he may draw when he must seek to determine those which he may attend and those which he must forego. Attendance at all operas has been interdicted for clerics in some of our dioceses.[66]

Let the cleric attend only the best. There is sufficient variety to make this possible. One well-known drama critic has written: "What a man hears in the theater is seldom as important as what he sees." For the priest there is the obligation to see *and* hear what is important, in the sense that all will benefit him and will not bring any discredit either to himself or to his fellow clerics.

F. Attendance of Clerics at Moving Pictures

The motion picture, the movies, the cinema, or the pictures — all names for the same entity — have become an integral and influential factor of modern life. Nowhere is that truer than in the United States. Among the four million who daily enter American motion-picture palaces there are to be numbered many clerics and priests. In itself the motion picture is either a great instrument for good or a powerful weapon for evil. Pope Pius XI (1922-1939) wrote in his Encyclical Letter on motion pictures:

> Good motion pictures are capable of exercising a profoundly moral influence upon those who see them. In addition to affording recreation, they are able to arouse noble ideals of life, to communicate valuable conceptions, to impart better knowledge of the history and beauties of the fatherland and other countries, to present truth and virtue under attractive forms, to create at least the flavor of understanding among nations...to champion the cause of justice...to contribute positively to the genesis of a just social order in the world.[67]

---

[66] *Statuta Diœceseos Pittsburghensis in Synodo Decima Quarta Lata*, n. 8, 2°; *Statuta Diœcesana in Synodo Prima Cheyennensi Lata*, n. 13. *Acta Synodi Roffensis Tertiæ*, n. 136. Also the *Third Diocesan Synod of Chicago* (n. 61) as quoted by Bouscaren-Ellis, *Canon Law*, p. 117.

[67] Litt. encycl. *Vigilanti cura*, 15 iul. 1936 — *AAS*, XXVIII (1936), 256; N.C.W.C. translation, p. 9.

And again:

Everyone knows what damage is done to the soul by bad motion pictures. They are occasions of sin; they seduce young people along the ways of life by glorifying the passions; they show life under a false light; they cloud the ideals, they destroy pure love, respect for marriage and affection for the family.[68]

This is the attitude of the Church toward motion pictures. It is easy to understand that the laws of the Church do not forbid motion pictures in themselves, but forbid clerics and priests to attend such motion pictures as are objectionable or unbecoming.

It has always been held as unbecoming for a cleric or a priest to attend motion pictures in the city of Rome. In 1918 a decree of the Vicariate of Rome, at the personal order of Pope Benedict XV (1914-1922), renewed an earlier ruling which had been given in July, 1909. By these rulings clerics were forbidden to attend the "cinema," even if the picture shown was of a religious nature.[69] Rectors of churches were ordered to publish the decree so that it would become known not only to the local clergy (secular and religious), but also to clerical *peregrini* who were also bound by it. The penalty was *suspensio a divinis ferendæ sententiæ.*

Michiels has argued from this decree that all laws forbidding clerics to attend motion pictures are laws which safeguard the public order.[70] Such a general conclusion would be valid if all of these laws *expressly* stated, as does this law, that travelers also are bound to its observance. However, if no mention is made of this in the law, and if it is not clear from other sources that it is a law which looks to the public order, the cleric may retain his liberty and attend a motion picture.

---

[68] Litt. encycl. *Vigilanti cura* — *AAS*, XXVIII (1936), 255; N.C.W.C. translation, p. 9.

[69] Vicariatus Urbis, *decr.*, 25 maii, 1918 — *AAS*, X (1918), 300; Bouscaren, *Digest*, I, 54.

[70] *Normæ Generales*, I, 321.

By the authority of Pope Pius XI (1922-1939), the Vicariate of Rome issued a similar decree in 1938.[71] This decree forbids clerics, seminarians, and students of ecclesiastical houses to attend, in the city of Rome, all public theaters, public spectacles, and motion pictures. If a group of young boys or men, from a school conducted by ecclesiastics, wish to attend any one of these events, they are to be accompanied, not by the ecclesiastics, but by responsible laymen. The same, *mutatis mutandis,* holds for women religious who conduct schools for girls.

A study of the particular statutes in other countries reveals that the prohibition is directed against the going of clerics to *public* theaters. In Belgium, for instance, clerics and priests, who have a domicile or a quasi-domicile there, are forbidden to attend motion pictures in public places, unless the motion picture is shown under Catholic auspices.[72] In Brazil, clerics may attend motion pictures only *"in aliqua pia vel religiosa domo."* Rarely, and then only with previously obtained permission of the local ordinary, may they attend a motion picture in a public place.[73]

With rare exceptions, the more or less general interpretation in our country (by individual bishops) has been to exempt motion pictures from the prohibition against attendance at public spectacles.[74]

---

[71] Sartori, *Enchiridion Canonicum* (7. ed., [1917-1944], Romæ: Ex Typographia Augustiana, 1944), p. 40.

[72] *Acta et Decreta Concilii Provincialis Mechliniensis,* n. 136.

[73] In the Statutes for Brazil (n. 27, § 3) as quoted by Duvieux, "Perigos do Cinema"—*Revista Ecclesiastica Brasiliera* (Petropolis, 1941-), I (1941), 239.

[74] Motion pictures are forbidden by the *Statutes of the Diocese of Crookston,* n. 17. Other synods forbid priests to attend motion pictures on Sunday (in public theaters): *Synodus Diœcesana Kansanopolitana Quarta* (Kansanurbe, 1928), *de vita clericorum,* n. 4; *Synodus Diœcesis Omahensis Quarta,* n. 19 (b). These statutes are to be obeyed even though they may seem more severe than the general law. The Holy See has given local ordinaries authority to judge what is and what is not proper in the conduct of the clergy of their jurisdiction.

The laity should see no evil in a priest's attending an occasional good motion picture. His movie-going should await the suitable occasion, and not become a habitual addition.[75] In making his choice of a picture the priest will always be guided by the ratings of the Legion of Decency.[76] The pictures which he views will be those on the A list. He will never attend a movie which has been classified as a Class C picture. It is hard to understand how a priest could ever attend a B picture without giving grave scandal, even though he himself may not suffer the least spiritual harm, at least when the objectionable element in the picture is of a sexual nature. From his presence many Catholics would conclude: "If it is all right for a priest to see this picture, it is certainly all right for me to do the same."[77]

Exempt religious are not subject to the disciplinary regulations of the local ordinary. To bring about the necessary uniformity of clerical conduct in the diocese it seems that the local ordinary and the major superior of the exempt religious should come to an agreement in the matter. If the secular clergy are forbidden to attend motion pictures, that same prohibition should extend to religious also. The general law on clerical obligations looks to both groups; particular law would do well to do the same, unless there be special reason to restrict the application of the law.

---

[75] Father Boylan, O.Cist.R., notes that an inordinate attachment to motion pictures can be an obstacle to a proper spiritual life. Constant exposure to the paganism of the cinema is not without its dangers. Equally dangerous is the inducement of passivity of mind and will, which arises from the fact that one's personal power of amusing oneself soon begins to atrophy. — "The Priest and Recreation" — *The Priest* (Huntington, 1944-), III (1947), No. 6, 434.

[76] This organization, to protect the morals of Catholics at the cinema, was formally instituted in April of 1934. The present Episcopal Committee of five is headed by Archbishop Keough of the Archdiocese of Baltimore.

[77] Connell, "How Should Priests Direct People Regarding the Movies?" — *American Ecclesiastical Review*, CXIV (1946), 248.

Article 2. The Attendance of Clerics at Dances

Those dances which violate the canons of morality and Christian decency need no special condemnation. No authentic declaration is required to keep clerics from such dances. That is a matter of divine and not merely of human law. Canon 140 treats of the presence of clerics at dances which are unbecoming. This does not imply necessarily that they need be or are immoral. This expression of the law as it now stands represents somewhat of a departure from the early absolute and only later qualified disapproval of dances, dancing, and those who engaged in it. It was not until the late Middle Ages that canonists and theologians were able to demonstrate that dancing was not immoral — that in and of itself it was licit, although it was not without its dangers.[78]

It is not to the purpose of these pages to enter into a treatment of the morality of dancing. The presumption accepted for this article is that dances and dancing *per se* are morally unobjectionable. It is best for the priest to assume, unless the opposite is manifest, that modern dancing, though on occasion a source of sin, is not to be regarded universally in itself as anything but legitimate recreation.[79]

A. The III Plenary Council of Baltimore

Under the chapter which treated of "forbidden methods of collecting funds for pious causes," the III Plenary Council urged priests to remove the abuse of sponsoring dances (Balls) in connection with banquets for the purpose of raising money.[80] From the wording of the law it is not clear whether the Council meant to forbid each and every

[78] St. Alphonsus called dancing an "actus lætitiæ secundum se, nisi malo fine fiat." — *Theologiæ Moralis*, lib. III, n. 429.

[79] "Questions and Answers" — *Clergy Review*, XVIII (1940), 350; Devane, "The Dance Hall" — *IER*, V. Series, XXXVII (1931), 172.

[80] "Mandamus quoque ut sacerdotes illum abusum, quo convivia parantur cum choreis (Balls) ad opera pia promovenda, omnino tollendum curent" — *Conc. Plen. III Acta et Decreta*, n. 290.

kind of dancing arranged by or for the parish. If the law be interpreted strictly, then the only types which it expressly forbids are those dances which are held in conjunction with dinners for the purpose of raising money. This original prohibition and its extent must be kept in mind as necessary for the interpretation of subsequent decrees from Rome on this point. This view is not without merit, for in many dioceses in this country there exists the practice of having dances, especially for the young teen-age boys and girls. These dances have become a recognized and useful part of the youth program. Their single aim is to give the young people a chance to have their recreation under proper supervision, where they may "meet their own," and that under the best circumstances possible. They are not intended as a means of realizing revenue. When admission is charged, it is only a nominal sum which is meant to help defray the expenses incurred in engaging an orchestra or in purchasing records. It cannot be argued from the Code that clerics are forbidden to attend these dances. There is nothing unbecoming about them, and certainly the young people are not scandalized when they have their priests present at their recreation.

B. Decrees of the Sacred Consistorial Congregation

There is some difficulty at hand when one attempts to reconcile present day practice with two decrees[81] which were issued for the United States and Canada by the Sacred Consistorial Congregation. These decrees, even though they antedate the Code, must be said to remain in force. They are particular law not contrary to the Code. The first of these decrees[82] interpreted and further enforced the decree (n. 290) of the Council of Baltimore. This prohibition had been ignored by many, and the practice of having these

---

[81] In assigning a cause for these decrees Coronata seems to hold the extreme view that dancing is immoral: "nec quod inhonestum est fieri ex bono fine planum est." — *Institutiones*, I, 233.

[82] S. C. Consist., *decr.*, 31 mart. 1916 — *Fontes*, n. 2092.

dances for the raising of funds had spread — even into Canada. In view of this, the Sacred Congregation ordered that all priests (secular and religious) were not to promote and encourage these dances no matter what their purpose.[83]

In employing the words *memoratas choreas,* the Sacred Congregation referred to specific dances, namely those dances which were held together with banquets. These are a far cry from the dances of the youth groups of our time. This decree seemed not to have clarified matters completely, for in the following year another decree was issued; this in response to a doubt submitted by one of the American bishops.[84]

The question was raised regarding the extent of the prohibition of the previous decree. The reply noted that the prohibition included all dances, even if held in the day or during the early hours of the night, and even if not protracted to a late hour, or if not accompanied with a dinner, and even if conducted after the manner of a picnic. All clerics are forbidden to sponsor or attend these dances. Bouscaren-Ellis, while holding these prohibitions still to be in effect, follow Vermeersch (1858-1936) in the suggestion that they be observed and enforced with prudence.[85]

This second decree apparently shut the door upon any attempt to have church-sponsored dances. The present contrary practice, however, may be explained on several scores. As Barrett notes,[86] the Sacred Congregation consulted with several bishops of this country before it made its decision. From the fact that the Holy See has previously been misinformed seriously about other conditions in this country, one may doubt whether the desired and necessary information was accurately presented to Rome. For example, the

---

[83] "... (Cardinales) decreverunt sacerdotes prohiberi quominus *memoratas choreas promoveant et foveant.*" (Italics inserted) — *Fontes,* n. 2092.

[84] S. C. Consist., *declar.,* 10 dec. 1917 — *AAS,* X (1917), 17; Bouscaren, *Digest,* I, 137.

[85] *Canon Law,* p. 118.

[86] *A Comparative Study,* p. 210.

Sacred Congregation speaks of the parish dances as being protracted *"ad multas noctis horas."* This is the result plainly of misinformation, for while it may have been true in some few cases, it was far from being the rule.[87]

It is reasonable to presume that, had Rome known the true conditions that prevailed, it would have legislated to correct the abuses with regard to these dances, and would not have banned the holding of dances themselves. Then again, when the law forbids priests to foster and promote these dances, it must mean an active promotion, for it does not forbid them to tolerate such dances. There seems to be no objection to these parish dances if the matter is entirely in the hands of the laity. Rome may have condemned dancing as sponsored or attended by priests, but it has not told them that they cannot bring wholesome social gatherings to their parish life. If these groups choose to hold dances, there should be no objection, although the priest should not assist actively. The presence of the priest who drops in to greet his people briefly seems not to do violence to the ruling of these decrees, nor to render impossible of attainment the goal at which they aim.

In some dioceses the local ordinary has established certain regulations with reference to the holding of dances. In some instances, it will fall to the lot of the clergy to see to it that these regulations are carried out; for example, when the dances are held on church property. While local ordinaries are not immune to all possibility of erroneous conscience, it seems to be a working presumption that no bishop would legislate favorably on a matter which he felt to be forbidden.[88]

---

[87] Woywod, "Answers to Questions" — *HPR*, XXXII (1932), 1080.

[88] "Catholic societies and clubs should take the lead in eliminating the practice of beginning dances late in the evening and continuing them until the early morning hours. All dances should conclude at midnight. Dances held under Catholic auspices are never to be scheduled on Saturday night or on the vigils of feast days." — *Statuta Archidiœceseos Indianapolitana* (I) *in Synodo Archidiœceseos Septima Lata* (Indianapolis: Standard Printing, 1947), n. 53.

Perhaps in the near future the bishops of this country will bring to Rome a complete and accurate presentation of the facts as they exist in this country. Doubtless, a more favorable ruling would be given. Conditions in this country are in many respects unique, finding no counterpart elsewhere, particularly not in Europe. The reluctance of our own canonists and commentators to discuss the point at any great length shows the need of greater clarification — and that preferably from Rome, the seat of authority.

Article 3. The Attendance of Clerics at Solemn Gatherings

The word *pompa,* from the Greek πομπή, means primarily a procession. It was applied to any solemn or public procession, such as those which were connected with weddings, funerals, military triumphs, public festivals, games, etc.[89] As it is used in canon 140 and in Church legislation of earlier times, it applies also to gatherings of a public or semi-public nature. Thus it embraces all those events which come under the term *spectacula.* There are some authors who give less prominence to the idea of publicity, and say that the word refers to parties (wedding parties), picnics, excursions, and even bazaars.[90] It seems that civic ceremonies of dedication and civil patriotic gatherings and celebrations are included under this word.[91]

Those principles which were valid in relation to the question of clerics and their attendance at sporting events and theatrical entertainments apply also to their attendance at *pompæ* and those gatherings which are not strictly private. The presumption is that these gatherings are not immoral, but that, under certain circumstances, they may

---

[89] It is in the sense of games that it was first used in the Council of Mainz (813), canon 10 — *MGH, Leges in 4°*, Sectio III, *Concilia Aevi Karolini,* Tom. II, pars I, 263.

[90] Ramstein, *A Manual of Canon Law,* p. 181; Ayrinhac, *General Legislation,* p. 307.

[91] Vermeersch-Creusen, *Epitome,* I, n. 255, 5.

become undignified or indecorous for clerics. The views of prudent men of the locality will have to be known and kept in mind. Suppose, for example, the case of a priest invited to a wedding breakfast. In most dioceses the priest is free to attend or to refuse, as he sees fit. Elsewhere it is the custom not to attend these affairs, because it is held unbecoming for a priest to be present at them.

Due consideration must also be accorded to the *purpose* of the gathering and the *type* of persons who are in attendance. This last point is not meant to indicate that priests will be friendly to some and will shun others. Christian charity militates against such conduct. However, people would be surprised and perhaps even scandalized to see their priests in public with people who are known publicly to be lacking in many of the Christian virtues. The purpose of the gathering is also an item of importance. Thus a priest is most certainly allowed to attend public functions which profess a charitable purpose, unless, of course, there is a prohibition established by diocesan legislation. Less clear is the matter of his lawful attendance at political rallies and gatherings, such as the national political conventions of the major parties. A priest may well accept an invitation to deliver the invocation or benediction at one of these conventions. He should never appear in a rôle which could lead people to think that he was actively engaged in politics.[92]

There are many occasions when a priest is called upon to attend one of the many events that qualify as *pompæ*. Before making a hasty decision, he should first weigh well the elements of public opinion, the purpose of the gathering, and the type of persons who will be present. If all of these are favorable, he may attend. In this matter, as in all matters which look to his recreation, the priest must take all necessary means to insure that his liberty will never be a stumbling block to the weak.

---

[92] This would bind with reservations in certain portions of Europe where priests are allowed to hold public office.

CONCLUSIONS

As a result of this study the following conclusions are offered:

1. The clergy as a community *(cœtus)* in the sense of a plurality of persons united by a common bond can introduce a custom against the general or particular law of the Church.

2. The law on clerical obligations was substantially formed by the time of the Council of Trent (1545-1563).

3. The major collections of law and the commentaries on the Decretals exercised the greatest influence on the clerical obligations as stated by the Council of Trent.

4. The earliest evidence of papal legislation on any of these obligations is the letter *"De Aleatoribus"* of Pope Saint Victor I (189-199) on gambling.

5. What constitutes an unbecoming trade or profession is largely determined by the conditions of the times and the general attitude of the public.

6. The non-exhaustive or merely illustrative listing of forbidden trades and professions in canon 138 is designed to furnish full freedom to diocesan legislation, which can meet particular exigencies.

7. Even to obtain the necessities of life a cleric cannot take up an unbecoming profession or trade.

8. The reason why priests and religious are forbidden to handle the technical arrangements of pilgrimages is equally applicable to arrangements regarding vacation or study travel-groups.

9. A cleric may sell for profit something which he has produced or composed in the fine arts in the pursuit of a hobby.

10. The *professional* practice of medicine as forbidden to clerics by the III Plenary Council of Baltimore (n. 82) and by the Code of Canon Law (c. 139, § 2) does not extend to the *study* of medicine.

11. A priest may practice psychiatry in connection with some diocesan agency, e.g., social service. He is not free to practice it as a profession for profit.

12. It was not until the fifteenth-sixteenth centuries that money was explicitly mentioned in conciliar legislation as an element in gambling.

13. The phrase *"ludus aleatorius"* refers only to games whose outcome depends entirely on chance. Any game with an element of skill is not forbidden by common law.

14. The phrase *"pecunia exposita"* is verified whether money is actually visible or not during the time of play. Equivalent to *pecunia* is anything which has a money value.

15. Any danger of scandal would warrant a prohibition to engage in card games otherwise permitted, or to bet on races or athletic events.

16. The first prohibition against clerics' attending of horse races dates from the seventh century. The law of the III Plenary Council of Baltimore (n. 79) which forbade American clerics to attend public horse races is still in effect.

17. Hunting is not scandalous in this country, nor is it clamorous. It is therefore allowed to priests and clerics.

18. A tavern is an establishment whose exclusive or principal service is the selling of wine, beer, and other alcoholic beverages. Only such places are forbidden to clerics.

19. It is forbidden to priests to drink in a bar or cocktail lounge of a private club or hotel.

20. The better opinion is that it is unbecoming for a priest to attend professional prize fights.

BIBLIOGRAPHY

SOURCES

Acta Apostolicæ Sedis, Commentarium Officiale, Romæ, 1909-1929; Civitate Vaticana, 1929- .

Beveregius, G. (Beveridge, William), *Codex Canonum Ecclesiæ Primitivæ Vindicatus ac Illustratus,* Londini, 1678.

Bizzarri, A., *Collectanea in usum Secretariæ S. C. Episcoporum et Regularium,* Romæ, 1885.

Bouscaren, T. Lincoln, *The Canon Law Digest,* 2 vols., Milwaukee: Bruce, 1934, 1943.

Bruns, Hermann T., *Canones Apostolorum et Conciliorum Sæculorum IV-VII,* 2 vols., Berolini, 1839.

Bullarum Diplomatum et Privilegiorum Sacrorum Romanorum Pontificum Taurinensis Editio, 24 vols. et Index, Augustæ Taurinorum, 1857-1872.

Codex Iuris Canonici Pii X Pontificis Maximi iussu digestus Benedicti Papæ XV auctoritate promulgatus, Romæ: Typis Polyglottis Vaticanis, 1917.

Codicis Iuris Canonici Fontes cura Emi Petri Card. Gasparri editi, 9 vols., Romæ (later Civitate Vaticana): Typis Polyglottis Vaticanis, 1923-1939. (Vols. VII-IX, ed. cura et studio Emi Iustiniani Serédi).

Corpus Iuris Canonici, Editio Lipsiensis II (Richter-Friedberg), 2 vols., Lipsiæ, 1879-1881.

Corpus Iuris Civilis, 3 vols., Berolini: Apud Weidmannos, 1928-1929; Vol. I, *Institutiones,* recognovit P. Krueger, 15. ed., 1929; *Digesta,* recognovit T. Mommsen, retractavit P. Krueger, 15. ed., 1929; Vol. II, *Codex Iustinianus,* recognovit et retractavit P. Krueger, 10. ed., 1929; Vol. III, *Novellæ,* recognovit R. Schoell et absolvit G. Kroll, 5. ed., 1928.

Decretales D. Gregorii Papæ IX, una cum Glossis Restitutæ, Romæ, 1582.

Decretum Gratiani Emendatum et Notationibus Illustratum una cum Glossis, Gregorii XIII, Pont. Max. iussu editum, 2 vols., Romæ, 1582.

District of Columbia, The Code of the, Washington, D. C.: Government Printing Office, 1930.

District of Columbia, The Code of the (1940 Edition), Washington, D. C.: Government Printing Office, 1940.

Fulton, John, *Index Canonum,* 4. ed., New York, 1883.

Hardouin, Jean, *Acta Conciliorum et Epistolæ Decretales ac Constitutiones Summorum Pontificum*, 12 vols., Parisiis, 1714-1715.

Enchiridion Clericorum, Romæ: Typis Polyglottis Vaticanis, 1938.

Haddan, A. – Stubbs, W., *Councils and Ecclesiastical Documents relating to Great Britain and Ireland*, 3 vols., Oxford, 1869-1873.

Ius Græco-Romanum, Vol. I, *Novellæ et Aureæ Bullæ Imperatorum post Iustinianum*, ed. K. E. Zachariæ von Lingenthal, nova editio, Athenis, 1930.

Jaffé, Philippus, *Regesta Pontificum Romanorum ab condita Ecclesia ad annum post Christum natum MCXCVIII* (2. ed. [Kaltenbrunner, Ewald, Loewenfeld]), 2 vols. in 1, Lipsiæ, 1885-1888.

Mansi, J. D., *Sacrorum Conciliorum Nova et Amplissima Collectio*, 53 vols. in 60, Parisiis, 1901-1927.

Monumenta Germaniæ Historica, 188 vols., incomplete, Hannoveræ, 1826- ; *Leges in 4°*, Sectio III (*Concilia)*, T. I, ed. F. Maassen, 1893; T. II, pars I et II, ed. A. Werminghoff, 1906-1908.

Pallottini, S., *Collectio Omnium Conclusionum et Resolutionum quæ apud Sacram Congregationem Cardinalium S. Conc. Trid. Interpretum Prodierunt ab eius Institutione anno MDLXIV ad annum MDCCCLX*, 18 vols., Romæ, 1868-1893.

Potthast, A., *Regesta Pontificum Romanorum inde ab anno post Christum natum MCXCVIII ad annum MCCCIV*, 2 vols. in 1, Berolini, 1874-1875.

Schroeder, H. J., *Disciplinary Decrees of the General Councils, Text, Translation and Commentary*, St. Louis: Herder, 1937.

Wilkins, David, *Concilia Magnæ Britanniæ et Hiberniæ a Synodo Verolamiensi* (A. D. CDXLVI) *ad Londinensem* (A. D. MDCCXVII), 4 vols., Londini, 1737.

Councils and Synods

Acta et Decreta Concilii Plenarii Americæ Latinæ, Romæ: Typis Vaticanis, 1900.

Acta et Decreta Concilii Plenarii Baltimorensis III, Baltimoræ: John Murphy, 1886.

Acta et Decreta Concilii Plenarii Hiberniæ apud Maynutiam anno 1927, Dublin: Typis Browne et Nolan, 1929.

Acta et Decreta Concilii Provincialis Mechliniensis Quarti anno MCMXX Mechliniæ Habiti, Mechliniæ: H. Dessain, 1923.

Acta et Decreta Synodi Diœcesanæ Quebecensis Secundæ anno 1940 Quebeci Celebratæ, Quebeci: Apud Cancellariam, 1940.

Acta et Decreta Synodi Diœcesanæ Toletanæ Primæ, Toleti: Apud Cancellariam Curiæ, 1941.

Acta Synodi Roffensis Tertiæ, Rochester: Typis J. P. Smith, 1914.

Canones et Decreta Sacrosancti Oecumenici Concilii Tridentini, ed., novissima, Romæ: Ex Typographia Polyglotta, 1882.

Concilia Provincialia Baltimori Habita ab anno 1829 usque ad annum 1849, 2. ed., Baltimori, 1851.

Concilii Plenarii Baltimorensis II Acta et Decreta, Baltimoræ: Joannes Murphy, 1868.

Constitutiones Diœceseos Novæ-Aureliæ in Synodo Diœcesana Sexta Lata, New Orleans: Sam Taylor Press, 1922.

Statuta Archidiœceseos Indianapolitanæ in Synodo Archidiœceseos (I) *Septima Lata*, Indianapolis: Standard Printing Co., 1947.

Statuta Archidiœceseos Sancti Francisci in Synodo Diœcesana Secunda Lata, San Francisco: The Monitor Publishing Co., 1936.

Statuta Diœcesana in Synodo Prima Cheyenniensi Lata, Omaha: Swartz Printing Co., 1913.

Statuta Diœceseos Pittsburgensis in Synodo Decima Quarta Lata, Pittsburgh: St. Joseph's Protectory Press, 1920.

Statuta Diœceseos Seattlensis in Synodo Quinta Lata, Seattle: Metropolitan Press Printing Co., 1938.

Statuta Diœceseos Trentonensis, Trentonii, 1897.

Statutes of the Diocese of Crookston, St. Louis: Herder, 1923.

Synodi Diœcesanæ Grandormensis Primæ Statuta, Grandormensi Civitate, 1903.

Synodus Diocesana Fargensis Prima, Milwaukiæ: Bruce, 1941.

Synodus Diœcesana Kansanopolitana Quarta, Kansanurbe, 1928.

Synodus Diœcesana Omahensis Quarta, Omaha: Typis Burkley Printing, 1934.

Synodus Diœcesana Sancti Ludovici Septima, Sancti Ludovici, 1929.

AUTHORS

Aertyns, Jos. - Damen, C. A., *Theologia Moralis Secundum Doctrinam S. Alphonsi*, 14. ed., 2 vols., Taurini: Marietti, 1944.

Aichner, S., *Compendium Juris Ecclesiastici*, 6. ed., Brixinæ, 1887.

Alphonsus Maria de Ligorio, S., *Theologia Moralis*, ed. novissima, 4 vols., Romæ, 1905-1912.

A New English Dictionary, 10 vols., edited by J. Murray, H. Bradley and Associates, Oxford: at the Clarendon Press, 1888-1928.

Aquinas, S. Thomas, *Summa Theologica*, 6 vols., Taurini: Marietti, 1937.

Augustine, Charles, *A Commentary on the New Code of Canon Law*, 2. ed., 8 vols., St. Louis: Herder, 1918-1924. Vol. I, 1918; Vol. II, 1919.

Ayrinhac, H. A., *General Legislation in the New Code of Canon Law*, New York: Benziger, 1923.

Ballerini, A. – Palmieri, D., *Opus Theologicum Morale*, 7 vols., Prati, 1889-1893.

Barrett, John Daniel, *A Comparative Study of the Councils of Baltimore and the Code of Canon Law*, The Catholic University of Amercia, Canon Law Studies, n. 83, Washington, D. C.: The Catholic University of America, 1932.

Bauduin, G., *De Consuetudine in Iure Canonico*, diss. canonica, Lovanii: Universitatis Catholicæ Typographi, 1888.

Benedictus XIV (Prosper Lambertini), *De Synodo Diœcesana*, 2 vols., Romæ, 1806.

Berardi, Carolus, *Gratiani Canones Genuini ab Apocryphis Discreti*, 3 vols. in 4, Venetiis, 1777.

Berutti, C., *Institutiones Iuris Canonici*, 6 vols., Vol. II, Pars I, Taurini-Romæ: Marietti, 1943.

Beste, U., *Introductio in Codicem*, ed. altera, Collegeville, Minn.: St. John's Abbey Press, 1944.

Blat, Albertus, *Commentarium Textus Codicis Iuris Canonici*, 5 vols. in 7, Vol. II, Pars I *(De Personis)*, 2. ed., Romæ: Ex Typographia Pontificis in Instituto Pii X, 1921.

Boich, Henricus, *In Quinque Decretalium Libros Commentaria*, ed. recognita, Venetiis, 1576.

Bonnar, A., *The Catholic Doctor*, 2. ed., New York: P. J. Kennedy, 1941.

Bouscaren, T. – Ellis, A., *Canon Law, A Text and Commentary*, Milwaukee: Bruce, 1946.

Brunini, J. B., *The Clerical Obligations of Canons 139 and 142*, The Catholic University of America Canon Law Studies, n. 103, Washington, D. C.: The Catholic University of America, 1937.

Cance, A., *Le Code de Droit Canonique*, 3 vols., Paris: Libraire Lecoffre, 1927-1929.

Cappello, F. M., *Summa Iuris Canonici in Usum Scholarum*, 3 vols., Vol. I, 3. ed., Romæ: Apud Aedes Universitatis Gregorianæ, 1938.

———, *Tractatus Canonico-Moralis de Sacramentis*, 3 vol. in 6, Vol. II, Pars III, Taurinorum Augustæ: Marietti, 1935.

Chelodi, Ioannes, *Ius Canonicum de Personis*, 3. ed., curavit P. Ciprotti, Trento: Libreria Moderna Editrice, 1942.

Cicognani, Amleto, *Canon Law*, trans. by J. O'Hara and F. Brennan, 2. ed., Philadelphia: The Dolphin Press, 1935.

Claeys-Bouuaert, F., et Simenon, G., *Manuale Juris Canonici*, 3 vols., Gandæ et Leodii: Dessain, Vol. I, 3. ed., 1930; Vol. II, 1931; Vol. III, 3. ed., 1931.

Cocchi, Guidus, *Commentarium in Codicem Iuris Canonici*, 8 vols. in 5, Taurinorum Augustæ: Marietti, Lib. I, 5. ed., 1938; Lib. II, Pars I, Sect. I, 4. ed., 1937.

Coronata, Mattheus Conte a, *Institutiones Iuris Canonici*, 5 vols., Vol. I, 2. ed., Romæ: Marietti, 1939.

———, *Tractatus Canonicus de Sacramentis*, 3 vols., Taurini: Marietti, 1943-1946. Vol. II, 1945.

Crnica, A., *Commentarium Theoretico-Practicum Iuris Canonici*, 2 vols., Sibenik: Typis Typographiæ „Kačić," 1940.

Cumont, Franz, *The Oriental Religions in Roman Paganism*, Chicago: Open Court Publishing Company, 1911.

Davis, Henry, *Moral and Pastoral Theology*, 3. ed., 4 vols., London: Sheed and Ward, 1938.

De Angelis, P., *Prælectiones Iuris Canonici*, 2. ed., 7 vols. in 5, Romæ, 1908.

D'Annibale, J., *Summula Theologiæ Moralis*, 5. ed., 3 vols., Romæ, 1908.

De Larranga, Francisco, *Prontuario di Teologia Moral*, ed. reconocida, Romæ, 1907.

Dictionnaire de Théologie Catholique, 14 vols., Paris: Libraire Letouzey et Ané, 1903-1939.

Donovan, D. A., *Compendium Theologiæ Moralis ad Mentem Ballerini*, 3 vols. in 1, S. Ludovici, 1895-1898.

Dubech, Lucien, Histoiré Genérale illustrée du Theâtre, 5 vols., Paris: Libraire du France, 1931-1934.

Enciclopedia Italiana di Scienze, Lettere ed Arti, 35 vols., Milano: Istituto Giovanni Trecanni, 1929-1937.

Eschbach, A., *Disputationes Physiologico-Theologicæ*, 2. ed., Romæ, 1901.

Fagnanus, Prosper, *Commentaria super Quinque Libros Decretalium*, 5 vols. in 3, Venetiis, 1709-1729.

Falco, M., *Corso di Diritto Ecclesiastico*, Padova: Tipographia del Seminario, 1930.

Fanfani, L., *De Iure Religiosorum ad Normam Codicis Iuris Canonici*, 2. ed., Taurini-Romæ: Marietti, 1925.

Ferraris, Lucius, *Prompta Bibliotheca Canonica, Juridica, Moralis, Theologica, necnon Ascetica, Polemica, Rubricistica, Historica*, 8 vols., Romæ, 1885-1892. Vol. IX, ed. Ian. Bucceroni, Romæ, 1899.

Ferreres, J. B., *Compendium Theologiæ Moralis*, 14. ed., 2 vols., Barcinone: Eugenius Subirana, 1928.

Forcellini-Corradini-Perin, *Lexicon Totius Latinitatis*, 4 tomes in 15, Padua, 1864-1887.

Fournier, J. – Le Bras, G., *Histoire de Collections Canoniques en Occident depuis les Fausses Décrétals jusqu 'au Décret de Gratien*, 2 vols., Paris: Recueil Sirey, 1931-1932.

Funk, F. X., *Didascalia et Constitutiones Apostolorum*, 2 vols., Paderbonæ, 1905.

Gasparri, Petrus Card., *Tractatus de Sacra Ordinatione*, 2 vols., Parisiis, 1893.

Genicot, E. – Salsmans, I., *Institutiones Theologiæ Moralis*, 10. ed., 2 vols., Bruxellis: Alb. Dewit, 1922.

Gonzalez-Tellez, Emmanuel, *Commentaria Perpetua in Singulos Textus Quinque Librorum Decretalium Greg. IX*, 5 vols. in 4, Venetiis, 1699.

Grannieto (Grana-Nieto), Antonius, *Catena Iurium sive in Decretalium Gregorii IX Librum II et III Commentarium*, ed. nova, Lugduni, 1678.

Grisar, Hartmann, *Geschichte Roms und der Päpste in Mittelalter*, Pars I, Freiburgi, 1901.

Guilday, Peter, *A History of the Councils of Baltimore* (1791-1884), New York: The Macmillan Co., 1932.

Guilfoyle, M., *Custom*, The Catholic University of America Canon Law Studies, n. 105, Washington, D. C.: The Catholic University of America, 1937.

Hammill, John Leo, *The Obligations of the Traveler According to Canon 14*, The Catholic University of America Canon Law Studies, n. 160, Washington, D. C.: The Catholic University of America Press, 1942.

Haring, J., *Grundzüge des katholischen Kirchenrechtes*, 3. ed., 2 vols., Graz: Verlag von Ulrich Moser's Buchhandlung, 1924.

Harper's, *A New Latin Dictionary*, edited by E. Andrews, revised, enlarged by C. Lewis and C. Short, New York, 1907.

Hefele, Karl – Le Clercq, Henri, *Histoire des Conciles*, 10 vols. in 19, Paris: Letouzey et Ané, 1907-1938.

Hostiensis, Cardinalis (Henricus de Segusio), *Commentaria in Quinque Decretalium Libros*, 5 vols. in 3, Venetiis, 1581.

Koch, Anthony – Preuss, Arthur, *A Handbook of Moral Theology*, 3. ed., 5 vols., St. Louis: Herder, 1925-1933. Vol. V, 1927.

Lehmkuhl, A., *Theologia Moralis*, 5. ed., 2 vols., Friburgi Brisgoviæ, 1888.

Levinson, Horace, *Your Chance to Win,* New York: Farrar and Rinehart, 1939.

Liddell, H. - Scott, R., *A Greek-English Lexicon,* new ed., revised and augmented by Jones, 2 vols., Oxford: at the Clarendon Press, 1940.

Lombardi, C., *Iuris Canonici Privati Institutiones,* 2. ed., 3 vols., Romæ, 1901.

Mann, Horace K., *The Lives of the Popes in the Early Middle Ages,* 18 vols., London: Herder, 1902-1932.

Marc, Clemens, *Institutiones Morales,* 6. ed., 2 vols., Romæ, 1891.

Maroto, Philippus, *Institutiones Iuris Canonici ad Normam Novi Codicis,* 2 vols., Vol. I, 3. ed., 1921.

McGrath, James, *The Privilege of the Forum,* The Catholic University of America Canon Law Studies, n. 242, Washington, D. C.: The Catholic University of America Press, 1946.

Mercante, F., *Compendio di Diritto Canonico con Illustrazioni Istorico-Dogmatiche,* 2. ed., 3 vols., Prato, 1832.

Merkelbach, Benedict H., *Summa Theologiæ Moralis ad Mentem D. Thomæ,* 3. ed., 3 vols., Parisiis: Typis Declée de Brouwer et Soc., 1938-1939.

Michiels, G., *Normæ Generales Iuris Canonici,* 2 vols., Lublin: Universitas Catholica, 1929.

Migne, J. P., *Patrologiæ Cursus Completus, Series Latina,* 221 vols., Parisiis, 1844-1864.

Moroni, G., *Dizionario di Erudizione Storico-Ecclesiastico,* 103 vols. in 52, Venezia, 1840-1861.

Mothon, Joseph, *Institutions Canoniques,* 3 vols., Vol. I, *Des Personnes,* Paris: Societé Saint Augustin, Desclée, de Brouwer, 1922.

Nicoll, Allardyce, *Masks, Mimes and Miracles: Studies in the Popular Theater,* New York: Harcourt, Brace and Co., 1931.

Noldin, H. - Schmitt, A., *Summa Theologiæ Moralis iuxta Codicem Iuris Canonici,* 22. ed., 3 vols., Oeniponte: Typis et Sumptibus F. Rausch, 1934.

Oesterle, G., *Prælectiones Iuris Canonici,* Vol. I, Romæ: Collegio S. Anselmi, 1931.

O'Hare, J. R., *The Socio-Economic Aspects of Horse-Racing,* The Catholic University of America Studies in Sociology, n. XII, Washington, D. C.: The Catholic University of America Press, 1945.

Ojetti, B., *Commentarium in Codicem Iuris Canonici,* 4 vols., Vol. II, *De Personis,* Romæ: Apud Aedes Universitatis Gregorianæ, 1928.

Panormitanus, Abbas (Nicholaus de Tudeschis), *Commentaria in Quinque Libros Decretalium,* 5 vols. in 7, Venetiis, 1588.

Phillips, George, *Kirchenrecht,* 7 vols., Regensburg, 1845-1872.

Pighi, J. B., *Cursus Theologiæ Moralis*, 4. ed., 3 vols., Veronæ, 1926.

Prümmer, Dominicus, *Manuale Theologiæ Moralis Secundum Principia S. Thomæ Aquinatis*, 10. ed., recognita a P. Dr. Muench, 3 vols., Barcelona: Editorial Herder, 1945-1946. Vol. II, 1945.

Rainer, E. G., *Suspension of Clerics*, The Catholic University of America, Canon Law Studies, n. 111, Washington, D. C.: The Catholic University of America, 1937.

Ramstein, Matthew, *A Manual of Canon Law*, Hoboken: Terminal Publishing Co., 1947.

Raus, J. B., *Institutiones Canonicæ*, 2. ed., Lugduni: Typis Emmanuel Vitte, 1931.

Regatillo, Eduardus, *Institutiones Iuris Canonici*, 2 vols., Santander: Sal Terræ, 1945-1946. Vol. I, 2. ed., 1946.

Reiffenstuel, Anacletus, *Ius Canonicum*, 5 vols. in 7, Parisiis, 1864-1870.

Richard, G., *Analysis Conciliorum Generalium et Particularium*, 5 vols., Augustæ Vindelicorum, 1778-1782.

Richeri, Thomas, *Dictionarium Iuris Civilis, Canonici et Feudalis necnon Delectus Regum Feudalium*, Taurini, 1792.

Ross, John Elliot, *Christian Ethics*, New York: Devin-Adair Co., 1924.

Ryan, Gerald, *Principles of Episcopal Jurisdiction*, The Catholic University of America Canon Law Studies, n. 120, Washington, D. C.: The Catholic University of America Press, 1939.

Sabetti, A. - Barrett, T., *Compendium Theologiæ Moralis*, 19. ed., Neo-Eboraci: F. Pustet, 1920.

Santi, Franciscus, *Prælectiones Iuris Canonici*, 4. ed., 5 vols. in 3, a Martino Leitner, Ratisbonæ, 1903-1905.

Sartori, C., *Enchiridion Canonicum*, 7. ed. (1917-1944), Romæ: Ex Typographia Augustiniana, 1944.

Schaefer (Schäfer), T., *De Religiosis ad Normam Codicis Iuris Canonici*, 3. ed., Romæ: Typis Polyglottis Vaticanis, 1040.

Schmalzgrueber, Franciscus, *Ius Ecclesiasticum Universum*, 5 vol. in 12, Romæ, 1843-1845.

Schulte, J. F. von, *Die Summa des Paucapalea*, Giessen, 1890.

———, *Die Summa des Stephanus Tornacensis*, Giessen, 1891.

Scott, S. P., *The Civil Law*, 17 vols. in 6, Cincinnati: The Central Trust Co., 1932.

Sebastianelli, G., *Prælectiones Iuris Canonici*, Vol. I, *De Personis*, 2. ed., Romæ, 1905.

Singer, Heinrich, *Die Summa Decretorum des Magister Rufinus*, Paderborn, 1902.

Sipos, S., *Enchiridion Iuris Canonici,* 3. ed., Pécs: Ex Typographia „Haladás R. T.," 1936.

Stocchiero, G., *Codice del Clero secondo Il Codex Iuris Canonici,* Vicenza: Società Anonima Tipografica, 1928.

Suarez, Franciscus, *Opera Omnia,* 28 vols., ed. Vivès, Parisiis: 1856-1861. Vols. V-VI, *De Legibus seu Legislatore Deo.*

Tanquerey, Ad., *Synopsis Theologiæ Moralis et Pastoralis,* 3 vols., Vol. II, 10. ed., 1936; Vol. III, 10. ed., 1937, Parisiis: Desclée et Socii.

Thaner, Fredericus, *Die Summa Magistri Rolandi, nachmals Papstes Alexander III,* Innsbruck, 1874.

Thesaurus Linguæ Latinæ, 8 vols., incomplete (to *M* partially), Lipsiæ, 1900- .

Thomassinus, Ludovicus, *Vetus et Nova Ecclesiæ Disciplina circa Beneficia et Beneficiarios,* 10 vols., Magontiaci, 1787.

Toso, A., *Ad Codicem Iuris Canonici...Commentaria Minora,* 5 vols., Romæ: Marietti, 1918-1927. Vol. I, 2. ed., 1921; Vol. II, 1922.

Van Hove, A., *Commentarium Lovaniense in Codicem Iuris Canonici,* Vol. I, Tom. I, *Prolegomena ad Codicem Iuris Canonici,* 2. ed., Mechliniæ-Romæ: H. Dessain, 1945; Vol. I, Tom. II, *De Legibus Ecclesiasticis,* 1930; Vol. I, Tom. III, *De Consuetudine, De Temporis Supputatione,* 1933.

Vecchiotti, S., *Institutiones Canonicæ,* 19. ed., 3 vols., Augustæ Taurinorum, 1886.

Vermeersch, A., *Theologiæ Moralis Principia-Responsa-Concilia,* 3. ed., 4 vols., Roma: Università Gregoriana, 1944-1947.

Vermeersch, A. - Creusen, J., *Epitome Iuris Canonici,* 6. ed., 3 vols., Romæ: H. Dessain, 1937-1946. Vol. I, 1937.

Vito, P., *Quistioni Canoniche,* 4 vols., Napoli: Tipografia Raffæle Picone, 1926-1930.

Von Neumann, John. - Morgenstern, Oskar, *The Theory of Games and Economic Behaviour,* Princeton: Princeton Univ. Press, 1944.

Wernz, F. X., *Ius Decretalium,* 2. ed., 6 vols., Romæ et Prati, 1906-1913.

Wernz, F. X.—Vidal, P., *Ius Canonicum,* 7 vols. in 8, cura A. P. Aguirre, Tom. I, 1938; Tom. II, 3. ed., Romæ: Universitas Gregoriana.

Winslow, M. M., Francis, *A Practical Commentary on the Apostolic Faculties,* New York: Field Afar Press, 1946.

Woywod, S., *A Practical Commentary on the Code of Canon Law,* 9. ed., revised by C. Smith, 2 vols., New York: Jos. F. Wagner, 1945.

Articles

Anonymous, "The Gambling Evil," — *The Homiletic Review,* XXII (1892), 381-383.

———, "Consentienti non fit iniuria," — *Revue Ecclésiastique de Liége,* XXIX (1937), 285-290.

———, "Se un sacerdote puo esercitare l'arte fotographica," — *Il Monitore Ecclesiastico,* XXV (1913-1914), 419-420.

Boylan, M. Eugene, "The Priest and Recreation," — *The Priest,* III (1947), No. 6, 432-436.

Browne, M. J., "Notes and Queries," — *IER,* V. Series, XLIV (1934), 526-527.

Brys, J., "De exercitio medicinæ clericis prohibito," — *Collationes Brugenses,* XXXV (1935), 364-366.

———, "De oblectamentis status clericalis decentiæ repugnantibus," — *Coll. Brug.,* XXXV (1935), 283-287.

Canestri, A., "De lege cum sanctione pœnali lata in peregrinos," — *Apollinaris,* VII (1934), 97-102.

Connell, F., "How Should Priests Direct People Regarding the Movies?" — *AER,* CXIV (1946), 241-253.

Coyle, Matthew A., "The Church and Theatre," — *ER,* XCII (1935), 561-577; XCIII (1935), 12-28; 133-142.

De Robeck, Nesta, "Nativity Plays in Italy," — *Dublin Review,* CXCVI (1935), 85-99.

Duvieux, F., "Perigos do Cinema," — *Revista Ecclesiastica Brasiliera,* I (1941), 236-240.

Goadby, L., "Dancing in Church," — *The Catholic Digest,* III (1939), No. 3, January, 31-33.

Kinane, J., "Clerical Obligations," — *IER,* V. Series, XI (1918), 468-483.

———, " 'Peregrini' and the laws which take care of the public order," — *IER,* V. Series, XLIII (1934), 113-125.

———, "The community capable of introducing a custom," — *IER,* V. Series, XXXVII (1931), 521-524.

———, "The Priest and Golf Competition," — *IER,* V. Series, XXXV (1930), 646.

Kuttner, S., "The Father of the Science of Canon Law," — *The Jurist,* I (1941), 3-19.

Lumbreras, P., "On Episcopal Censures," — *HPR,* XLVIII (1948), 844-847.

Mahoney, E., "The Vatican Council and Priestly Sanctity," — *ER,* LXXXIV (1931), 113-123.

Myers, C., "Theatre Law of the Old Province of Westminster", — *Clergy Review,* III (1932), 89-105.

O'Brien, J., "The Morality of Gambling," — *ER,* CIX (1943), 401-411.

Pereda, J., "La Iglesia y los Toros," — *Razón y Fe,* CXXX (1944), 505-525.

———, "La Moral y los Toros," — *Razón y Fe,* CXXXII (1945), 291-305.

"Queries and Minor Notes," — *The Journal of the American Medical Association,* CXXXVI (1948), No. 13, March, 907.

Roelker, E. G., "The Traveler and Local Statutes," — *The Jurist,* II (1942), 105-119.

Ryder, H., "Harnack on the 'De Aleatoribus,' " — *Dublin Review,* XII (1889), 82-98.

Sheehan, A., "Dancing before the Lord," — *The Catholic Digest,* X (1946), No. 9, July, 22-24.

Van Hove, A., "Leges quæ ordini publico consulunt," — *ETL,* I (1924), 153-167.

Vermeersch, A., "De significatione vocis tabernæ in c. 138," — *Periodica,* XI (1922), 19.

———, "Quæstiones," — *Jus Pontificium,* I (1921), 11.

Wauck, Le Roy A., "On Casting Out a Devil," — *America,* LXXVIII (1947), 181-182.

Woywod, S., "Answers to Questions," — *HPR,* XXXII (1932), 1080.

PERIODICALS

America, New York, 1909-

American Ecclesiastical Review, The, Vols. I-XXXII, Philadelphia, 1895-1905; from 1905: *The Ecclesiastical Review,* Vols. XXXIII-CIX, Philadelphia, 1905-1943; from 1944: *The American Ecclesiastical Review,* Washington, D. C., Vol. CX, 1944-

Apollinaris, Romæ, 1928-

Catholic Digest, The, St. Paul, 1936-

Clergy Review, The, London, 1931-

Collationes Brugenses, Bruges, 1896-

Dublin Review, The, London, 1836-

Ephemerides Theologicæ Lovanienses, Brugis, 1924-

Homiletic and Pastoral Review, The, New York, 1900-

Homiletic Review, The, New York, 1877-

Irish Ecclesiastical Record, The, Dublin, 1864-

Journal of the American Medical Association, The, Chicago, 1883-

Jurist, The, Washington, D. C., 1941-

Jus Pontificium, Romæ, 1921-1940

Monitore Ecclesiastico, Il, Romæ, 1876-

Periodica de Re Canonica et Morali Utili præsertim Religiosis et Missionariis: Periodica de Religiosis et Missionariis, Brugis, 1905-1919; *Periodica de Re Canonica et Morali Utili præsertim Religiosis et Missionariis*, Brugis, 1920-1927; *Periodica de Re Morali, Canonica, Liturgica*, Brugis, 1927-1936, et Romæ, 1937-

Priest, The, Huntington, 1944-

Razón y Fe, Madrid, 1901-

Revista Ecclesiastica Brasiliera, Petropolis, 1941-

Revue Ecclésiastique de Liége, Liége, 1908-

Theological Studies, Woodstock, Md., 1940-

Time, New York, 1923-

Abbreviations

AAS — *Acta Apostolicæ Sedis.*
AER — *American Ecclesiastical Review.*
Bruns — *Canones Apostolorum et Conciliorum sæc. IV-VII*, ed. Bruns.
Coll. Brug. — *Collationes Brugenses.*
ER — *The Ecclesiastical Review.*
ETL — *Ephemerides Theologicæ Lovanienses.*
Fontes — *Codicis Iuris Canonici Fontes cura...Gasparri editi.*
Hardouin — *Acta Conciliorum, etc.*
HPR — *Homiletic and Pastoral Review.*
IER — *The Irish Ecclesiastical Record.*
JE — Jaffé, *Regesta Pontificum Romanorum* (edited by P. Ewald: from 590 to 882).
Mansi — *Sacrorum Conciliorum Nova et Amplissima Collectio.*
MGH — *Monumenta Germaniæ Historica.*
MPL — Migne, *Patrologia Latina.*
Periodica — *Periodica de Re Morali, Canonica, Liturgica.*
Potthast — *Regesta Pontificum Romanorum, etc.*
S. C. C. — Sacra Congregatio Concilii.
S. C. Consist. — Sacra Congregatio Consistorialis.
S. C. de Prop. Fide — Sacra Congregatio de Propaganda Fide.
S. C. Ep. et Reg. — Sacra Congregatio Episcoporum et Regularium.
S. C. S. Off. — Suprema Congregatio Sancti Officii.

INDEX

BIOGRAPHICAL NOTE

JOHN THOMAS DONOVAN was born in Milwaukee, Wisconsin, on August 14, 1918. He received his primary education at Immaculate Conception parochial school, Milwaukee. He completed his high school and early college studies at Saint Francis Seminary, Milwaukee, Wisconsin. In October, 1938, he was appointed to the North American College, Rome, Italy, to make his philosophical and theological studies at the Pontifical Gregorian University from which he received the Baccalaureate in Philosophy in 1940. Returning to this country because of the war, in September of that same year he entered the Theological College of the Catholic University of America, where he received the degree of Licentiate in Sacred Theology in May, 1944. He was ordained to the Holy Priesthood on May 20, 1944, in Milwaukee, and then was assigned as an assistant pastor at Saint Thomas Aquinas Church, Milwaukee. In September of 1945 he was enrolled in the School of Canon Law at the Catholic University of America, where he received the Baccalaureate Degree in Canon Law in May, 1946, and the degree of the Licentiate in Canon Law in May, 1947.

CANON LAW STUDIES[1]

1. FRERIKS, REV. CELESTINE A., C.PP.S., J.C.D., Religious Congregations in Their External Relations, 121 pp., 1916.
2. GALLIHER, REV. DANIEL M., O.P., J.C.D., Canonical Elections, 117 pp., 1917.
3. BORKOWSKI, REV. AURELIUS L., O.F.M., J.C.D., De Confraternitatibus Ecclesiasticis, 136 pp., 1918.
4. CASTILLO, REV. CAYO, J.C.D., Disertacion Historico-Canonica sobre la Potestad del Cabildo en Sede Vacante o Impedida del Vicario Capitular, 99 pp., 1919 (1918).
5. KUBELBECK, REV. WILLIAM J., S.T.B., J.C.D., The Sacred Penitentiaria and Its Relation to Faculties of Ordinaries and Priests, 129 pp., 1918.
6. PETROVITS, REV. JOSEPH J. C., S.T.D., J.C.D., The New Church Law on Matrimony, X-461 pp., 1919.
7. HICKEY, REV. JOHN J., S.T.B., J.C.D., Irregularities and Simple Impediments in the New Code of Canon Law, 100 pp., 1920.
8. KLEKOTKA, REV. PETER J., S.T.B., J.C.D., Diocesan Consultors, 179 pp., 1920.
9. WANENMACHER, REV. FRANCIS, J.C.D., The Evidence in Ecclesiastical Procedure Affecting the Marriage Bond, 1920 (Printed 1935).
10. GOLDEN, REV. HENRY FRANCIS, J.C.D., Parochial Benefices in the New Code, IV-119 pp., 1921 (Printed 1925).
11. KOUDELKA, REV. CHARLES J., J.C.D., Pastors, Their Rights and Duties According to the New Code of Canon Law, 211 pp., 1921.
12. MELO, REV. ANTONIUS, O.F.M., J.C.D., De Exemptione Regularium, X-188 pp., 1921.
13. SCHAAF, REV. VALENTINE THEODORE, O.F.M., S.T.B., J.C.D., The Cloister, X-180 pp., 1921.
14. BURKE, REV. THOMAS JOSEPH, S.T.D., J.C.D., Competence in Ecclesiastical Tribunals, IV-117 pp., 1922.
15. LEECH, REV. GEORGE LEO, J.C.D., A Comparative Study of the Constitution "Apostolicæ Sedis" and the "Codex Juris Canonici," 179 pp., 1922.

---

[1] All published numbers are available from the Catholic University of America Press, 621 Michigan Avenue, N.E., Washington 17, D. C., except the following: Numbers 1-114 inclusive, and numbers 116, 118, 120, 122, 123, 136, 162, and 198.

16. MOTRY, REV. HUBERT LOUIS, S.T.D., J.C.D., Diocesan Faculties According to the Code of Canon Law, II-167 pp., 1922.

17. MURPHY, REV. GEORGE LAWRENCE, J.C.D., Delinquencies and Penalties in the Administration and the Reception of the Sacraments, IV-121 pp., 1923.

18. O'REILLY, REV. JOHN ANTHONY, S.T.B., J.C.D., Ecclesiastical Sepulture in the New Code of Canon Law, II-129 pp., 1923.

19. MICHALICKA, REV. WENCESLAUS CYRILL, O.S.B., J.C.D., Judicial Procedure in Dismissal of Clerical Exempt Religious, 107 pp., 1923.

20. DARGIN, REV. EDWARD VINCENT, S.T.B., J.C.D., Reserved Cases According to the Code of Canon Law, IV-103 pp., 1924.

21. GODFREY, REV. JOHN A., S.T.B., J.C.D., The Right of Patronage According to the Code of Canon Law, 153 pp., 1924.

22. HAGEDORN, REV. FRANCIS EDWARD, J.C.D., General Legislation on Indulgences, II-154 pp., 1924.

23. KING, REV. JAMES IGNATIUS, J.C.D., The Administration of the Sacraments to Dying Non-Catholics, V-141 pp., 1924.

24. WINSLOW, REV. FRANCIS JOSEPH, M.M., J.C.D., Vicars and Prefects Apostolic, IV-149 pp., 1924.

25. CORREA, REV. JOSE SERVELION, S.T.L., J.C.D., La Potestad Legislativa de la Iglesia Catolica, IV-127 pp., 1925.

26. DUGAN, REV. HENRY FRANCIS, A.M., J.C.D., The Judiciary Department of the Diocesan Curia, 87 pp., 1925.

27. KELLER, REV. CHARLES FREDERICK, S.T.B., J.C.D., Mass Stipends, 167 pp., 1925.

28. PASCHANG, REV. JOHN LINUS, J.C.D., The Sacramentals According to the Code of Canon Law, 129 pp., 1925.

29. PIONTEK, REV. CYRILLUS, O.F.M., S.T.B., J.C.D., De Indulto Exclaustrationis necnon Sæcularizationis, XIII-289 pp., 1925.

30. KEARNEY, REV. RICHARD JOSEPH, S.T.B., J.C.D., Sponsors at Baptism According to the Code of Canon Law, IV-127 pp., 1925.

31. BARTLETT, REV. CHESTER JOSEPH, A.M., LL.B., J.C.D., The Tenure of Parochial Property in the United States of America, V-108 pp., 1926.

32. KILKER, REV. ADRIAN JEROME, J.C.D., Extreme Unction, V-425 pp., 1926.

33. MCCORMICK, REV. ROBERT EMMETT, J.C.D., Confessors of Religious, VIII-266 pp., 1926.

34. MILLER, REV. NEWTON THOMAS, J.C.D., Founded Masses According to the Code of Canon Law, VII-93 pp., 1926.

35. ROELKER, REV. EDWARD G., S.T.D., J.C.D., Principles of Privilege According to the Code of Canon Law, XI-166 pp., 1926.

36. BAKALARCZYK, REV. RICHARDUS, M.I.C., J.U.D., De Novitiatu, VIII-208 pp., 1927.

37. PIZZUTI, REV. LAWRENCE, O.F.M., J.U.L., De Parochis Religiosis, 1927. (Not Printed.)

38. BLILEY, REV. NICHOLAS MARTIN, O.S.B., J.C.D., Altars According to the Code of Canon Law, XIX-132 pp., 1927.

39. BROWN, MR. BRENDAN FRANCIS, A.B., LL.M., J.U.D., The Canonical Juristic Personality with Special Reference to its Status in the United States of America, V-212 pp., 1927.

40. CAVANAUGH, REV. WILLIAM THOMAS, C.P., J.U.D., The Reservation of the Blessed Sacrament, VIII-101 pp., 1927.

41. DOHENY, REV. WILLIAM J., C.S.C., A.B., J.U.D., Church Property: Modes of Acquisition, X-118 pp., 1927.

42. FELDHAUS, REV. ALOYSIUS H., C.PP.S., J.C.D., Oratories, IX-141 pp., 1927.

43. KELLY, REV. JAMES PATRICK, A.B., J.C.D., The Jurisdiction of the Simple Confessor, X-208 pp., 1927.

44. NEUBERGER, REV. NICHOLAS J., J.C.D., Canon 6 or the Relation of the Codex Juris Canonici to the Preceding Legislation, V-95 pp., 1927.

45. O'KEEFE, REV. GERALD MICHAEL, J.C.D., Matrimonial Dispensations, Powers of Bishops, Priests, and Confessors, VIII-232 pp., 1927.

46. QUIGLEY, REV. JOSEPH A. M., A.B., J.C.D., Condemned Societies, 139 pp., 1927.

47. ZAPLOTNIK, REV. JOHANNES LEO, J.C.D., De Vicariis Foraneis, X-142 pp., 1927.

48. DUSKIE, REV. JOHN ALOYSIUS, A.B., J.C.D., The Canonical Status of the Orientals in the United States, VIII-196 pp., 1928.

49. HYLAND, REV. FRANCIS EDWARD, J.C.D., Excommunication, Its Nature, Historical Development and Effects, VII-181 pp., 1928.

50. REINMANN, REV. GERALD JOSEPH, O.M.C., J.C.D., The Third Order Secular of Saint Francis, 201 pp., 1928.

51. SCHENK, REV. FRANCIS J., J.C.D., The Matrimonial Impediments of Mixed Religion and Disparity of Cult, XVI-318 pp., 1929.

52. COADY, REV. JOHN JOSEPH, S.T.D., J.U.D., A.M., The Appointment of Pastors, VIII-150 pp., 1929.

53. KAY, REV. THOMAS HENRY, J.C.D., Competence in Matrimonial Procedure, VIII-164 pp., 1929.

54. TURNER, REV. SIDNEY JOSEPH, C.P., J.U.D., The Vow of Poverty, XLIX-217 pp., 1929.

55. KEARNEY, REV. RAYMOND A., A.B., S.T.D., J.C.D., The Principles of Delegation, VII-149 pp., 1929.

56. CONRAN, REV. EDWARD JAMES, A.B., J.C.D., The Interdict, V-163 pp., 1930.

57. O'NEILL, REV. WILLIAM H., J.C.D., Papal Rescripts of Favor, VII-218 pp., 1930.

58. BASTNAGEL, REV. CLEMENT VINCENT, J.U.D., The Appointment of Parochial Adjutants and Assistants, XV-257 pp., 1930.

59. FERRY, REV. WILLIAM A., A.B., J.C.D., Stole Fees, V-136 pp., 1930.

60. COSTELLO, REV. JOHN MICHAEL, A.B., J.C.D., Domicile and Quasi-Domicile, VII-201 pp., 1930.

61. KREMER, REV. MICHAEL NICHOLAS, A.B., S.T.B., J.C.D., Church Support in the United States, VI-136 pp., 1930.

62. ANGULO, REV. LUIS, C.M., J.C.D., Legislation de la Iglesia sobre la intencion en la application de la Santa Misa, VII-104 pp., 1931.

63. FREY, REV. WOLFGANG NORBERT, O.S.B., A.B., J.C.D., The Act of Religious Profession, VIII-174 pp., 1931.

64. ROBERTS, REV. JAMES BRENDAN, A.B., J.C.D., The Banns of Marriage, XIV-140 pp., 1931.

65. RYDER, REV. RAYMOND ALOYSIUS, A.B., J.C.D., Simony, IX-151 pp., 1931.

66. CAMPAGNA, REV. ANGELO, PH.D., J.U.D., Il Vicario Generale del Vescovo, VII-205 pp., 1931.

67. COX, REV. JOSEPH GODFREY, A.B., J.C.D., The Administration of Seminaries, VI-124 pp., 1931.

68. GREGORY, REV. DONALD J., J.U.D., The Pauline Privilege, XV-165 pp., 1931.

69. DONOHUE, REV. JOHN F., J.C.D., The Impediment of Crime, VII-110 pp., 1931.

70. DOOLEY, REV. EUGENE A., O.M.I., J.C.D., Church Law on Sacred Relics, IX-143 pp., 1931.

71. ORTH, REV. CLEMENT RAYMOND, O.M.C., J.C.D., The Approbation of Religious Institutes, 171 pp., 1931.

72. PERNICONE, REV. JOSEPH M., A.B., J.C.D., The Ecclesiastical Prohibition of Books, XII-267 pp., 1932.

73. CLINTON, REV. CONNELL, A.B., J.C.D., The Paschal Precept, IX-108 pp., 1932.

74. DONNELLY, REV. FRANCIS B., A.M., S.T.L., J.C.D., The Diocesan Synod, VIII-125 pp., 1932.

75. TORRENTE, REV. CAMILO, C.M.F., J.C.D., Las Procesiones Sagradas, V-145 pp., 1932.

76. MURPHY, REV. EDWIN J., C.PP.S., J.C.D., Suspension Ex Informata Conscientia, XI-122 pp., 1932.

77. MACKENZIE, REV. ERIC F., A.M., S.T.L., J.C.D., The Delict of Heresy in its Commission, Penalization, Absoluton, VII-124 pp., 1932.

78. LYONS, REV. AVITUS E., S.T.B., J.C.D., The Collegiate Tribunal of First Instance, XI-147 pp., 1932.

79. CONNOLLY, REV. THOMAS A., J.C.D., Appeals, XI-195 pp., 1932.

80. SANGMEISTER, REV. JOSEPH V., A.B., J.C.D., Force and Fear as Precluding Matrimonial Consent, V-211 pp., 1932.

81. JAEGER, REV. LEO A., A.B., J.C.D., The Administration of Vacant and Quasi-Vacant Episcopal Sees in the United States, IX-229 pp., 1932.

82. RIMLINGER, REV. HERBERT T., J.C.D., Error Invalidating Matrimonial Consent, VII-79 pp., 1932.

83. BARRETT, REV. JOHN D. M., S.S., J.C.D., A Comparative Study of the Councils of Baltimore and the Code of Canon Law, X-223 pp., 1932.

84. CARBERRY, REV. JOHN J., PH.D., S.T.D., J.C.D., The Juridical Form of Marriage, X-177 pp., 1934.

85. DOLAN, REV. JOHN L., A.B., J.C.D., The Defensor Vinculi, XII-157 pp., 1934.

86. HANNAN, REV. JEROME D., A.M., S.T.D., LL.B., J.C.D., The Canon Law of Wills, IX-517 pp., 1934.

87. LEMIEUX, REV. DELISE A., A.M., J.C.D., The Sentence in Ecclesiastical Procedure, IX-131 pp., 1934.

88. O'ROURKE, REV. JAMES J., A.B., J.C.D., Parish Registers, VII-109 pp., 1934.

89. TIMLIN, REV. BARTHOLOMEW, O.F.M., A.M., J.C.D., Conditional Matrimonial Consent, X-381 pp., 1934.

90. WAHL, REV. FRANCIS X., A.B., J.C.D., The Matrimonial Impediments of Consanguinity and Affinity, VI-125 pp., 1934.

91. WHITE, REV. ROBERT J., A.B., LL.B., S.T.B., J.C.D., Canonical Ante-Nuptial Promises and the Civil Law, VI-152 pp., 1934.

92. HERRARA, REV. ANTONIO PARRA, O.C.D., J.C.D., Legislacion Eclesiastica sobra el Ayuno y la Abstinencia, XI-191 pp., 1935.

93. KENNEDY, REV. EDWIN J., J.C.D., The Special Matrimonial Process in Cases of Evident Nullity, X-165 pp., 1935.

94. MANNING, REV. JOHN J., A.B., J.C.D., Presumption of Law in Matrimonial Procedure, XI-111 pp., 1935.

95. MOEDER, REV. JOHN M., J.C.D., The Proper Bishop for Ordination and Dimissorial Letters, VII-135 pp., 1935.

96. O'MARA, REV. WILLIAM A., A.B., J.C.D., Canonical Causes for Matrimonial Dispensations, IX-155 pp., 1935.

97. REILLY, REV. PETER, J.C.D., Residence of Pastors, IX-81 pp., 1935.

98. SMITH, REV. MARINER T., O.P., S.T.LR., J.C.D., The Penal Law for Religious, VIII-169 pp., 1935.

99. WHALEN, REV. DONALD W., A.M., J.C.D., The Value of Testimonial Evidence in Matrimonial Procedure, XIII-297 pp., 1935.

100. CLEARY, REV. JOSEPH F., J.C.D., Canonical Limitations on the Alienation of Church Property, VIII-141 pp., 1936.

101. GLYNN, REV. JOHN C., J.C.D., The Promoter of Justice, XX-337 pp., 1936.

102. BRENNAN, REV. JAMES H., S.S., M.A., S.T.B., J.C.D., The Simple Convalidation of Marriage, VI-135 pp., 1937.

103. BRUNINI, REV. JOSEPH BERNARD, J.C.D., The Clerical Obligations of Canons 139 and 142, X-121 pp., 1937.

104. CONNOR, REV. MAURICE, A.B., J.C.D., The Administrative Removal of Pastors, VIII-159 pp., 1937.

105. GUILFOYLE, REV. MERLIN JOSEPH, J.C.D., Custom, XI-144 pp., 1937.

106. HUGHES, REV. JAMES AUSTIN, A.B., A.M., J.C.D., Witnesses in Criminal Trials of Clerics, IX-140 pp., 1937.

107. JANSEN, REV. RAYMOND J., A.B., S.T.L., J.C.D., Canonical Provisions for Catechetical Instruction, VII-153 pp., 1937.

108. KEALY, REV. JOHN JAMES, A.B., J.C.D., The Introductory Libellus in Church Court Procedure, XI-121 pp., 1937.

109. MCMANUS, REV. JAMES EDWARD, C.SS.R., J.C.D., The Administration of Temporal Goods in Religious Institutes, XVI-196 pp., 1937.

110. MORIARTY, REV. EUGENE JAMES, J.C.D., Oaths in Ecclesiastical Courts, X-115 pp., 1937.

111. RAINER, REV. ELIGIUS GEORGE, C.SS.R., J.C.D., Suspension of Clerics, XVII-249 pp., 1937.

112. REILLY, REV. THOMAS F., C.SS.R., J.C.D., Visitation of Religious, VI-195 pp., 1938.

113. MORIARTY, REV. FRANCIS E., C.SS.R., J.C.D., The Extraordinary Absolution from Censures, XV-334 pp., 1938.

114. CONNOLLY, REV. NICHOLAS P., J.C.D., The Canonical Erection of Parishes, X-132 pp., 1938.

115. DONOVAN, REV. JAMES JOSEPH, J.C.D., The Pastor's Obligation in Prenuptial Investigation, XII-322 pp., 1938.

116. HARRIGAN, REV. ROBERT J., M.A., S.T.B., J.C.D., The Radical Sanation of Invalid Marriages, VIII-208 pp., 1938.

117. BOFFA, REV. CONRAD HUMBERT, J.C.D., Canonical Provisions for Catholic Schools, VII-211 pp., 1939.

118. PARSONS, REV. ANSCAR JOHN, O.M.CAP., J.C.D., Canonical Elections, XII-236 pp., 1939.

119. REILLY, REV. EDWARD MICHAEL, A.B., J.C.D., The General Norms of Dispensation, XII-156 pp., 1939.

120. RYAN, REV. GERALD ALOYSIUS, A.B., J.C.D., Principles of Episcopal Jurisdiction, XII-172 pp., 1939.

121. BURTON, REV. FRANCIS JAMES, C.S.C., A.B., J.C.D., A Commentary on Canon 1125, X-222 pp., 1940.

122. MIASKIEWICZ, REV. FRANCIS SIGISMUND, J.C.D., Supplied Jurisdiction According to Canon 209, XII-340 pp., 1940.

123. RICE, REV. PARTICK WILLIAM, A.B., J.C.D., Proof of Death in Prenuptial Investigation, VIII-156 pp., 1940.

124. ANGLIN, REV. THOMAS FRANCIS, M.S., J.C.D., The Eucharistic Fast, VIII-183 pp., 1941.

125. COLEMAN, REV. JOHN JEROME, J.C.D., The Minister of Confirmation, VI-153 pp., 1941.

126. DOWNS, REV. JOSEPH EMMANUEL, A.B., J.C.D., The Concept of Clerical Immunity, XI-163 pp., 1941.

127. ESSWEIN, REV. ANTHONY ALBERT, J.C.D., Extrajudicial Penal Powers of Ecclesiastical Superiors, X-144 pp., 1941.

128. FARRELL, REV. BENJAMIN FRANCIS, M.A., S.T.L., J.C.D., The Rights and Duties of the Local Ordinary Regarding Congregations of Women Religious of Pontifical Approval, V-195 pp., 1941.

129. FEENEY, REV. THOMAS JOHN, A.B., S.T.L., J.C.D., Restitutio in Integrum, VI-169 pp., 1941.

130. FINDLAY, REV. STEPHEN WILLIAM, O.S.B., A.B., J.C.D., Canonical Norms Governing the Deposition and Degradation of Clerics, XVII-279 pp., 1941.

131. GOODWINE, REV. JOHN, A.B., S.T.L., J.C.D., The Right of the Church to Acquire Property, VIII-119 pp., 1941.

132. HESTON, REV. EDWARD LOUIS, C.S.C., PH.D., S.T.D., J.C.D., The Alienation of Church Property in the United States, XII-222 pp., 1941.

133. HOGAN, REV. JAMES JOHN, A.B., S.T.L., J.C.D., Judicial Advocates and Procurators, XIII-200 pp., 1941.

134. KEALY, REV. THOMAS M., A.B., LITT.B., J.C.D., Dowry of Women Religious, IX-152 pp., 1941.

135. KEENE, REV. MICHAEL JAMES, O.S.B., J.C.D., Religious Ordinaries and Canon 198, V-164 pp., 1942.

136. KERIN, REV. CHARLES A., S.S., M.A., S.T.B., J.C.D., The Privation of Christian Burial, XVI-279 pp., 1941.

137. LOUIS, REV. WILLIAM FRANCIS, M.A., J.C.D., Diocesan Archives, X-101 pp., 1941.

138. MCDEVITT, REV. GILBERT JOSEPH, A.B., J.C.D., Legitimacy and Legitimation, X-247 pp., 1941.

139. MCDONOUGH, REV. THOMAS JOSEPH, A.B., J.C.D., Apostolic Administrators, X-217 pp., 1941.

140. MEIER, REV. CARL ANTHONY, A.B., J.C.D., Penal Administrative Procedure Against Negligent Pastors, XI-240 pp., 1941.

141. SCHMIDT, REV. JOHN ROGG, A.B., J.C.D., The Principles of Authentic Interpretation in Canon 17 of the Code of Canon Law, XII-331 pp., 1941.

142. SLAFKOSKY, REV. ANDREW LEONARD, A.B., J.C.D., The Canonical Episcopal Visitations of the Diocese, X-197 pp., 1941.

143. SWOBODA, REV. INNOCENT ROBERT, O.F.M., J.C.D., Ignorance in Relation to the Imputability of Delicts, IX-271 pp., 1941.

144. DUBE, REV. ARTHUR JOSEPH, A.B., J.C.D., The General Principles for the Reckoning of Time in Canon Law, VIII-299 pp., 1941.

145. MCBRIDE, REV. JAMES T., A.B., J.C.D., Incardination and Excardination of Seculars, XX-585 pp., 1941.

146. KROL, REV. JOHN T., J.C.D., The Defendant in Ecclesiastical Trials, XII-207 pp., 1942.

147. COMYNS, REV. JOSEPH J., C.SS.R., A.B., J.C.D., Papal and Episcopal Administration of Church Property, XIV-155 pp., 1942.

148. BARRY, REV. GARRETT FRANCIS, O.M.I., J.C.D., Violation of the Cloister, XII-260 pp., 1942.

149. BOLDUC, REV. GATIEN, C.S.V., A.B., S.T.L., J.C.D., Les Etudes dans les Religions Cléricales, VIII-155 pp., 1942.

150. BOYLE, REV. DAVID JOHN, M.A., J.C.D., The Juridic Effects of Moral Certitude on Pre-Nuptial Guarantees, XII-188 pp., 1942.

151. CANAVAN, REV. WALTER JOSEPH, M.A., LITT.D., J.C.D., The Profession of Faith, XII-143 pp., 1942.

152. DESROCHERS, REV. BRUNO, A.B., PH.L., S.T.B., J.C.D., Le Premier Concile Plénier de Québec et le Code de Droit Canonique, XIV-186 pp., 1942.

153. DILLON, REV. ROBERT EDWARD, A.B., J.C.D., Common Law Marriage, X-148 pp., 1942.

154. DODWELL, REV. EDWARD JOHN, PH.D., S.T.B., J.C.D., The Time and Place for the Celebration of Marriage, X-156 pp., 1942.

155. DONNELLAN, REV. THOMAS ANDREW, A.B., J.C.D., The Obligation of the Missa pro Populo, VII-131 pp., 1942.

156. ELTZ, REV. LOUIS ANTHONY, A.B., J.C.D., Coöperation in Crime, XII-208 pp., 1942.

157. GASS, REV. SYLVESTER FRANCIS, M.A., J.C.D., Ecclesiastical Pensions, XI-206 pp., 1942.

158. GUINIVEN, REV. JOHN JOSEPH, C.SS.R., J.C.D., The Precept of Hearing Mass, XIV-188 pp., 1942.

159. GULCZYNSKI, REV. JOHN THEOPHILUS, J.C.D., The Desecration and Violation of Churches, X-126 pp., 1942.

160. HAMMILL, REV. JOHN LEO, M.A., J.C.D., The Obligations of the Traveler According to Canon 14, VIII-204 pp., 1942.

161. HAYDT, REV. JOHN JOSEPH, A.B., J.C.D., Reserved Benefices, XI-148 pp., 1942.

162. HUSER, REV. ROGER JOHN, O.F.M., A.B., J.C.D., The Crime of Abortion in Canon Law, XII-187 pp., 1942.

163. KEARNEY, REV. FRANCIS PATRICK, A.B., S.T.L., J.C.D., The Principles of Canon 1127, X-162 pp., 1942.

164. LINAHEN, REV. LEO JAMES, S.T.L., J.C.D., De Absolutione Complicis In Peccato Turpi, 114 pp., 1942.

165. MCCLOSKEY, REV. JOSEPH ALOYSIUS, A.B., J.C.D., The Subject of Ecclesiastical Law According to Canon 12, XVII-246 pp., 1942.

166. O'NEILL, REV. FRANCIS JOSEPH, C.SS.R., J.C.D., The Dismissal of Religious in Temporary Vows, XIII-220 pp., 1942.

167. PRINCE, REV. JOHN EDWARD, A.B., S.T.D., J.C.D., The Diocesan Chancellor, X-136 pp., 1942.

168. RIESNER, REV. ALBERT JOSEPH, C.SS.R., J.C.D., Apostates and Fugitives from Religious Institutes, IX-168 pp., 1942.

169. STENGER, REV. JOSEPH BERNARD, J.C.D., The Mortgaging of Church Property, 186 pp., 1942.

170. WALDRON, REV. JOSEPH FRANCIS, A.B., J.C.D., The Minister of Baptism, XII-197 pp., 1942.

171. WILLETT, REV. ROBERT ALBERT, J.C.D., The Probative Value of Documents in Ecclesiastical Trials, X-124 pp., 1942.

172. WOEBER, REV. EDWARD MARTIN, M.A., J.C.D., The Interpellations, XII-161 pp., 1942.

173. BENKO, REV. MATTHEW ALOYSIUS, O.S.B., M.A., J.C.D., The Abbot *Nullius*, XVI-148 pp., 1943.

174. CHRIST, REV. JOSEPH JAMES, M.A., S.T.L., J.C.D., Dispensation from Vindicative Penalties, XIII-285 pp., 1943.

175. CLANCY, REV. PATRICK M. J., O.P., A.B., S.T.LR., J.C.D., The Local Religious Superior, X-229 pp., 1943.

176. CLARKE, REV. THOMAS JAMES, J.C.D., Parish Societies, XII-147 pp., 1943.

177. CONNOLLY, REV. JOHN PATRICK, S.T.L., J.C.D., Synodal Examiners, and Parish Priest Consultors, X-223 pp., 1943.

178. DRUMM, REV. WILLIAM MARTIN, A.B., J.C.D., Hospital Chaplains, XII-175 pp., 1943.

179. FLANAGAN, REV. BERNARD JOSEPH, A.B., S.T.L., J.C.D., The Canonical Erection of Religious Houses, X-147 pp., 1943.

180. KELLEHER, REV. STEPHEN JOSEPH, A.B., S.T.B., J.C.D., Discussions with Non-Catholics: Canonical Legislation, X-93 pp., 1943.

181. LEWIS, REV. GORDIAN, C.P., J.C.D., Chapters in Religious Institutes, XII-169 pp., 1943.

182. MARX, REV. ADOLPH, J.C.D., The Declaration of Nullity of Marriages Contracted Outside the Church, X-151 pp., 1943.

183. MATULENAS, REV. RAYMOND ANTHONY, O.S.B., A.B., J.C.D., Communication, a Source of Privileges, XII-225 pp., 1943.

184. O'LEARY, REV. CHARLES GERARD, C.SS.R., J.C.D., Religious Dismissed After Perpetual Profession, X-213 pp., 1943.

185. POWER, REV. CORNELIUS MICHAEL, J.C.D., The Blessing of Cemeteries, XII-231 pp., 1943.

186. SHUHLER, REV. RALPH VINCENT, O.S.A., J.C.D., Privileges of Religious to Absolve and Dispense, XII-195 pp., 1943.

187. ZIOLKOWSKI, REV. THADDEUS STANISLAUS, A.B., J.C.D., The Consecration and Blessing of Churches, XII-151 pp., 1943.

188. HENEGHAN, REV. JOHN JOSEPH, S.T.D., J.C.D., The Marriages of Unworthy Catholics: Canons 1065 and 1066, XVI-213 pp., 1944.

189. CARROLL, REV. COLEMAN FRANCIS, M.A., S.T.L., J.C.L., Charitable Institutions.

190. CIESLUK, REV. JOSEPH EDWARD, PH.B., S.T.L., J.C.D., National Parishes in the United States, VI-178 pp., 1944.

191. COBURN, REV. VINCENT PAUL, A.B., J.C.D., Marriages of Conscience, XII-172 pp., 1944.

192. CONNORS, REV. CHARLES PAUL, C.S.SP., A.B., J.C.D., Extra-Judicial Procurators in the Code of Canon Law, X-94 pp., 1944.

193. COYLE, REV. PAUL RAYMOND, A.B., J.C.D., Judicial Exceptions, IX-142 pp., 1944.

194. FAIR, REV. BARTHOLOMEW FRANCIS, A.B., S.T.L., J.C.D., The Impediment of Abduction, XII-122 pp., 1944.

195. GALLAGHER, REV. THOMAS RAPHAEL, O.P., A.B., S.T.LR., J.C.D., The Examination of the Qualities of the Ordinand, X-166 pp., 1944.

196. GANNON, REV. JOHN MARK, S.T.L., J.C.D., The Interstices Required for the Promotion to Orders, VII-100 pp., 1944.

197. GOLDSMITH, REV. J. WILLIAM, B.C.S., S.T.L., J.C.D., The Competence of Church and State Over Marriage — Disputed Points, X-128 pp., 1944.

198. GOODWINE, REV. JOSEPH GERARD, A.B., S.T.B., J.C.D., The Reception of Converts, XIV-326 pp., 1944.

199. KOWALSKI, REV. ROMUALD EUGENE, O.F.M., A.B., J.C.D., Sustenance of Religious Houses of Regulars, X-174 pp., 1944.

200. MCCOY, REV. ALAN EDWARD, O.F.M., J.C.D., Force and Fear in Relation to Delictual Imputability and Penal Responsibility, XII-160 pp., 1944.

201. MCDEVITT, REV. VINCENT JOHN, PH.B., S.T.L., J.C.L., Perjury.

202. MARTIN, REV. THOMAS OWEN, PH.D., S.T.D., J.C.D., Adverse Possession, Prescription and Limitation of Actions: The Canonical "Præscriptio," XX-208 pp., 1944.

203. MIKLOSOVIC, REV. PAUL JOHN, A.B., J.C.L., Attempted Marriages and Their Consequent Juridic Effects.

204. MUNDY, REV. THOMAS MAURICE, A.B., S.T.L., J.C.D., The Union of Parishes, X-164 pp., 1944.

205. O'DEA, REV. JOHN COYLE, A.B., J.C.D., The Matrimonial Impediment of Nonage, VIII-126 pp., 1944.

206. OLALIA, REV. ALEXANDER AYSON, S.T.L., J.C.D., A Comparative Study of the Christian Constitution of States and the Constitution of the Philippine Commonwealth, XII-136 pp., 1944.

207. POISSON, REV. PIERRE-MARIE, C.S.C., A.B., PH.L., TH.L., J.C.L., Droits Patrimoniaux des Maisons et des Eglises Religieuses.

208. STADALNIKAS, REV. CASIMIR JOSEPH, M.I.C., J.C.D., Reservation of Censures, X-141 pp., 1944.

209. SULLIVAN, REV. EUGENE HENRY, S.T.L., J.C.D., Proof of the Reception of the Sacraments, X-165 pp., 1944.

210. VAUGHAN, REV. WILLIAM EDWARD, J.C.D., Constitutions for Diocesan Courts, X-210 pp., 1944.

211. PARO, REV. GINO, S.T.D., J.C.L., The Right of Apostolic Delegation.

212. BALZER, REV. RALPH FRANCIS, C.P., J.C.D., The Computation of Time in a Canonical Novitiate, X-227 pp., 1945.

213. Dougherty, Rev. John Whelan, A.B., S.T.L., J.C.D., De Inquisitione Speciali, XII-195 pp., 1945.

214. Dziob, Rev. Michael Walter, J.C.D., The Sacred Congregation for the Oriental Church, XII-181 pp., 1945.

215. Eidenschink, Rev. John Albert, O.S.B., B.A., J.C.D., The Election of Bishops in the Letters of Pope Gregory the Great, VII-200 pp., 1945.

216. Gill, Rev. Nicholas, C.P., J.C.D., The Spiritual Prefect in Clerical Religious Houses of Study, X-140 pp., 1945.

217. Hynes, Rev. Harry Gerard, S.T.L., J.C.D., The Privileges of Cardinals, XII-183 pp., 1945.

218. McDevitt, Rev. Gerard Vincent, S.T.L., J.C.D., The Renunciation of an Ecclesiastical Office, XIV-179 pp., 1945.

219. Manning, Rev. Joseph Leroy, J.C.D., The Free Conferral of Offices, VIII-116 pp., 1945.

220. Meyer, Rev. Louis G., O.S.B., A.B., S.T.B., J.C.D., Alms-gathering by Religious, XII-163 pp., 1945.

221. O'Donnell, Rev. Cletus Francis, M.A., J.C.D., The Marriage of Minors, XII-268 pp., 1945.

222. Prunskis, Rev. Joseph, J.C.D., Comparative Law, Ecclesiastical and Civil, in Lithuanian Concordat, X-161 pp., 1945.

223. Sweeney, Rev. Francis Patrick, C.SS.R., J.C.D., The Reduction of Clerics to the Lay State, X-199 pp., 1945.

224. Vogelpohl, Rev. Henry John, J.C.D., The Simple Impediments to Holy Orders, XVI-190 pp., 1945.

225. Brockhaus, Rev. Thomas Aquinas, O.S.B., J.C.D., Religious Who Are Known as *Conversi*, X-127 pp., 1945.

226. Griese, Rev. N. Orville, S.T.D., J.C.D., The Marriage Contract and the Procreation of Offspring, XVI-224 pp., 1946.

227. Boudreaux, Rev. Warren Louis, J.C.D., The *"ab acatholicis nati"* of Canon 1099, § 2, XII-110 pp., 1946.

228. Bowe, Rev. Thomas Joseph, A.B., J.C.D., Religious Superioresses, VIII-206 pp., 1946.

229. Diederichs, Rev. Michael Ferdinand, S.C.J., J.C.D., The Jurisdiction of the Latin Ordinaries Over Their Oriental Subjects, XIV-153 pp., 1946.

230. Dingman, Rev. Maurice John, A.B., S.T.L., J.C.L., The Plaintiff in Contentious Trials.

231. Frison, Rev. Basil, C.M.F., M.Mus., J.C.D., The Retroactivity of Law, X-221 pp., 1946.

232. Galvin, Rev. William Anthony, M.A., J.C.D., The Administrative Transfer of Pastors, XII-288 pp., 1946.

233. GORACY, REV. JOSEPH C., J.C.L., The Diriment Matrimonial Impediment of Major Orders.

234. HALE, REV. JOSEPH FRANCIS, M.A., S.T.L., J.C.L., The Pastor of Burial.

235. HENRY, REV. JOSEPH ARTHUR, A.B., J.C.D., The Mass and Holy Communion: Inter-Ritual Law, XII-138 pp., 1946.

236. LINENBERGER, REV. HERBERT, C.PP.S., J.C.L., The False Denunciation of an Innocent Confessor.

237. LOWRY, REV. JAMES MARTIN, A.B., J.C.D., Dispensation from Private Vows, XII-266 pp., 1946.

238. LYNCH, REV. GEORGE EDWARD, A.B., S.T.L., J.C.D., Coadjutors and Auxiliaries of Bishops, X-107 pp., 1947.

239. LYNCH, REV. TIMOTHY, M.S.SS.T., J.C.D., Contracts Between Bishops and Religious Congregations, XIV-232 pp., 1946.

240. MCCLUNN, REV. JUSTIN DAVID, A.B., S.T.L., J.C.D., Administrative Recourse, VII-142 pp., 1946.

241. LOHMULLER, REV. MARTIN NICHOLAS, A.B., J.C.D., The Promulgation of Law, XII-140 pp., 1947.

242. MCGRATH, REV. JAMES, A.B., J.C.D., The Privilege of the Canon, XII-156 pp., 1946.

243. MARBACH, REV. JOSEPH FRANCIS, A.B., J.C.D., Marriage Legislation for the Catholics of the Oriental Rites in the United States and Canada, XIV-314 pp., 1946.

244. SHIMKUS, REV. BERNARD ALOYSIUS, A.B., J.C.L., The Determination and Transfer of Rite.

245. SMITH, REV. VINCENT MICHAEL, A.B., S.T.L., J.C.L., Ignorance Affecting Matrimonial Consent.

246. WACHTRLE, REV. PAUL ANTHONY, A.B., J.C.L., The Baptism of of the Children of Non-Catholics.

247. CROTTY, REV. MATTHEW MICHAEL, J.C.D., The Recipient of First Holy Communion, X-142 pp., 1947.

248. EAGLETON, REV. GEORGE, J.C.L., The Quinquennial Faculties, Formula IV.

249. GIBBONS, REV. MARION LEO, C.M., LL.B., J.C.D., Domicile of the Wife Unlawfully Separated from Her Husband, XIV-171 pp., 1947.

250. KELLY, REV. BERNARD MATTHEW, S.T.L., J.C.D., The Functions Reserved to Pastors, XII-141 pp., 1947.

251. KILCULLEN, REV. THOMAS JOHN, LL.M., J.C.D., The Collegiate Moral Person as Party Litigant, X-150 pp., 1947.

252. LAFONTAINE, REV. GERMAIN JOSEPH, W.F., J.C.L., Relations Canoniques entre le Missionnaire et Ses Superieurs.

253. LANE, REV. LORAS THOMAS, A.B., S.T.L., J.C.L., Matrimonial Procedure in the Ordinary Court of Second Instance.

254. LOVER, REV. JAMES FRANCIS, C.SS.R., J.C.D., The Master of Novices, X-168 pp., 1947.

255. MCNICHOLAS, REV. TIMOTHY JOSEPH, J.C.L., The *Septimæ Manus* Witness.

256. MAROSITZ, REV. JOSEPH JOHN, M.S.C., J.C.D., Obligations and Privileges of Religious Promoted to the Episcopal or Cardinalatial Dignities, XII-180 pp., 1947.

257. MURPHY, REV. FRANCIS JOSEPH, A.B., J.C.D., Legislative Powers of the Provinical Council, XII-158 pp., 1947.

258. O'BRIEN, REV. ROMAEUS WILLIAM, O.CARM., J.C.D., The Provincial Superior in Religious Orders of Men, X-294 pp., 1947.

259. PFALLER, REV. BENEDICT AUGUSTINE, O.S.B., J.C.L., The *Ipso Facto* Effected Dismissal of Religious.

260. POPEK, REV. ALPHONSE SYLVESTER, M.A., J.C.D., The Rights and Obligations of Metropolitans, XVIII-460 pp., 1947.

261. RISTUCCIA, REV. BERNARD JOSEPH, C.M., J.C.L., Quasi-Religious.

262. SONNTAG, REV. NATHANIEL LOUIS, O.F.M.CAP., J.C.D., Censorship of Special Classes of Books, XII-147 pp., 1947.

263. STADLER, REV. JOSEPH NICHOLAS, J.C.L., Frequent Holy Communion.

264. SZAL, REV. IGNATIUS JOSEPH, J.C.L., The Communication of Catholics with Schismatics.

265. WAGNER, REV. URBAN STANLEY, O.F.M.CONV., J.C.D., Parochial Substitute Vicars and Supplying Priests, X-126 pp., 1947.

266. QUINN, REV. JOSEPH, M.A., J.C.L., Documents Required for the Reception of Orders.

267. BENNINGTON, REV. JAMES CLEMENT, A.B., J.C.L., The Recipient of Confirmation.

268. BLAHER, REV. DAMIAN JOSEPH, O.F.M., A.B., J.C.L., The Ordinary Processes in Causes of Beatification and Canonization.

269. CLUNE, REV. ROBERT BELL, B.A., J.C.L. Judicial Interrogation of the Parties.

270. COURTEMANCHE, REV. BASIL F., B.A., J.C.L., The Total Simulation of Matrimonial Consent.

271. DLOUHY, REV. MAUR JOHN, O.S.B., A.B., J.C.L., The Ordination of Exempt Religious.

272. DONOVAN, REV. JOHN THOMAS, PH.B., S.T.L., J.C.L., The Clerical Obligations of Canons 138 and 140.

273. FREKING, REV. FREDERICK W., A.B., S.T.B., J.C.L., The Canonical Installation of Pastors.

274. FULTON, REV. THOMAS B., J.C.L., Prenuptial Investigation.

275. GODLEY, REV. JAMES P., J.C.L., The Time and the Place for the Celebration of Mass.

276. KANE, REV. THOMAS A., A.B., B.S., J.C.L., Jurisdiction of Patriarchs until 1439.

277. KENNEDY, REV. ANDREW A., J.C.L., The Annual Pastoral Report to the Local Ordinary.

278. KONRAD, REV. JOSEPH GEORGE, J.C.L., Transfer of Religious.

279. KRESS, REV. ALPHONSE, J.C.L., Contumacy in Ecclesiastical Trials.

280. MCCARTNEY, REV. MARCELLUS ANTHONY, O.F.M., M.A., J.C.L., Faculties of Regular Confessors.

281. MCCASLIN, REV. EDWARD PATRICK, M.A., S.T.L., J.C.L., The Division of Parishes.

282. MCELROY, REV. FRANCIS J., A.B., J.C.L., The Privileges of Bishops.

283. QUINN, REV. STEPHEN, M.S.SS.T., J.C.L., Relation between the Local Ordinary and Religious of Diocesan Approval.

284. SCHNEIDER, REV. EDELHARD LOUIS, S.D.S., M.A., J.C.L., The Status of Secularized Ex-Religious Clerics.

285. THOMPSON, REV. CHESTER J., A.B., J.C.L., The Simple Removal from Office.

www.ingramcontent.com/pod-product-compliance
Lightning Source LLC
LaVergne TN
LVHW050242080826
844660LV00012B/581

* 9 7 8 0 8 1 3 2 2 4 5 0 3 *